EKKLESIA

TRI◎◎S

Each TRIOS book addresses an important theme in critical theory, philosophy, or cultural studies through three extended essays written in close collaboration by leading scholars.

EKKLESIA

THREE INQUIRIES
IN CHURCH AND STATE

PAUL CHRISTOPHER
Johnson

PAMELA E.
Klassen

WINNIFRED FALLERS
Sullivan

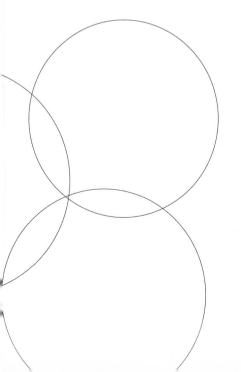

The University of Chicago Press
Chicago and London

The University of Chicago Press, Chicago 60637
The University of Chicago Press, Ltd., London
© 2018 by The University of Chicago
All rights reserved. No part of this book may be used or reproduced in any
manner whatsoever without written permission, except in the case of brief
quotations in critical articles and reviews. For more information, contact the
University of Chicago Press, 1427 East 60th Street, Chicago, IL 60637.
Published 2018
Printed in the United States of America

27 26 25 24 23 22 21 20 19 18   1 2 3 4 5

ISBN-13: 978-0-226-54544-8 (cloth)
ISBN-13: 978-0-226-54558-5 (paper)
ISBN-13: 978-0-226-54561-5 (e-book)
DOI: https://doi.org/10.7208/chicago/9780226545615.001.0001

Library of Congress Cataloging-in-Publication Data

Names: Container of (work): Johnson, Paul C. (Paul Christopher), 1964–
   People and the law of the hound at Canudos. | Container of (work): Klassen,
   Pamela E. (Pamela Edith), 1967– Spiritual jurisdictions. | Container of
   (work): Sullivan, Winnifred Fallers, 1950– Banning bibles.
Title: Ekklesia : three inquiries in church and state / Paul Christopher
   Johnson, Pamela E. Klassen, Winnifred Fallers Sullivan.
Other titles: Trios (Chicago, Ill.)
Description: Chicago : The University of Chicago Press, 2018. | Series: Trios |
   Includes bibliographical references.
Identifiers: LCCN 2017028653 | ISBN 9780226545448 (cloth : alk. paper) |
   ISBN 9780226545585 (pbk. : alk. paper) | ISBN 9780226545615 (e-book)
Subjects: LCSH: Church and state—Brazil. | Church and state—Canada. |
   Church and state—United States.
Classification: LCC BR500 .E35 2018 | DDC 322/.1—dc23
LC record available at https://lccn.loc.gov/2017028653

♾ This paper meets the requirements of ANSI/NISO Z39.48-1992 (Permanence of
Paper).

CONTENTS

William Edmondson, *Church Lady* (1933/37). Limestone, 49.5 × 20 × 20 cm. Through prior acquisition of the George F. Harding Collection (2014.4). Art Institute of Chicago. Photograph: Art Institute of Chicago / Art Resource, New York.

INTRODUCTION

Paul Christopher Johnson, Pamela E. Klassen,
and Winnifred Fallers Sullivan

The inaugural issue of the *Journal of Church and State* in 1959
began by citing the grand claim of the Swiss theologian Emil
Brunner: "The relation between Church and State is the greatest
subject in the history of the West."[1] Today, more than fifty years
later, these capitalized rubrics seem less discrete and their relations less self-evidently important, while also seeming oddly
unavoidable. What other words are there? As a great subject,
the Christian particularity of the pairing of church and state
has been both obvious and misrecognized, much in the same
way that the word "religion" often connotes a universality that
obscures its Christian template. Resisting Brunner's triumphal-
ism, as well as any position that views church and state as natu-
rally occurring institutions, we nevertheless begin with several
basic assumptions: we agree that attending to church and state
remains necessary; we believe each to be both inescapable and
radically contingent; and finally, we regard the two as necessarily entangled. We intervene to offer new perspectives from the
Americas on these issues.[2]

   We investigate this constellation of issues under the rubric
ekklesia. "Ekklesia" bears an etymology stemming from both
ancient Athenian citizen assemblies and, later, early Christian
churches; each was a local congregation gathered in the name
either of the polis or the body of Christ, of the demos or of God.

In each case ekklesia implied exclusion, having profound effects on those not understood to be similarly collected: slaves, women, pagans, Jews. Jean-Luc Nancy notes that the word ekklesia was "drawn from" or gestured to institutions of the Greek city yet marked the birth of a new mode of assembly distinct from the social or political, in that sense signaling at once the twin origin and "essential separation" of church and state.[3] It is the tension between the two clauses *drawn from* and *essential separation* that attracts our attention and that we seek to hold in focus. That ekklesia shares roots in the two kinds of assemblies that furnish the origins of state and church in Western imaginations and political theory—namely the Greek city-state and the early Christian church—and yet persists in wildly different settings provokes our reflections in this book. We give attention both to the attempted separation of religion and politics, church and state—their "essential separation"—and to the richly diverse failures of such an attempt, the ways one form "draws from" the other. These essays foreground the infiltrations of religion, especially in Christian forms, into legal and political spheres too easily read as solely matters of state as well as the always present effect of the legal and the political in matters of religion.

THINKING THROUGH CHURCHSTATENESS

"The state" has been often described and theorized, but "the church" less so, at least beyond ecclesiastical contexts too indebted perhaps to its sense as given. The phenomenon of their often enmeshed and intercalibrated forms—a crossed and intertextual churchstateness—requires more detached and empirically grounded description and conceptualization. This volume returns to the old saw of "church and state" to render it strange and to specify the niches in which New World redactions of churchstateness have struggled to be realized. We seek to underline the persistent hybridity, mutuality, and yet incompleteness of Christian, colonial, and state power in the Americas.

"Old World" and preconquest forms of jurisdiction haunt the phenomenon of churchstateness: enabled in distinctive ways by the brutishness of the Atlantic passage and challenged by indigenous laws and visions of authority, the claims of church and state in the Americas, as elsewhere, rest on foundational violence.

Insisting on being surprised anew by the odd persistence and irregularity of the patterns and powers of churchstateness in the Americas, we seek to intervene in academic conversations in religious studies, legal studies, history, anthropology, political science, and indigenous studies. We use ekklesia to open an inquiry into the ways collectives in the Americas have been forged from an ill-defined yet powerful churchstateness composed of the interpenetrating and mutually constitutive forces of religion, law, and politics. Christian ideas and motivations have played a fundamental role in generating these collectives, the body of Christ and the body politic together working to constitute the people as chosen, celebrated, and accorded the right to exercise will.

Church and state are analytical markers or pivots around which cluster distinct but overlapping techniques of convening the people.[4] They name institutions and disciplinary conventions of converting human beings into self-conscious collectives capable of acting together. One might imagine—in the distinctive European American voice of political philosophy—that the first acts that generated the sense of being a collective might have arrived in public ceremonial form, "acting and speaking together," as Hannah Arendt put it—triumphant songs; recitations; choreographed gestures of hand, head, arm or leg; wearied pilgrimages to sanctified sites.[5] It would be difficult to specify whether these were religious or political, church or state. Who could say? They were both.

Judith Butler, building on Arendt, argues that "the people" continue to emerge through plural assembly that is performative and embodied. This corporeality, gathered together, Butler argues, can challenge "reigning notions of the political" precisely because of the willingness of people to exercise a "plural and performative right to appear."[6] For our purposes, the power of the people lies in its effectiveness as a metaphor of assembly that binds and excludes individuals and that makes and dissolves corporeality. Sometimes a challenge to the state, and sometimes required by the state, plural assembly is also embodied in the Christian obligation to congregate, together constituting the people.

Assemblies are characterized by mixed qualities of what we are provisionally calling churchness, stateness, and church-stateness. Ekklesia are, so to speak, convened under a transcendent sovereignty. As ekklesia, the people appear "surrounded by a numinous haze," gathered over a sensibility of foundation rendered perceptible in ritual and authorized in law.[7] As members of ekklesia, or groups with foundation authorized to act, individual persons are shaped into agents with transformative potential. Church and state are joined at the hip in the historical cultivation of many of the most obvious techniques of making such communities: the use of ritual and symbolic forms to transform masses of individuals into a body, the conversion of work and suffering into the civil terms of duty and virtue, the ceremonial assemblies of glory and acclamation that establish strata of rank and prestige, the activation of charity and caregiving, the fostering of distinct and overlapping subjectivities, and the economies of violent sacrifice through which abstract ideals like "the nation" and "the faithful" are made manifest in the flesh.

But just how are they joined at the hip? The familiar phrase, church and state, marks a codependence or symbiosis only poorly understood, perhaps particularly in its present uses. As an opening sally perhaps one might provisionally propose, even while insisting on the problems caused by such a separation of function, that churches rely on states for definition, protection, infrastructure, recognition, and financial or legal rights, while states take from the church the aesthetics of monumentality and permanence, the solemnity of legal-ritual formalities to grant legitimacy to governance and the transmission of power, and the time-weathered aura of tradition. In so doing, states gain and communicate a past and are made to appear as a natural inheritance accrued in sediments of time, history, territory, and blood.

Continuing with this rough profile, one might then note that at specific historical junctures, church and state collapse into each other to become virtual isomorphs. This course has been not infrequently recommended by classical political theorists, from positions as different as those presented in Rousseau's fusion called "civil religion" and Hobbes's politicoreligious Leviathan. Here one could name manifold historical examples, stretching the notion of church beyond its Christian referents: imperial cults from Rome to Japan and divine kings from Oyo (in today's Nigeria) to Tenochtitlan, as well as other formations such as pre-Communist Tibet. The king's authority was staged as descended from heaven, the queen's touch deployed as the hand of God.

At other moments king and cleric drifted from the other's sphere, as rival and combatant. There is usually an implicit inevitability to this genre of the story: even a pope like Gregory II, attired as feudal lord with castle, land, and army, could never fully become an earthly sovereign and had to astutely leverage one king against another to thrive. Of these cycles of approximation and distance—but mostly told today with a telos of the ultimate separation of political and religious spheres—every student of church history can recite examples. Historians of religions, stocked with comparative examples from outside the West, wait ready with more. But even to recite these stories is to belie their interested presumptions, excluding as they do the messiness of religious and political life, giving too much to the voices of the powers that be, too much distinctness to entities only ever imagined as separate. Who experienced such tidy stories?

Theorists questioning the relation of church and state frequently work on a comparative Atlantic axis, in which the question of the "separation" of church and state in the United States is juxtaposed with political histories in Europe and Great Britain.[8] When naturalized, that is, when not recognized, this transatlantic juxtaposition can have the effect of converting a couple of parochial examples into a seemingly universally relevant historical juggernaut, as Emil Brunner would have had it. While clearly a conjunction that has profoundly shaped theories—and practices—of religion, politics, and secularity on both sides of the Atlantic, the twinning of church and state must also be investigated at a much more local scale, closer to the ground, through a consideration of the fuzziness of the borders and of the political wrangling that takes place in courts of law, via public discourse, and between bodies on land. Bringing together a local scale of analysis with a broader "statewide" and comparative approach is especially important for another necessary denaturalization of church and state, one that reveals how the sovereignty of colonial nation-states has been premised on labor-intensive rituals, laws, and acts of "legal violence," to take Walter Benjamin's phrase, often legitimated in the name of a Christian God.[9]

In other words, in many cases church and state conjures a mutually consolidated system of rule, a closed system of vertically integrated institutional power over a certain territory, whose long narrative we all know and understand only too well. It can be traced back to the Constantinian revolution and forward through to the emergence of the early modern nation-states of Europe, the fascist governments of the twentieth century, and the security states of the twenty-first. The texts of this narrative include Augustine, Rousseau, Hobbes, Kantorowicz, Gramsci, Schmitt, and Agamben as well as those of Bhabha, Fanon, and Said, postcolonial critics of the modern state and of its only too complicit partner, Christianity. Church and state in this reading are symbiotically joined twins, to a degree even made in each other's image. One completes or stands in for the other, supplying missing or fading powers as needed. In the "secularization" version of this way of thinking, the church declines in northern Europe when the state assumes the church's previous functions such as social welfare, marriage, and education. In countries like Syria, Egypt or Nigeria, conversely, the state is read as weakened because religious movements (which, insisting on troubling the power of the received story, we are naming "the church" even though these movements are not all Christian) have assumed powers previously granted to the state, such as the legitimate right to violence. For example, outside observers often express concern about the effects of Orthodox Jewish leaders on the state in Israel. The point is that the rise or fall of church or state is presented as always corollary to, or even a function of, the opposing movement of the other, as though in a zero-sum game or a controlled vacuum.

This book tells a different story. We see stateness and churchness as analytically distinct but as, in practice, also an interlocking series of documents, procedures, practices, discursive registers, buildings, uniforms, lawlike rules, sounds, and ways of seeing.[10] *Churchstateness* designates partly isomorphic patterns of materials, practices, and procedures that join only apparently discrete domains. Specific historical cases reveal distinct calibrations of hybrid churchstateness. Noah Shusterman, riffing on James Scott, used the phrase "seeing like a church" to describe how the revolutionary French regime replicated church actions in its regulation of holidays, the calendar, and the proper use of time.[11] States might likewise be understood to "see like a church" when legal courts begin to cast themselves as experts on religious authenticity.[12] State and religion became entwined, paradoxically, with liberal and secular reform—as transpired in Brazil in 1890, in India beginning in 1955, in the United States during the civil rights movement, or in South Africa after 1994. Moving in the other direction, the church might be seen to "see like a state" when it seeks to undercut what James Scott called *metis*, or local cunning, to universalize its own influence.[13] Yet such seeings also reproduce a distinction that this volume resists. As both a conceptual and a historical tangle, the rubric "churchstateness" points to a scrum of fictions about authorizing presence and foundations for intervention.

THE PEOPLE

The wide-angle frame has been helpful to track patterns of governance from the foundation of the sacred king to, in the seventeenth and eighteenth centuries, a foundation from which to build the sacred people. While some have pushed the time frame earlier,[14] the more familiar tale perhaps is that the new assemblage called the people was born between the time of Rousseau's *Social Contract* (1760) and the end of the "long" Age of Revolution, extending to around 1840. In the context of the American Revolution, for example, the people starred equally in pamphlets by conservative writers like Edmund Burke and revolutionaries like Thomas Paine. The king was dead as inheritor and benefactor who, through his bodily person, anchored the power of right. The new foundation, whether of law, contract, or social bond, was the more abstract people.

The people in a modern sense, then, came into being in the eighteenth century through discourses, most prominently in claims of (putatively) universal human rights that appear in England's Charter, the United States' Bill of Rights, France's Revolutionary Constitution, Poland's May 3 Constitution of 1791, Haiti's revolution from 1791 to its 1804 Declaration of Independence, and declarations of independence in formerly Spanish America from 1811 (Venezuela) to 1831 (Colombia), to name only a few. Claims to authority predicated on divine providence from beyond the terrestrial hum continued in force, not least in antislavery documents and in slave rebellions from Nat Turner's in the United States (1831) to the largest Brazilian slave rebellion, carried out mostly by Muslim Hausa in Bahia (1835). And the treaties signed between Indigenous nations and the British and Americans depended on sacralized authority on both sides of the agreements. Despite the religious ideals invoked during this "long" Age of Revolution, the power of providential claims of God-given rights hung on the degree to which they were yoked to an enforcing state and national body of "citizens." This latter term signals how the people were always, in practice if not in ideal, distinguished from people, the faceless multitude in the distance beyond recognized authenticity or legal right.

Nothing in this is very original, at least not among philosophers of political theology who have given the closest scrutiny to the story of the transfer of foundational power from the king to the people. Scholars from Carl Schmitt and Ernst Kantorowicz to Michel Foucault, Giorgio Agamben, Eric Santner, and Claude Lefort have all observed that the entity called the people is possessed of key contradictions. Lefort, for example, pointed out the contradiction between "the people" as the proletariat versus "the people" as the nation and the way that "the people," in the moment of reifying a social bond simultaneously abstracts it into "a plurality of atoms," a statistic.[15] The Anglo tradition's emphasis on the term's reference to specific individuals and their rights stands in some contrast to the French tilt toward collectivist formulations of the people, or the nineteenth-century German idealization of *Volk*. Even more fundamental is the fracture between inclusion and exclusion, between democratic extension and its specified limit. *The* people are surrounded by *other* people. In that sense, the people is an ideal that is also a boundary splitting center from periphery; it indexes at once a given citizenry and an encompassing sea of only potential people, and non-people who wait amassed beyond a given frontier—selectively given the freedom to enter, or banned altogether.[16] These latter are invalid, illegitimate, juridically disempowered noncitizens, sometimes thought of as subjects, most often distinguished by their gender, race, class, or religion.[17] They are simply not, as Hegel had it, "in history." Thinkers including Schmitt, Hacking, and Santner examined the biopolitical management of the bifurcations of People/people as a social and political form.

These thinkers also thought they saw a historical process through which the gap between the king's two bodies, between his flesh-and-blood form and his immortal, sovereign one, as Kantorowicz detailed—and the enormous labor expended on making those bodies cohere—was transferred to a new body in a kind of ontological rupture. The new rupture was between people and the people, calling forth efforts to bridge and justify the chasm separating actual human bodies from the social and even transcendent ideal of the people. To this end, Agamben outlined a dual genealogy that juxtaposed terms like "demos"— the citizens—in contradistinction to bare-life urbs and plebs, the multitude, the *massa*, the *ochlos*.[18] Even more, he described how religion offers one way that people are converted into the people, via the ekklesia, bodies joined in liturgies of glorious acclamation.[19]

Political theologians have taken great care in conceptualizing the shift from one form of gap to another. Still, to play the gnat in the ears of giants for a moment, the on-the-ground work of discerning, archiving, and analyzing *processes* of this great shift from the problematic of the king, or queen, to that of the people, has been taken up with less urgency. Insofar as that processual work has been undertaken, moreover, it yields suggestive if opaque leads. When Santner asserts that the king's two bodies "*morph* into" the person-office opposition, or "it [a structural interregnum or void] *passed* from the court and into the heart of the People," or that juridical speech "*comes to replace*" liturgical speech as the locus of magic, new questions are posed.[20] How might we move closer to, or even explore the inner recesses of, these transitional verbs and phrases like "morph, "pass into," or "come to replace" in order to better view their cogs and tunings, their stutters and gaps? They are anything but self-evident; they are certainly not completed.

THE AMERICAS

Any guise of self-evidence or the obvious in the frame of church and state rests in the fact that the thrust of the political-theological story, at least from the vantage point of the Americas, has been mostly too captive to Europe.[21] Perhaps we could say with only a little exaggeration that the Americas, when they appear in works of contemporary political theology, serve mostly as utopic horizon in the vein of Locke's famous phrase "In the beginning, all the world was America," with but little thereafter on the consequences of the Americas' colonial interpellation *as* a place imagined to mimic Europe's "beginning."[22] So, for example, Locke's philosophical "New World" utopia masks his own part in the dispossession of Indigenous nations and in instituting slavery in the Americas as legal right.[23] Almost two centuries later, Tocqueville's descriptions are still comically romantic: "In America, the principle of the sovereignty of the people is not either barren or concealed, as it is with some other nations; it is recognised by the customs and proclaimed by laws; it spreads freely, and arrives without impediment at its most remote consequences."[24] In Tocqueville's America the air is wholesome and the forests primeval. Slavery appears but mostly painted with a light brush and pastel hue, even in chapter 5, "How Democracy Affects the Relations of Master and Servants." And Tocqueville was hardly alone in looking past slavery while contemplating "the people."

Hegel too utterly effaced *actual* slaves and their revolution in Saint-Domingue / Haiti from his famous passage on the dialectic of the master and the slave in *Phenomenology of Spirit*, as Susan Buck-Morss shows.[25] This was so even though he worked on the passage from 1803 to 1805 in Jena, every day reading the newspaper, calling it his "morning prayer."[26] The news in his morning prayers covered the revolution in France's most prosperous colony, the loss of some fifty thousand of Napoleon's troops, and Haiti's declaration of independence by a former slave, Jean-Jacques Dessalines, in 1804. Surely Buck-Morss is correct, then, to say that Hegel configured the master-slave dialectic (and probably also his idea of *Volksgeist*, the "spirit of the people" that moves toward unity with the state through religion), in part through a reading of the Americas that insistently misrecognized it as absent of any use beyond "echo of the Old World" or "land of the future."[27] In particular, the United States' lack of religious unity—the "acme of absurdity"—and its lack of genuine stateness seemed to him to go hand in hand.[28]

In Tocqueville and Hegel's versions of primitivism, like many others, the Americas remained marginal, even the exception that proved the rule, to the dominant "church and state" narrative.[29] The assumption seemed to be that the separations of church and state that characterize the modern democracies of the New World are wholly distinct from the pattern of the Old World, a pattern characterized by the persistence of state churches—even if they mostly now serve the role of "heritage" or national patrimony—and secularized and embedded in the institutions of the contemporary welfare state. In popular discourse at home and abroad, and even in some scholarly accounts, religion and politics in the Americas are cast as somehow free, and free of each other, each retaining its particular charisma, but without mutual interpenetration.[30]

The New World stories we tell here challenge the standard narratives of church and state in unexpected ways. Each essay in the volume complicates the stories of church-state assemblages, seeing in the settler states of North and South America messy alternative patterns of conjoined religious and political power, patterns resulting from the undertow produced by other gods and other fantasies of sovereignty.[31] These often highly specific local and persistently material challenges have led to an always incomplete and continuously contested attempt at the realization of churchstateness. The incomplete realization of each, the shifting borders of the separation, and the episodic conjoining of church and state, took new forms in both theory and practice. One was translated into the other. Bruno Latour used "translation" to describe how the qualities of one entity are at once projected into and taken up by a second entity. Thus politics and science become bundled as once-discrete projects like *waging war* and *slowing down neutrons* are yoked; or rather, it turns out that politics and science were never discrete to begin with.[32] We argue for revisiting "church and state" in a similar key, paying close attention to their translation in and through the Americas.

"THE PEOPLE" IN THE AMERICAS

Notwithstanding Walter Benjamin's gesture toward the problem of the frontier in the institution of sovereign power, the radically different spaces of the Americas have too seldom registered in political theology.[33] The transfer of sovereign power from the king to the people unfolded differently, and more unevenly, in the Americas than in Europe, in part because the king was only occasionally or virtually present and rarely real. The difference is significant because, at the same time as the mapping of a frontier is crucial to the project of establishing the people at the metropolitan center, rival sovereignties *already* existed in the Americas. The Americas were "the frontier" for European metropolitans, but territories in the Americas also had their own centers and peripheries that set the geographic and anthropological edge and end of stateness. Colonial proclamations of law and state power were often shallow and ever more difficult to enforce the further from the capital city they ranged. As Timothy Mitchell described, the nation-state as an "almost transcendental entity" came into being, in part, through the making of frontiers, which themselves can be broken down into practices and processes like "barbed-wire fencing, passports, immigration laws, inspections, currency control," not to mention through classifications exercised in thought and speech.[34] At the frontier, rival sovereignties contravened and unsettled the idea of the European state as the sole or primary horizon of affiliation or law. The rule of law had been invented but was always left unrealized.[35] "A key feature of the colonial world," wrote Thomas Blom Hansen and Finn Stepputat, "was that different kinds and registers of sovereignty coexisted and overlapped."[36]

Most obvious among rival polities to nation-states are Indigenous nations and alliances, the subject of Klassen's essay,
which have expressed a continuing and competing sovereignty
across both continents. There were also temporarily existing
sovereignties of runaway slaves established within colonies,
known in Brazil as *quilombos*. The most famous of these, Palmares, had its own king, lands, and army and endured for most
of the seventeenth century. When it was finally conquered by
the Portuguese colonial state, they beheaded Palmares's king
and paraded his head in the capital on a pike, not unlike the fate
of Nat Turner's head in the United States. It was a grim acknowledgment of a bona fide rival sovereign, or at least a potential
one, in need of a carefully staged public death. Still another form
of polity gathered and governed "outside the state" was that of
dissident religious communities, often including slaves or ex-
slaves, sometimes joining forces with Indigenous or marginal-
ized mixed-race groups—mestizos, caboclos, métis—who insti-
tuted their own structures of law and government. Most famous
of these in Brazil was the town of Canudos in the 1890s, about
which Johnson writes in this volume. The prophet of Canudos
was also beheaded, the resulting trophy sent to coastal cities for
patriotic huzzahs gathered to ritualize republican state power.
The Métis politician Louis Riel, an activist and a mystic, led both
"legitimate" Canadian governments and Métis/Indigenous rebellions in the prairies. His eventual refusal to accept Canadian
sovereignty in the terms on which Anglo-Protestants insisted
led to his execution at the hands of the state, in 1885.[37] Rival sovereignties and legal orders can be found throughout US history,
including the robust nations of Indian country, occasional slave
polities, homegrown religiopolitical orders such as the Mormon
Church, as well as always myriad new and persistent separatist
communities resistant to assimilation to dominant social, political, and cultural norms.[38]

The seeming portability of church and state as categories of
analysis that can be applied to realms that have neither Chris-

tians nor singularly authoritative jurisdictions should give pause to theorists of religion and secularity who are attentive to colonial histories. Theorist of law and empire Lauren Benton's concept of "multijurisdictional legal orders" is particularly helpful for tacking between the theoretical and the local in a critical analysis of churchstateness. Benton argues that contests over jurisdiction were rooted in differing foundations for law and political collectivity, often based in diverse visions of transcendence: "We perceive this clearly in territories of colonial and imperial expansion, where culturally and religiously different peoples employed legal strategies that exploited (and further complicated) unresolved jurisdictional tensions, particularly those between secular and religious authorities."[39] As legal scholar John Borrows shows, churchstateness, in its broadest sense as we use it here, was just one version of how jurisdiction could and should work, albeit a very powerful approach to the blending of legal, Christian, and ritual practice.[40]

In the Americas, then, diverse rival social orders and polities existed prior to colonial states, and even alongside colonial states on their frontiers. The Americas forced European settler regimes to grapple with different and additional challenges of governance than those they faced at home. The problem was not just the constitution of the people out of the decapitated corpse—or the rejected, still-breathing body—of the sovereign and his kingdom, but rather the effort at the deliberate *unmaking* of the orders in the already-existing societies of the Americas. Only then would settlers gain the capacity of forging and performing sovereign power by, as Benjamin posited, pressing law into unmarked frontiers. At the borders, the settler state would convert the inhabitants or—applying the right to violence with impunity—replace them with proper subjects, ones with socially informed bodies able to incorporate and reproduce stateness.[41] The risk was that "religious" sovereignties would remain active and in force even when spatially encompassed by stateness, which was precisely what transpired at Canudos in Brazil (as Johnson's essay details), on Indigenous lands that made treaty with the Canadian Crown (as Klassen describes), and in death penalty jury rooms in the United States (as Sullivan's essay explains).

What was required was not just the technology of converting humans into the people, then, but the inverse too, the technologies of *unmaking* extant, parallel, and rival sovereignties. But how to best achieve this unmaking—via which discursive and material techniques and procedures? Agamben famously described how power is made and maintained by separating and expelling a part of its own social body, the *homo sacer* who demonstrates the sovereign exception as the right to kill not as sacrifice but in and for power itself. In the cases presented here, sovereignty was and is constituted by discovering and naming completely discrete Others, recognized and acknowledged as genuine rival ekklesia, paradoxically, through the violence, even total war, waged against them. These previously sovereign social orders and humans resident to the Americas were then often incorporated into colonial or modern states as victims or corpses, converted and initiated into national heritage and public memory—a new piling of foundation—exactly through their ceremonial destruction.

THE ESSAYS

The goal here is not to argue that resistance and disruption by the forms of hybrid churchstateness found in the Americas have been or are a more reliable source of justice. Instead, using a method that combines theory with close-range examples, we offer three inquiries in church and state that reveal how religious and political authorities are coconstituted both in their separation and in their union. Our set of topics is close to the ground, with an ear out for the messy peculiar vernaculars of these places, seeking to bring into relief their strange and stubborn irregularities. With chapters on Brazil, Canada, and the

United States, the book takes up the topic of church and state, testing its resilience in relation to specific national histories and locations in the Americas.

Through the engagement with three sites of particularity in the Americas, we call attention to recurring themes that make these sites and stories worthy of comparison. Steady base notes sustain and connect otherwise dissonant chords and runs. First and most important is the unfinished question of the Americas, who are *the people*? The question is specifically complicated by the American phenomenon of the rival sovereignties of Indigenous nations, and the precariously enslaved sovereignties of African descendants. Second, the question of the significance of ekklesia in the formation of the people is further destabilized by the notion of the frontier in the Americas, zones of inexistent or fragile states where dissident collective compositions often forged through rival versions of religious authority, including Christian ones, grew, thrived, and resisted. At the frontier, subaltern sovereignties continued to exert force even when they were absorbed into states, yielding vivid church-state transculturations.[42]

Third, all three of our essays engage the issue of violence as exercised by states in *unmaking* extant rival sovereignties. We consider the acts of sacrifice called upon in the making of states via the unmaking of other social collectives and affinities, as well as in the communicative nature of violence, as republics announced and defined themselves through spectacular destructive power and erasure. Fourth, all the cases here address the complex weave of recognition and rejection, that is, the ways "uncivil religion" gets converted, distorted, and incorporated into usable forms like "heritage" and "tradition." Fifth, we all signal the import of sensorial, material, informal religion in the sustaining of subaltern versions of churchstateness: spoken and performed scripture, song and soundscapes, and the engagement of objects with lively force, including Bibles, buildings, staffs, paper proclamations, pipes, rosary beads, bells, stones, clothes, clay, the paraphernalia of execution, weapons, and parts of dead bodies.

Johnson's essay, "The People and the Law of the Hound at Canudos," offers a new interpretation of the religiopolitical ekklesia known as Canudos, in Brazil, and their massacre in 1896–97. In this event, nearly thirty thousand peasants led by the Catholic prophet Antônio Conselheiro were annihilated by soldiers recently chartered in the founding of the republic in 1890. The essay looks closely at the settlement's actual practices as they constituted peasants as the people, even as it interrogates republican techniques and technologies for unmaking them.

The prophet, Antônio Conselheiro, had advocated for the restoration of church power over the state, especially in relation to immediate concerns of the control of cemetery grounds, burial rites, and marriage, which had abruptly been shifted to state control. In poetry they left behind at the site, the rebels decried this new state, the republic and its regime, as "the law of the hound." Their Catholicism included few official rites or masses but many material exchanges with saints, frequent visits with the spirits of the dead, a rich sonics, and abundant amulets and images. The lowly enthusiasts represented ekklesia in its popular form as it had been constituted over three previous centuries, but in 1896 this rich religious ensemble was dismissed as an erratic and uncontrollable "crowd" and crushed by the state in alliance with a newly ascendant version of the church.

In the events at Canudos and thereafter, church and state collaborated to forge the new rules of authoritative mediation that would undergird the republic. Law and land, like ritual benefits related to baptism, marriage, death, and burial, would thereafter be administered through the proper state channels rather than through the diffuse and, so to speak, crowded practices of churchness. In its newly purified edition, the official Roman Catholic Church gained for the first time a durable institutional profile. It could be and was variously joined to the Brazilian state, likewise a new invention just prior to the turn of the twentieth century. The shift from churchness as broker of interpersonal contracts to the church as broker of institutional and international power allowed its cooption toward strong-arm nationalist aims between 1930 and the Second World War but also gave it leverage as the key site of institutional resistance thereafter.[43]

Too many accounts of Brazilian history cast churchstateness in the mold of the European march toward the separation of spheres, to wit: "Brazil offered a classic case of church and state intertwined in colonial society. . . . Separation of church and state became effective with separation from Portugal (1889) and the beginning of the Republic (1890)."[44] Johnson's essay argues the opposite. Church and state were institutionally poorly defined and mostly absent of conflict during most of Brazil's history.[45] In fact "the Church" only became significant after the founding of the republic in 1890. This was achieved through campaigns of purification that pressed the church into existence as a religiopolitical institution distinct from the diffuse range of popular practices expressed at Canudos. Finally, the essay explores how, in spite of the Canudos dissidents' refusal to submit to the dictates of the newborn republic, they were ultimately pulled into its history, heritage, and foundation against their will, through their destruction and posthumous redemption.

In "Spiritual Jurisdictions: Treaty People and the Queen of Canada," Pamela Klassen argues that jurisdiction—quite literally, "saying the law"—offers a range of scales for addressing the messy vernaculars of churchstateness. She argues that convictions about the separation of church and state have helped settler-colonial nations, including fiercely republican ones, to obscure the fragility of their claims to sovereignty in the name of both Christianity and the Crown. Klassen's chapter analyzes how new ekklesia came into being through local and national practices that emerged as Indigenous nations responded to and resisted becoming "possessions" of colonial British America. Indigenous responses to colonial power in Canada have long called attention to the "and" in church and state—that is, to their twinned power. In Canada, church and state allied in the creation of the 1876 "Indian Act," a set of laws that consolidated more than one hundred years of colonial regulation and classification of "Indian subjects." Even earlier, the Royal Proclamation of 1763 acknowledged that Indigenous nations had title to their lands. This means that a proclamation issued by King George III, a man who mediated the authority of both head of state and head of the church (and who still provides a foremost exemplar of tyranny in the United States), undergirds all treaty relations between Indigenous nations and the Canadian government.[46] The Royal Proclamation continues to be heralded as the underlying legal document with which all subsequent Canadian laws related to Indigenous peoples must accord.[47] Even today, Indigenous nations continue their tradition of putting the "God" in government, by insisting that their negotiations are with the Crown: the Queen and her representative in Canada, the Governor General.

Canada rarely merits a mention in theories of secularity or of church-state relations, but its status as a modern polity that both willingly retains a monarch as the head of state and recognizes at least the limited sovereignty of Indigenous peoples makes it an important example to think with. In Anglophone contexts, the more common contrast when thinking of church and state is between the "established church" of Great Britain, where the Church of England has privileged political status, and that of the "disestablished" religions of the United States of America, where religion supposedly has no bearing on one's eligibility for elected office. Bringing Canada into the picture introduces an alternative approach to churchstateness that represents neither Christian establishment nor a (supposedly) strict separation of the two. In the Canadian case, "multiculturalism" is legally mandated, and few would publicly assert that Canada is a "Christian nation." Nevertheless, Christian symbols and narratives continue to shape the "heritage" of even the most committedly secular of polities, as the crucifix hanging in the National Assembly of Quebec attests. And while the Queen is far away in both miles and memories for many Canadians, she remains etched onto the money and into the structures of governance.

During the long process by which European colonizers sought to name and claim the Americas through the divinely mandated "doctrine of discovery," Indigenous peoples worked with their own understandings of spiritual jurisdiction, which led them to agree to enter into treaty relations with the new arrivals to their continents, both claiming their sovereignty and sharing their land. In both Canada and the United States, colonial ideas about who could rightfully claim to own the land and to belong to the land were premised on origin myths written in the Christian Bible, declared by the pope and refined by early modern political theorists.[48] Whether involving the Edenic paradise in Genesis or the states of nature underwriting the social contracts of Hobbes and Locke, claiming the land required stories and rituals of possession.[49] Indigenous nations have also substantiated their claims of ownership and belonging through stories and rituals, which despite more than a century of Canadian attempts to ignore or deny them, persist as ways of claiming the land through spiritual jurisdiction.

Between the Royal Proclamation of 1763 and the current Canadian government's stated openness to "Nation-to-Nation" relations lies a complicated tangle of multijurisdictional church-stateness in relation to Indigenous nations and people. Considering the question of church and state with attention to Indigenous protocols and power turns the Atlantic axis askew in another direction, by showing that the church and the state were not the only assemblies through which spiritual jurisdiction was imagined or enacted. In Canada and the United States, treaties with Indigenous nations depended on political negotiations that proceeded according to specific Indigenous ritual protocols; they were relationships realized through rituals conducted across visions of Indigenous and Christian spiritual legitimation. Both in the past and the present, the sovereignty of colonial nation-states in the Americas has depended on the vexed relationship between church and state, not only as ideas in which power is housed but also as rituals, protocols, and material possessions through which authority flows. If treaties made new peoples, they also initiated obligations to regularly reconsider what the relationships embedded in treaties mean for both Indigenous and Canadian sovereignty. Treaties are, in part, ritualized claims to jurisdiction in which bodies or land became infused both with what we are calling churchstateness and with Indigenous forms of spiritualized sovereignty through the memorial properties of texts, beads, and metal.

Winnifred Sullivan's essay, "Banning Bibles: Death-Qualifying a Jury," makes visible the ways in which ekklesia in the United States are never constituted by the separation of church and state but are instead characterized by an unstable mixture of political, economic, and religious motives and imaginative resources, an informal Christendom that has only infrequently been safely institutionally consolidated in entities properly denoted as a church or a state. Taking the increased effort to ban Bibles and scriptural references from death penalty courtrooms and jury rooms as a starting place, her essay considers the political theological pressure thereby placed on the churchstateness of the jury that decides between life and death.

Comparing separation of church and state in the United States and Europe, comparative legal historian James Whitman has argued that a key difference is in the US failure to ban religion from public discourse. He takes as an exemplary case the quotation of the Bible in the US capital courtroom. For Whitman the Bible in a courtroom is matter out of place. Sullivan's essay argues that this modernist iconoclasm, of a piece with a more extensive effort to rationalize and secularize the jury's task, distracts our attention from the ongoing work that do-it-yourself religion plays in the United States. Bibles and other scriptures are not symbols of a stable and dogmatic church authority, as critics would have it, but sites of vernacular philosophizing and the continuous creation of new ekklesia. What so disturbs Whitman and others, the use of biblical analogies in closing arguments in capital cases in the United States or the introduction of biblical language into the jury room, cannot be handled by a better separation of church and state in the United States. They seem to misunderstand religion in the United States as something that could be disestablished if only the will were there. It is in fact much more intractable than that. There is no "there" there to be separated. There is rather a shadowy shapeshifting churchness taken from the flotsam and jetsam of religious life washed up on the US shore, ever adaptable to sustain national projects or to resist them. Controlling American religion through banning Bibles is very much like whack-a-mole. As Eric Santner says, the decapitation of the king resulted in the inability to secure the body of the people.[50] It also resulted in an inability to secure the body of the church.

The death penalty has had wide public support in the United States, across religious communities and outside them. The death penalty persists in the United States notwithstanding widespread decline in other parts of the world. David Garland accounts for US exceptionalism in this area as being the result of a distinctive history and form of democratic politics and cultural heritage characterized by lack of strong state formation, preference for individualism and local control, high levels of interpersonal violence, the racial logic of slavery, and the politics of law-and-order populism. He gestures only indirectly to US religious exceptionalism in his account. Yet, as Sullivan shows, post-*Furman* reform of its administration, focusing as it does on individuation of the jury's decision, withdrawing formal legal and religious guidance from the jurors, demands of them, as representatives of the people, a decision as to whether to expel the defendant permanently from the ekklesia. Here, in the holy of holies, arguably at the dark center of US exceptionalism, required to make a moral decision for which each juror is asked to take entire personal responsibility, the death penalty jury in the penalty phase can be seen to, in effect, be abandoned by the state and the church, forced to constitute a temporary tiny churchstate for the purposes only of the case before them, the result dependent on the accidental psychological, religious, and experiential biographies of twelve persons. The postapocalyptic bleakness of this place, penetrated with little light, by design, even at a time in which actual executions are rapidly declining, continues to do the work of constituting the people. The predicament of the American jury in the penalty phase reveals the paradoxically empty and lawless place at the heart of popular sovereignty / free religion, a place of irreducible surplus and entanglement—and suffering.

By framing our three inquiries in church and state with the concept of ekklesia, we are not suggesting that this term somehow escapes a peculiarly Christian historicity, that is, a sense of the past and its uses for the present. Neither church nor state is a neutral term of empirical description that is universally applicable to all forms of human convening. But on their own and joined as ekklesia, they continue to carry with them a power that is embedded in the land and the people of the Americas.

NOTES

1. "Editorial," *Journal of Church and State* 1, no. 1 (1959): 2.

2. While we each specialize in the study of parts of the Americas, we regard our efforts as an invitation to dialogue with those studying other parts of the world, viewing our angle on the subject not as exclusive to the Americas, but as suggestive of approaches that might prove fruitful to rethink the great subject both in the Americas and elsewhere.

3. Jean-Luc Nancy, "Church, State, Resistance," in *Political Theologies: Public Religions in a Post-Secular World*, ed. Hent de Vries and Lawrence Eugene Sullivan (New York: Fordham University Press, 2006), 106.

4. "Church" and "State" each opens out to a broad range of phenomena. "State" may refer to "pre, para- and post-political" forms and practices of government variously permeated by religion, to take Hent de Vries' phrase. The same is true of "Church," which may refer to pre-, para- and post-religious formations, their management by the legal, and their infiltration by the political. Hent de Vries, Introduction to *Political Theologies: Public Religions in a Post-Secular World*, ed. Hent de Vries and Lawrence Eugene Sullivan (New York: Fordham University Press, 2006), 1–88.

5. Hannah Arendt, *The Human Condition*, 2nd ed. (Chicago: University of Chicago Press, 2013), 198, 202.

6. Judith Butler, *Notes Toward a Performative Theory of Assembly* (Cambridge, MA: Harvard University Press, 2015), 11.

7. The phrase is Margaret Canovan's, from "The People," in *The Oxford Handbook of Political Theory*, ed. John S. Dryzek, Bonnie Honig, and Anne Phillips (New York: Oxford University Press, 2008), 357.

8. See, e.g., James Whitman, "Separating Church and State: The Atlantic Divide," *Historical Reflections* 34, no. 3 (2008): 86–104. In the United States it is not only theorists who do this. Separationism is deeply embedded in a vernacular political discourse that sees European and British ways of churchstateness as deeply alien.

9. Walter Benjamin, "Critique of Violence," in *Reflections: Essays, Aphorisms, Autobiographical Writings*, trans. Edmund Jephcott (New York: Schocken Books, 1986), 280.

10. As Timothy Mitchell writes, "The state should be addressed as an effect of detailed processes of spatial organization, temporal arrangement, functional specification, and supervision and surveillance." Timothy Mitchell, "The Limits of the State: Beyond Statist Approaches and Their Critics," *American Political Science Review* 85, no. 1 (1991): 95. Churchness can similarly be seen as an effect of processes and practices, and *churchstateness* as their overlap, cross-referencing, replication, and patterns of exchange and isomorphism.

11. Noah Shusterman, *Religion and the Politics of Time* (Washington, DC: Catholic University of America Press, 2010). See also

John Durham Peters, "Calendar, Clock, Tower," in *Deus in Machina: Religion, Technology, and the Things in Between*, ed. Jeremy Stolow (New York: Fordham University Press, 2012), 25–42. By contrast, the church has, at times, tried not to see like a state, endorsing the devotion to saints and developing the "inculturated mass" with its Afro-Brazilian drumming, exchange, and style. See John Burdick, *Blessed Anastácia: Women, Race and Popular Christianity in Brazil* (New York: Routledge, 1998). Here also consider the ways church-stateness becomes a hybrid that is hidden, and hegemonic, by being renamed as "civilization." As Charles Taylor writes, this thing, "civilization," entailed a state, law and order, and a regime of internal discipline made of Christian morals, work ethic, and self-control. Charles Taylor, *A Secular Age* (Cambridge, MA: Harvard University Press, 2007), 394.

12. See, among others, Winnifred Fallers Sullivan, *Paying the Words Extra: Religious Discourse in the Supreme Court of the United States* (Cambridge, MA: Harvard University Press, 1995); Winnifred Fallers Sullivan, *The Impossibility of Religious Freedom* (Princeton, NJ: Princeton University Press, 2005); Partha Chatterjee, *The Politics of the Governed* (New York: Columbia University Press, 2006).

13. James Scott, *Seeing Like a State: How Certain Schemes to Improve the Human Condition Have Failed* (New Haven, CT: Yale University Press, 1998).

14. For example, Philip S. Gorski pushes the impetus toward nationalism and a self-conscious sensibility of being "a people" back to the Calvinism of the 1550s and the kinds of disciplinary order it instilled, manifesting in social welfare policies, efficient sociopolitical bureaucracies, and many other features of successful states. Philip S. Gorski, *The Disciplinary Revolution: Calvinism and the Rise of the State in Early Modern Europe* (Chicago: University of Chicago Press, 2003). See also Lorna Jane Abray, *The People's Reformation: Magistrates, Clergy, and Commons in Strasbourg, 1500–1598* (Ithaca, NY: Cornell University Press, 1985). Earlier formations could also be posited. Already in the fifteenth century, by the end of the Hundred Years' War, France and England are such formations. One

might cite the Tudor consolidation of the British state or Joan of Arc dying to preserve France for the French.

15. Claude Lefort, "The Permanence of the Theologico-Political?," in *Political Theologies: Public Religions in a Post-Secular World*, ed. Hent de Vries and Lawrence Eugene Sullivan (New York: Fordham University Press, 2006), 161, 167.

16. With rare exceptions—the United Nations People's Assembly perhaps offers a cosmopolitan limit case for the conceptualization of the people as a fully global and inclusive entity. Canovan, "The People," 354. The neologism the Anthropocene also makes such a gesture, in a more negative vein.

17. Mahmood Mamdani, *Citizen and Subject: Contemporary Africa and the Legacy of Late Colonialism* (Princeton, NJ: Princeton University Press, 1996).

18. Giorgio Agamben, *The Kingdom and the Glory: For a Theological Genealogy of Economy and Government*, trans. Lorenzo Chiesa (Stanford, CA: Stanford University Press, 2011), 174–75. The citizen's body presents another bifurcation, since on the one hand it enjoys rights and privileges, while on the other hand it may abruptly "disappear" into torture camps and other forms of indefinite incarceration. This has been particularly in evidence since 9/11. See Thomas Blom Hansen and Finn Stepputat, "Sovereignty Revisited," *Annual Review of Anthropology* 35, no. 1 (2006): 295–330. Malik W. Ghachem pointed to the disjuncture between the slave's two bodies as articulated in James Madison's *Federalist Papers* No. 54, consisting of a moral body liable before the law, and a body as property that could be bought and sold. Malick W. Ghachem, "The Slave's Two Bodies: The Life of an American Legal Fiction," *William and Mary Quarterly*, 3rd series, 60, no. 4 (2003): 809–42.

19. Agamben, *The Kingdom and the Glory*, 169–74.

20. Eric Santner, *The Royal Remains: The People's Two Bodies and the Endgames of Sovereignty* (Chicago: University of Chicago Press, 2011), 45, 160, 36. Michel Foucault details similar transformations. See Michel Foucault, *Wrong-Doing, Truth-Telling: The Function of Avowal in Justice*, ed. Fabienne Brion and Bernard Harcourt, trans.

Stephen Sawyer (Chicago: University of Chicago Press, 2014); Michel Foucault, *Security, Territory, Population: Lectures at the College de France, 1977–78*, ed. Arnold Davidson, trans. Graham Burchell (London: Palgrave Macmillan, 2009).

21. With important exceptions—such as the recent work of Paul Kahn and Roberto Blancarte—or, in an older US Cold War context, of Reinhold Niebuhr, John Courtney Murray and Leo Strauss, among others. See, e.g., Paul Kahn, *Political Theology: Four New Chapters on the Concept of Sovereignty* (New York: Columbia University Press, 2012); Reinhold Niebuhr, *Moral Man and Immoral Society: A Study in Ethics and Politics* (New York: Scribner, 1932); Reinhold Niebuhr, *The Irony of American History* (New York: Scribner, 1952); and John Courtney Murray, *We Hold These Truths: Catholic Reflections on the American Proposition* (New York: Sheed and Ward, 1960). One could also cite such religiopolitical works as Susan B. Anthony, *The Woman's Bible*; Jane Addams, *Twenty Years at Hull House*; Martin Luther King, "The Letter from the Birmingham Jail"; *The Autobiography of Malcolm X*; Thomas Merton, *Contemplation in a World of Action*; Francis Schaeffer, *How Should We Then Live? The Rise and Decline of Western Thought and Culture*; and Dee Brown, *Bury My Heart at Wounded Knee*. There have been a number of efforts since the early republic and the work of Justice Story to describe the religiopolitical fusion that is American disestablished religion. One notable example is Will Herberg, *Protestant, Catholic, Jew: An Essay in American Religious Sociology* (Chicago: University of Chicago Press, 1955).

22. John Locke, *Second Treatise of Government*, 1689, IV: §49. The line is invoked in Giorgio Agamben, *Homo Sacer: Sovereign Power and Bare Life*, trans. Daniel Heller-Roazen (Stanford, CA: Stanford University Press, 1998), 36.

23. In the service of Lord Ashley, Locke drafted the constitution of the Lords Proprietors of the Carolinas and profited by being a stakeholder in the Royal Africa Company and the Bahamas Adventurers. See James Farr, "Locke, Natural Law, and New World Slavery," *Political Theory* 36, no. 4 (2008): 495–522; and William Uzgalis,

"'An Inconsistency Not to Be Excused': On Locke and Racism," in *Philosophers on Race: Critical Essays*, ed. Julie Ward and Tommy Lott (Oxford: Blackwell, 2002), 81–100. Locke also supported the hybrid practices of Christian mission and land speculation in the twin pursuit of dispossessing Indigenous peoples of their territory. See Jack Turner, "John Locke, Christian Mission, and Colonial America," *Modern Intellectual History* 8, no. 2 (2011): 267–97.

24. Alexis de Tocqueville, *Democracy in America*, vol. 1, trans. Henry Reeve (London: Longman and Roberts, 1862), 48.

25. Susan Buck-Morss, "Hegel and Haiti," *Critical Inquiry* 26, no. 4 (2000): 821–65.

26. Ibid., 844.

27. Georg Wilhelm Friedrich Hegel, *The Philosophy of History*, trans. John Sibree (London: Dover, 1956), 85–86.

28. Ibid., 85.

29. There is also a late modern America that makes a frequent appearance in political theology, namely that of Abu Ghraib and Guantánamo, the America of the "war on terror" and the state of exception. Perhaps these premodern and late modern depictions of the Americas are flipsides of the same coin; both express an alleged lack of history and serious political philosophy.

30. But the work of scholars such as Walter Mignolo, Nelson Maldonado-Torres, Jean O'Brien, Glen Coulthard, and others shows us that the work of "coloniality," both before and after revolution and independence, has been done by both church and state, nurtured by political philosophy, local histories, and religious imaginations. Walter Mignolo, *The Darker Side of the Renaissance: Literacy, Territoriality, and Colonization* (Ann Arbor: University of Michigan Press, 2003); Nelson Maldonado-Torres, *Against War: Views from the Underside of Modernity* (Durham, NC: Duke University Press, 2008); Jean M. O'Brien, *Firsting and Lasting: Writing Indians Out of Existence in New England* (Minneapolis: University of Minnesota Press, 2010); Glen Sean Coulthard, *Red Skin, White Masks: Rejecting the Colonial Politics of Recognition* (Minneapolis: University of Minnesota Press, 2014).

31. See, e.g., Pamela Klassen, "Fantasies of Sovereignty: Civic Secularism in Canada," *Critical Research on Religion* 3, no. 1 (2015): 41–56.

32. Bruno Latour, *Pandora's Hope: Essays on the Reality of Science Studies* (Cambridge, MA: Harvard University Press, 1999); see also Emily Martin, *Flexible Bodies: Tracking Immunity in American Culture from the Days of Polio to the Age of AIDS* (Boston: Beacon, 1994).

33. Benjamin, "Critique of Violence," 296. The frontier, the edge, is always at question in measuring the depth and extension of the state. Here, for example, is Gorski's definition of state power: "the capacity to defend and expand a sovereign territory and govern the human and natural resources within it." Gorski, *The Disciplinary Revolution*, 35.

34. Mitchell, "The Limits of the State," 94.

35. Keally McBride, *Mr. Mothercountry: The Man Who Made the Rule of Law* (Oxford: Oxford University Press, 2016).

36. Hansen and Stepputat, "Sovereignty Revisited," 297. See also Lauren Benton, *Law and Colonial Cultures: Legal Regimes in World History, 1400–1900* (New York: Cambridge University Press, 2002).

37. Jennifer Reid, *Louis Riel and the Creation of Modern Canada: Mythic Discourse and the Postcolonial State* (Albuquerque: University of New Mexico Press, 2008).

38. Robert Cover, "Nomos and Narrative." *Harvard Law Review* 97 (1983): 4–68.

39. Benton, *Law and Colonial Cultures*, 6.

40. John Borrows, *Recovering Canada: The Resurgence of Indigenous Law* (Toronto: University of Toronto Press, 2002). See also Justin Richland, "Hopi Tradition as Jurisdiction: On the Potentializing Limits of Hopi Tribal Sovereignty." *Law & Social Inquiry* 36 (2011): 201–234.

41. Benjamin, "Critique of Violence," 295. The phrase "socially informed body" is from Pierre Bourdieu, *Outline of a Theory of Practice*, trans. Richard Nice (Cambridge, MA: Cambridge University Press, 1977), 124. On sovereignty defined as "the ability to kill, punish and discipline with impunity," including in its post-

colonial insurgent forms, see Hansen and Stepputat, "Sovereignty Revisted," 296. Also see Max Weber's classic definition of the state: "a human community that (successfully) claims the monopoly of the legitimate use of physical force within a given territory." Max Weber, "Politics as a Vocation," in *From Max Weber*, translated and edited by Hans Gerth and C. Wright Mills (New York: Oxford University Press, 1946).

42. "Transculturation" is apposite here in part not least because of its American roots. The neologism first appeared in Fernando Ortiz's *Cuban Counterpoint: Tobacco and Sugar* (originally published 1940 as *Contrapunteo cubano del tabaco y del azúcar*). Transculturation nuanced "acculturation" by insisting that even cultural losses, and the responses to loss, continued to inform the experience of a new territory and generate new forms both among the colonized and the colonizers. Thus metropolitan modes of representation are continually transformed in contact zones of the periphery. Fernando Ortiz, *Cuban Counterpoint: Tobacco and Sugar*, trans. Harriett de Onís (Durham, NC: Duke University Press, 1995).

43. For example, to the state dictatorship of 1964–84. Brazil's council of bishops, first convened in 1952, was unusual compared with other South American councils, often co-opted or unsuccessful in resisting dictatorships, and became a key node of the global Catholic left. See Anthony Gill, *Rendering Unto Caesar: The Catholic Church and the State in Latin America* (Chicago: University of Chicago Press, 1998). On Chile, see William Cavanaugh, *Torture and Eucharist* (Oxford: Blackwell, 1998).

44. Edward Cleary, "The Brazilian Catholic Church and Church-State Relations: Nation-Building," *Journal of Church and State* 39, no. 2 (1997): 255.

45. With certain key exceptions, as in the episode called "The Religious Question" of 1882, when Emperor Dom Pedro II clashed with the church over the right of priests to also practice as Freemasons.

46. The Royal Proclamation was issued in the wake of the British victory over the French in the Seven Years' War.

47. Jim Aldridge, *Keeping Promises: The Royal Proclamation of*

1763, Aboriginal Rights, and Treaties in Canada (Montreal: McGill-Queen's University Press, 2015).

48. James (Sákéj) Youngblood Henderson, "The Context of the State of Nature," in *Reclaiming Indigenous Voice and Vision*, ed. Marie Battiste (Vancouver: University of British Columbia Press, 2000); James Tully, *Strange Multiplicity: Constitutionalism in an Age of Diversity* (Cambridge: Cambridge University Press, 1995).

49. J. Edward Chamberlin, *If This Is Your Land, Where Are Your Stories? Finding Common Ground* (New York: Random House, 2004); Thomas King, *The Truth about Stories: A Native Narrative* (Toronto: House of Anansi, 2003).

50. Santner, *Royal Remains*.

THE PEOPLE AND THE LAW OF THE HOUND AT CANUDOS

Paul Christopher Johnson

> Backed up by the law,
> Those evil ones abound,
> We keep the law of God,
> They keep the law of the *hound*!
>
> Text recovered in the ruins of Canudos[1]

In Brazil as elsewhere, many citizens now see the state as a fragile shell. The republic seems hollowed out; there is no "there" there. In September 2015 the lawyer and professor Janaína Paschoal submitted a motion to launch impeachment proceedings against Brazil's president, Dilma Rousseff. On April 4, 2016, in a video that went viral, she took the podium at a rally to describe the government in diabolical terms. "When we succeed at impeaching Dilma," she shouted into the microphone, "We will destroy the Republic of the Serpent!" Two weeks later Brazil's lower house in congress voted to begin impeachment proceedings against the president. Fifty-nine deputies prominently invoked God in the televised process of declaring their vote, including the (then) president of congress, Eduardo da Cunha. God was rolled

into verbal screeds against corruption, and not without justifi-
cation. The country was in economic turmoil, with many federal
and state employees long unpaid. Yet as one congressional dep-
uty after another found themselves accused of corruption and
bribery or were discovered to hold secret offshore bank accounts
or rely on illegal "box number two" (*caixa dois*) campaign funds,
the political and economic impasse mutated into a moral crisis
of trust.[2]

On the feast day of Santo Antonio, June 13, the Convent of
Saint Anthony in the center of Rio de Janeiro was filled to over-
flowing. Usually the faithful petition Saint Anthony for marriage, lasting love, and children. That year, said Cardinal Orani
Tempesta, "people's biggest worry is the question of their getting
paid at the end of the month. Obviously we ask for intercession
so the state will have jobs and be able to pay people."[3] The cardinal implied that even divine aid needs the state for its administration and distribution, while the state, for its part, needs some
transcendent guarantee. But if the congress that impeached the
president is itself packed with thieves, where is the solid body
around which justice settles and gathers force? What guarantees
the wages of those who work for the state? Where is stateness at
all and, given its elusiveness, how will the church help to broker
its benefits?

Fears that the republic was a fragile mirage caused concern
not least because in August the Olympics would begin, and
the bright lights of international media would be turned on
Rio. The former capital city required at least the look and infrastructure, the "metaphysical effect" of a republican state.[4] It
needed to pop on television screens with the sounds and col-
ors of national unity, security, tradition, and competence, with
foundation. Instead the state appeared febrile and thin, a trompe
l'oeil propped up by the army now called in to protect arriving
tourists on normal city streets. On the eve of the games, the
unfinished husks of apartments at the Olympic village and the
still-idle new metro line testified more to the obscurity than
the presence of stateness.

When the games were done, the political clouds massed and stacked again. On August 30, 2016, the yearlong felling of a regime was a fait accompli when the senate voted to confirm the president's dismissal. Dilma, criticized from the right as an atheist, even sought last-minute help from God, or at least the godly.[5] Yet, far from settling matters, the impeachment launched new debates and marches on the fate of democracy in Brazil and, tangentially, the place of religion and religious discourse in that future. The jurist Janaína Paschoal, who had helped to launch the charge, weighed in again as she summarized and sealed the case before the senate on the eve of the last vote: "It was God who made various people perceive, all at once, what was happening to our country, and who gave them courage to get up and do something about it."[6] Paschoal clarified that she was a not an evangelical but a spiritist: "I'm devoted to St. George, St. Michael the Archangel, and Iemanjá [the Yoruba and Afro-Brazilian goddess of the sea and maternity] . . . If I was a Pastor or a Mãe de Santo [priestess of Candomblé], would my request for impeachment be less legitimate? . . . I think it's necessary to talk about God, because materialism, intrigue, indifference, falsity and dissimulation have taken over the country."[7]

Some senators echoed the need for religion to repair the republic. They too hoped to play Saint George slaying the serpent.[8] Despite Paschoal's presentation of a stereotypically Brazilian-style ecumenism, many of those echoing her position in bringing God into Brazilian politics hail from the so-called *bloco evangélico* (evangelical block), a cross-party alliance of evangelical congresspersons who mostly vote in chorus and who had aggressively rallied for the "leftist" Dilma's demise.

In the press appeared familiar wry laments: given the anemic condition of the nation's *futebol*, usually the favored totem (it was never the church or the republic), only the long-running telenovelas would be left to convene collective civil life. Once upon a time a backlands town named Canudos was the subject of such a telenovela, in 1997. It flickered on screens in almost every home. A century before that, in 1897, the real Canudos and its destruction served as a narrative pivot of the nation, through the medium of newspapers.[9] In that moment, the new republic was similarly suspected of being possessed of a demonic quality manifested by the serpent or, as the people of Canudos called it, the Law of the Hound.

Here I take up a question raised in the introduction on the techniques of making and unmaking social orders that install new renditions of the People. The essay takes the reader to Brazil and the first decade after a confluence of key events: the abolition of slavery (1888), the founding of the republic (1889), the exile (1889) and then death (1891) of the emperor, Pedro II, and the separation of church and state (1890). The paradoxical event I explore is the appearance of a powerfully weaponized church-state alliance that emerged just a few years after the official separation of church and state. In fact, the separation of church and state helped to generate a more forceful and aggressive edition of the church than had existed before.

Looking at churchstateness through the window afforded by Brazil's first republican decade and, within it, the ekklesia of Canudos and the astonishing war waged against it by the new government, offers a rare opportunity. In just a few years unfolded a radical national reimagination of the people in relation to church and state. The reporter Euclides da Cunha called it a "revoltation" (*revoltação*)[10]—more than a revolt but not quite a revolution—the neologism struggling to name a wide-ranging transition compressed into a single riveting decade. Among the first challenges to the republic and its ideals was the emergence of a large frontier town in the middle of "nowhere" a thousand miles from the federal capital in Rio de Janeiro.[11] Its name was Canudos, or, as its religious and political leader Antonio Conselheiro (Anthony the Counselor) renamed it in 1893, "Belo Monte." There, in a shantytown that swelled to as many as fifty-two hundred houses[12] and approached thirty thousand persons, a specific politics of refusal erupted: the refusal of the republic's separation of church and state and a refusal of the idea that a lawful polity and governance could not exist outside the republican state. They imagined the republic as the Antichrist and its laws as the Law of the Hound. In the 1890s, Antonio exhorted the faithful to resist the new republic and its signs—civil marriage, state burials, federal taxation, the national census, and the forced exile of the emperor. He did not seek military conflict but did not shy from it when it came. He described visions of four wars, of victory in three followed by a fourth conflagration whose terminus was unknown, but that would bring change.

Over the course of a year, from 1896 to 1897, the humble villagers of Canudos—the plebs, the serfs, the frontier, the fanatic horde, as they were called—defeated the republic's well-equipped military three times. The fourth expedition brought six thousand soldiers reinforced later by several thousands more, Krupp cannons, and mounted machine guns. It brought fire and the total destruction of the city, almost all its inhabitants, and the Counselor himself. But it also authorized the republic in acclamation, in glory, and in blood. The journalist Euclides da Cunha was direct on this score in his diary entry: "What is being destroyed is not Canudos—it's our unnerving apathy, our morbid indifference about the future, our ill-defined religiosity spread through strange superstitions."[13] The total war on Canudos was waged to destroy a renegade people—their religion, polity, and polis—and advance a still-precarious stateness to the edge of the territorial and religious frontier. The republican state succeeded, at least superficially: the head of Canudos's sovereign, Antonio Conselheiro, was carried back to Bahia for craniometrical evaluation at the Faculty of Medicine: a thorough conversion to a state-informed body indeed.[14]

My wager is that the case of Canudos can move us closer, even into, the oblique processes of transition from sacred king to sacred state—this "pass into," that "comes to replace" named in the introduction—by revealing how the republic no less than the people or the king depend for their efficacy on their capacity to take hold of emotions and direct actions, to grip persons and quicken them toward certain affinities and predispositions. Santner called this this the "jointure of the somatic and the normative."[15] Through the events at Canudos we may be able to see how the loss of the king and the arrival of the republic helped produce the church/state dyad and what that actually meant in the lives and deaths of a people at the frontier, how it signified in, through, and on the ground. How did the normative get into the bones and sinews, to become somatic? In this essay I give attention to how republican state and church came to possess subjects or, conversely, be resisted and cast out—that is, respectively, as ecstasy and as excess. It was reported of the Counselor that, at a certain hour each day, he entered into an ecstatic state in order to communicate directly with God. In response, one Brazilian official wrote of the rebellion, "The urgent challenge is to make the *jagunços* [more or less, "ruffians," the standard name given to the backland rebels] feel the relevance of their duties as citizens."[16] The civic challenge in the view of this state bureaucrat was to make the prophet and his community know ecstasy *as* excess, to drain ecstasy and fill them rather with duty, to leave their bodies infused by the spirit of the state.[17]

Much has been written, told, and filmed about the war at Canudos, from the journalist Euclides da Cunha's canonical 1902 *Os Sertões* (*Rebellion in the Backlands*) that became a classic of Brazilian literature to Mario Vargas Llosa's massive 1981 *War of the End of the World* to various films and a television miniseries. The study of Canudos, too, has passed through multiple cycles.[18] To cut into this mass of histories and afterlives, the first part of the present treatment revisits the much-told story from a particular point of view, attuned to everyday religious practices as they constituted an ekklesia. The essay then turns to republican techniques of unmaking a people who did not conform to the new order of churchstateness. Here I pay close attention to the mundane modes of civil religion at the front—its music, chants, burials, and flags.

The first technique of unmaking, detailed below, was through the sensorial eclipse of Canudos's religious practices by republican sounds and sights. Like Klassen in this volume, I foreground the sensorium in how the normative becomes somatic—the sonic vibrations and felt textures. It was through the sensorium that republican claims were pressed on one side and countered by an older version of churchstateness on the other. Then the essay turns to the second and third techniques of unmaking by caricaturizing of the followers of the Counselor as dangerously mixed—religiously, socially, and racially—and so illegible and illegitimate as candidates to join the republic. The next and related technique was casting this ekklesia as a fanatical *horde*.[19] For, after the republican transformation, in Brazil as elsewhere, all social groups came to be perceived through the lens of the people, either as positive exemplars of it or deviants or rebels against it. By discursively rendering, and then killing, those at Canudos as a delirious crowd, a flawed and illegitimate ekklesia, these persons were unhinged from the (Brazilian) people until their postmortem rehabilitation and redemption, as sacrificed citizens of the republic. The fourth technique of unmaking was the spectacularization of the machinery of war and the demolition of Canudos. Related to Sullivan's essay in this volume on the death penalty in the United States, I emphasize in this part how the republic's separation of church and state summoned its own rites of terror, how it, for example, relied on performative beheadings of the rebels as a form of enunciation and communication. In the end the republican army took with it the Counselor's severed head less as a totem of republican society, as a Durkheimian formulation might have it, than as signature of the religious group's radical outsideness—its completed detachment, as in the French revolutionary model. Later, the victims were posthumously converted into honorary citizens, as sacred corps and corpse.

Before turning to these techniques of unmaking, I begin by glossing the story of the emergence and then destruction of Canudos and its prophet, Antonio Conselheiro (fig. 1).

FIGURE 1. Parque Estadual de Canudos, Bahia, Brazil (opened in 1986). The photographs, enlarged and mounted, were installed on the former battle-ground and are specific faces from an 1897 photograph by Flávio de Barros, originally entitled *400 jagunço prisoneiros* (see fig. 3 below). The reservoir in the background was created by the state and inundated the original site of the former settlement in 1969. Photograph by Paul Christopher Johnson.

PILGRIM'S PROGRESS

The arid northeast of Brazil suffered massive changes in the second part of the nineteenth century. The centers of prosperity shifted to the south's burgeoning coffee valleys and to the northwest with its rubber extraction in Amazonia. Sugar, the traditional anchor of the northeast, declined. The interior's familiar role in raising cattle for the dried beef (*carne seca*) to feed the coastal slave-labor force, was likewise in doubt.[20] The plantations that managed to remain prosperous underwent drastic mechanization, with fifty refining factories built in a single decade from 1875 to 1885. Factory men wielding new British technologies began to overshadow the centuries-old seigneurial landowning class. Rails and telegraph lines were set, laying the groundwork for an emergent "national culture" for the first time, but also pitting urban bourgeoisie, industrial, and military classes in Rio de Janeiro and São Paulo against rural landowners of the northeast, who until then ruled their vast estates like autonomous lords.

Even against this backdrop of dramatic change, life for the poor laborer remained little altered. Workers on large ranches and farms were serfs and semislaves even after abolition in 1888. Bound in debt and patronage relations with land barons, they had few options other than peonage, banditry, or a state of permanent nomadism, a dangerous risk given the threat of drought and starvation. Droughts lasting several years without any rainfall whatsoever occurred from 1877 to 1879, a decade later, in 1888–89, and yet again in 1893–95.[21] The future chief of police of Salvador, Durval Vieira de Aguiar, traveled the region in 1882 and drafted a description: its people were peaceful if often in need, he wrote. The commerce was insignificant; the industry consisted of nothing but the curing of leather and making of nets. Worrisome for Durval was that the forms of "moral equivalence" that had for centuries woven the social fabric of the region, despite the poverty and periodic drought, had unraveled.[22]

Within such precarity, the church provided a crucial social frame. This was churchness writ large, an ensemble of folk traditions and Iberian practices dating back centuries, godparenthood networks, pilgrimages, cultivation of relations with saints, the influence of Amerindian and African shamanism, and the expectation of miracles as well as charismatic figures who could bring them about.[23] In the late nineteenth century, the church undertook an aggressive program of reform that aimed to severely trim this ample and malleable repertory. Ralph Della Cava summarized the reform as threefold: a return of the church to the people; a reorganization of ecclesiastic jurisdiction and structure; and a spiritual revival among both laity and clergy.[24] The first of these, the return to the people, is especially noteworthy for my purposes. The "return" cues us to the previous long-standing disinterest in the poor, who had mostly been left to their own devices in improvising a folk Catholicism now derided as childish and superstitious. Also conspicuous is the tension between the "return to the people" and what Della Cava cast as the third part of the reform, ultramontane reforms and revivals. This top-down regulation of the church's theology and orthopraxy rendered a "return to the people" anything but straightforward. The people, after all, were loyal to their own strongly rooted forms of practice, and mostly accustomed to making do without actual priests.

EMERGENCE

Let's now bring the Counselor onstage. Antonio had already achieved a certain popular fame by 1874. He was forty-six. With his steady gait and intense, chary gaze, he calls attention even in silence: long beard and hair, attired like a prophet, in a long blue cotton tunic and rough sandals. His earlier life doesn't matter much for our purposes: Raised in the rural province of Ceará; well educated compared with most, including some Latin; a shaky family life made worse by ferocious intermittent drought; entrenched conflicts with family rivals. As a younger man he lost the family business and then his wife and finally fled the pressures of debt, grief, drought, and the law. His worldly goods were confiscated and sold at auction. He wandered and worked as an itinerant stonemason and builder. At the beginning, one of his followers, Honório Vilanova, recalled he was "strong as a bull" and wore a straw hat over eyes full of fire.[25] Others, less sympathetic, called his eyes "fevered and agitated" with "sparks of terrible hate."[26] Later, after decades of living on the barest of alms, he turned gaunt, but the fire in his eyes remained.

At one point he was known as Antonio dos Mares, Anthony of the Seas. People also called him *Beato*, the blessed, or even Santo Antonio Aparecido (Saint Anthony of the Appearance).[27]

A few addressed him as Brother or Father. By the 1890s he was often known as *Bom Jesus* (Good Jesus) and seen by some as a representative or extension of Christ himself, though he himself asked to be called Pilgrim (*Peregrino*).[28] It was the title of Antonio Conselheiro, the Counselor, that stuck.

The Counselor ranged from village to village dodging caatinga thorn bushes across dust and red rock. He spoke and ate little, slept on the ground, and carried almost no possessions beyond a small wooden box with a crucifix in it, stopping in small villages to rebuild chapels and cemetery walls. Sometimes he preached at night to a ragged cast of followers alongside the locals who cared to listen. A word repeatedly appearing in descriptions of his physical profile was "cadavérico," cadaver-like; another was "somnambulesco," like a sleepwalker or one hypnotized or in trance;[29] and yet another was "autômato," the word suggesting that he was directed by powers other than his own and disinterested in most of what motivated others to act.[30] The Counselor seemed rather to be *en*acted, or spoken through. Laborers saw him as poor and plain spoken, like them, yet also as completely different, a man endowed with special gifts. When he walked, worked, and spoke, the effect on those who observed and listened was charismatic. In Talcott Parsons's translation of Max Weber, those gathered around a charismatic leader become "a corporate group . . . based on an emotional form of communal relationship."[31] Weber's term for such a group was *Gemeinde*, and though Parsons called it untranslatable, I note its dual uses as a jurisdiction or borough and a parish. "Gemeinde" communicates a churchstate hybrid, a community stitched by acting together in rituals both religious and political, not unlike ekklesia. Something like that double skin was starting to accrete to Antonio.

By 1876 the Counselor and his nomadic band drew sufficient attention in Bahia that the police arrested him on a trumped-up charge of having killed his mother and sister.[32] When asked to name his livelihood, he told them, "My occupation is to pick up stones on paths to build churches."[33] If the charges were false, his self-description was true—between 1880 and 1892 he built or rebuilt at least nine churches and five cemeteries—one reason he was often welcomed by local priests.[34] Nevertheless he stood accused of "increasing superstition among the people to a dangerous point of fanaticism," and planting seeds of disrespect toward the landowners and managers.[35] He appeared again in 1879 to visit an old friend, João Brigido, in Ceará. The friend, now become a reporter, found him strikingly changed from his youth, with the appearance of a holy man, and asked about his plans. Antonio said he had to fulfill an obligation, but that after that he would drift "wherever the unfortunate call me."

By 1882 church officials in Bahia took notice of the drifter. An official pastoral was issued prohibiting his delivery of sermons and performance of "other religious acts" on church properties. The document complained of his excessive morality that weakened parochial authorities. The accusation of *excess* was recurrent—he was too pious, too ascetic, too critical, and attracted too many followers. In 1886 the archbishop of Bahia wrote to the provincial governor, João Capistrano Bandeira de Mello, that he "preached subversive doctrines, doing harm to religion and to the state, distracting the people from their work and tearing them away from their work to follow him, trying to convince them that he is the Holy Spirit."[36] That phrase, "harm to religion and to the state," appears often in the record; it alerts us to a new twin birth—church/state as previously separate modes of assembly now allied and animated as bicephalon in a perceived moment of crisis.

Pressed by the archbishop, Governor Capistrano of the province of Bahia tried to have Antonio committed to an insane asylum based on "religious monomania, which impels him to preach subversive doctrines . . . and thus doing great harm to religion and the state"—there is the phrase again—but the court sanitarium in the capital of Rio de Janeiro, the Hospício Dom Pedro II, had no vacancies.

As late as 1889, the Counselor appeared in travel writing about Bahia, still cast as lightweight provincial color.[37] Until then, he appeared to have around two hundred devotees, bolstered by more who came on occasion to hear his words. From 1893 forward, though, he attracted more stringent attention. For now the crowds were growing, and not only in response to his religious leadership. He seemed to be making himself into a genuine *political* problem, based on his alleged condemnation of the precarious new republic. For example, municipalities were granted the right by the federal government to collect taxes in the rural interior, and signs announcing the new taxes were posted in plazas. In one such village, Bom Conselho, Antonio took part in a rebellion that burned the taxation announcements in the central square. Still, the idea that he posed a serious political threat was exaggerated, as he was hardly the only such tax resister. Moreover, a majority of the rural population may have been "monarchists" by default, who viewed the republic, not unreasonably, as a distant, urban elite project of the military class.[38] Yet, that particular tax protest and the response to it marked a new ravel of religion and politics in his message and the alliance of church and state against him.

Alongside the call to piety and faithful work, the Counselor's messages henceforth often criticized the republic.[39] Antonio's denunciation was not of the government tout court but rather of a series of specific grievances: that the burial of the dead and the marriage of the living were no longer sacred events but rather state managed and that taxes were supposed to be paid by the poorest of the poor for these new "rights." Other issues, too, awakened his suspicion and that of his followers. Measurements were standardized according to a mysterious international "metric system." Herders who formerly could range their goats across the wide expanse were suddenly to observe demarked property lines. Fears of the Law of the Hound multiplied.

After all, had it not been the saintly Princess Isabel, daughter of the emperor, who had finally, in 1888, abolished slavery once and for all? She had acted as the hand of God. Perhaps this new regime was asking so many questions, collecting "census data," and critical of the princess, because they planned to reinstate slavery![40] The Counselor gave words to such suspicions. He called the republic an empty fraud; its currency was likewise vacuous and without backing. The emperor would return and the union of church and state would be restored. In the meantime, he and his followers would serve as the godly vanguard. When thirty police were sent to arrest the Counselor in the town of Masseté, his disciples defended him and repelled the police. From that day forward he was on high alert, a wanted man, and the Counselor sought a protected enclave where he and the community could build the ekklesia, safe from outside interference.

In June 1893 Antonio and his flock arrived in the valley of Canudos.[41] It consisted of a tiny village with a chapel and perhaps fifty huts built of mud and straw. When there was rain, a river called the Vaza-Barris flowed on one side, and beyond the river, hills sheltered the valley. The Counselor knew the site, having passed there before, but now he returned to build and settle. They set to work repairing the old church named, like him, for Santo Antonio. Soon they laid the foundation for a new and larger church, built to last. It would have granite towers and thick walls made from stones dragged by men pulling an oxcart from as far as thirty-six kilometers away. The Counselor made the stones light with a touch of his hand.[42]

The new church doubled as fortress and also served as meetinghouse. With word spreading of free land to settle and the Counselor's successful resistance to the republic's taxes and police, increasing numbers migrated to join, and the new church had space to accommodate them all. They came for the opportunity, and because there was protection living in a large community. Some grew manioc, corn, and beans; others raised chickens and goats. Many arrived as campesinos seeking a better life, quite apart from their religious convictions, leaving behind positions as peons on estates.[43] They came for independence and the possibility of owning something of their own. Others were eager to join an egalitarian community under the wing and words of the Counselor himself. They came to hear the truth and be near him. In addition, there were followers of Antonio who lived apart from the town. Among them was Francisco Cardoso de Macedo, who lived on a ranch near enough to hear the bell toll and who came to Canudos periodically to hear the Counselor speak and take part in ritual events.[44] Fifty years later he still called Antonio a saint.

The Counselor's vision of a self-sufficient community beholden to no owner, and inspired by an ascetic devotion to Jesus and the saints, offered an alternative to the existing churchstate alliance—or rather, the alliance between church and landowners. These latter typically themselves had little love for the state, preferring to organize their own fiefdoms without interference. The greatest landholder and boss of the region was Cícero Dantas Martins, uncle of the titleholder of Canudos. Known as the "Baron of Jeremoabo," he owned fifty-nine farms in Bahia and two more in a neighboring province.[45] This rural lord and his kin—related both by blood and by godparenthood—comprised the ruling caste of the entire region.

The Counselor did not explicitly aim to threaten this order. Nevertheless, the depopulation of plantations and estates by laborers fleeing to Canudos was devastating, and the alarm appeared in the baron's correspondence. One friend of the baron wrote in January 1894 that between sixteen and twenty families had left his ranch only that week to reach Canudos. Another penned a letter in February describing the "veritable depopulation, a torrential exodus" that even the governor was powerless to stop.[46] The baron's letters reveal both the vigilance with which landowners followed Canudos and their attempts to leverage political connections against the movement, including attempts to spur a military intervention. Interviewed by a newspaper in March 1897, the baron was quoted as saying that "the people are

abandoning their houses and duties en mass to accompany Antonio Conselheiro. The population lives as though in ecstasy . . .
neither landowners nor ranchers can count on their fieldhands
and cowboys."[47]

The Counselor's reputation took on strange new shapes as it
expanded to the capital city of Rio de Janeiro, a thousand miles
away. There were rumors of a monarchy restoration movement
in the north, led by a bearded fanatic and probably abetted by
foreign agents and British weapons arriving via Minas Gerais
or Argentina.

THE WARS

The baron's wish was granted when an official military reply was
issued.[48] The Counselor had ordered and prepaid for a shipment
of wood to be used in the building of the new church. When
the wood failed to appear without account, the Counselor sent
word to the town of Joazeiro that he and his men were coming
to claim it. The town's magistrate, Dr. Arlindo Leoni, issued an
emergency telegraph to the governor declaring the town to be
under attack. In response the governor dispatched one hundred
soldiers. Alerted ahead of time, the counselorists waylaid them
en route. Armed with only the simplest weapons, singing and
carrying banners of the saints, they rushed the soldiers head-
long, suffering 150 dead compared with only 10 soldiers. Yet by
faith they had won, and they celebrated victory over the Dog.

Within days a new regiment was sent to sack Canudos, this
time with 543 soldiers, 14 officers and 3 surgeons. After two
battles, this army was likewise vanquished after its supply of
ammunition ran thin. Again the counselorists launched un-
daunted numbers at superior firepower, suffering grave losses
of 135 compared with only a few soldiers, but sending the army
into retreat nonetheless. God was surely with them.

Two weeks later a third expedition was launched. It included
thirteen hundred men, armed with machine guns and Krupp

cannons. This republican army was led by the famous General Moreira César, who, despite his epileptic seizures, had built a stellar reputation by putting down recent antirepublic uprisings in the southern state of Santa Catarina. He pressed his army to a fast march, and the men arrived exhausted and dehydrated after weeks of crossing scorched land with little water. In a fit of vainglorious mania, Moreira César commanded his troops to invade Canudos immediately upon their arrival. They would eat lunch in Canudos without firing a gun, he crowed. Things went awry when he himself was mortally wounded, slumping in the saddle of his conspicuous white horse. When second in command Colonel Tamarindo was likewise killed, a chaotic retreat ensued. As they fled, the republican troops left behind large quantities of guns and ammunition, including advanced weaponry the rebels had never handled before but quickly mastered.[49] This new loss, suffered by one of Brazil's most famous generals commanding a large and well-equipped force, inspired real panic in the capital. Riots took over certain Rio streets. Three newspapers known for their monarchist sympathies had their offices ransacked.[50]

A short month later, the fourth and final republican expedition assembled and lumbered into motion. General Arthur Oscar de Andrade Guimarães commanded six brigades of one thousand men each. This would be total war, with nothing and no one spared, designed and prosecuted to communicate total dominance in the most spectacular fashion possible. The troops surrounded and laid siege to Canudos in early July 1897, burying the town under a daily fusillade. Two months later, on September 6, the new church's tower and bell toppled after weeks of heavy cannon fire. The Counselor died on September 22, apparently of dysentery. The final assault took the settlement on October 1, and what remained of the town was burned to ash. At dawn on October 6, 1897, the body of Antonio Conselheiro was found, exhumed, photographed, and beheaded, and the trophy taken back to the coast.

Reports from the front—for the role of "war correspondent"

in Brazil originated with Canudos—were run on foot to the nearest city, Monte Santo, and then sent by telegraph back to Rio de Janeiro, when the jagunços did not succeed at cutting the lines.[51] Still, due to the military's process of censoring and redacting stories—including granting privileges to certain journalists while banning others deemed too critical—news routinely took at least ten days and often longer to appear in the press.[52] The report of victory was an exception; it arrived in the capital on the same day via submarine cablegram, to the office of one of Rio's main dailies, the *Jornal de Notícias*: "Rio/Urgent/Bahia/Canudos taken counselor not found forts salute victory barracks prepare celebrations public and private buildings with flags widespread rejoicing."[53] It reads at once as a notification and a needed cue to the proper, republican response: Rejoice! Prepare parties! Hang flags!

When the soldiers departed, "the streets were carpeted with cadavers," reported journalist Favila Nunes on October 8, 1897.[54] Soon "clouds of vultures" and stray dogs descended to feast, until a farmer, Ângelo dos Reis, came with thirteen friends and relatives from Formosa, seventy-eight kilometers distant, to bury the dead.[55]

COMPETING SENSORIA

In the first decades of the Pilgrim's sojourn, many priests were sympathetic. His Catholicism was familiar in its "return to the people," even if his mortifications seemed grandstanding. Not a few priests defended him as a model of orthodoxy. The churches filled when the Pilgrim came to town. The message emphasized disciplined asceticism, Marian devotion, and a passionate devotion to the sacraments and the saints. Penitent work was the center of his daily routine. Some said it was to atone for a terrible sin in his past, perhaps the matricide he'd been accused of in 1876. Yet his skill in stonework and eagerness to build were invaluable. Church maintenance was the task of the imperial administration, whose seat was in distant Rio, which meant that many churches long sat in idle decay and disrepair. What is more, with the arrival of the republic and the official separation of church and state, the Counselor gave voice to distress over the church's disenfranchisement in ways its officials—who were part of the region's governance and administration—mostly could not.

Such ambivalence about the Counselor disappeared by 1895, at least within the official church administration. In that year two Capuchin priests arrived in Canudos, sent by the archbishop of Bahia, Dom Jerônimo Tomé da Silva, acting in league with the new governor of Bahia, Dr. Rodrigues Lima. Their names were João Evangelista de Monte Marciano and Caetano de Leo. Neither was well prepared for the situation, the latter only recently arrived in Brazil from Italy. Their Portuguese was imperfect and their sense of the region's dialect even worse. Even with the best preparation, the mandate was hard: they were to persuade the inhabitants to disperse and return to their former homes and jobs on the estates they had abandoned. What transpired was a disaster of revealing miscues, yet their report offers precious insight into the religious life of the community.

The two Capuchins were accompanied by a local priest, Padre Sabino, a longtime friend of Canudos who had married and buried many of its residents. The trio arrived on May 13, 1895, at 10:00 a.m. The Italians' first recorded impression was surprise that many in the community were armed, even during mass. Republican money was not allowed to circulate. Exchange was either in barter and trade or using older imperial coin. Strict order and discipline ruled. Petty crime was nil. For such disputes as arose, the Counselor served as judge and jury. The interdiction of alcohol was firm—though the sixty-year-old artisan called Master Faustino had a reputation for importing clandestine nips.[56] Everyone in the community greeted each other with "Praise be to Our Lord Jesus Christ." Many addressed Antonio as "my father counselor" (*meu pai conselheiro*); he called them, in turn, "brothers" and "sisters." As coreligionists they composed a kind of extended family.[57] The sense of belonging was perhaps aided by the relative uniformity of dress, as luxury clothing was burned.[58]

The Counselor told the visiting priests, "In the time of the monarchy I allowed myself to be captured because I recognized the government. Not anymore, because I do not recognize the Republic." Residents, they reported, raised loud praises to the Most Holy Trinity, to the Good Jesus, to the Holy Spirit, and to Antonio Conselheiro. Every time he appeared in the door he was received with loud acclaim.

PEOPLE'S CHURCH

The visiting priests conceded that the Counselor never performed official sacraments for which he was not authorized. In fact, they reported, he did not approach the sacraments at all. Rather, he acted as though he were neither in need of them nor of priests. Moreover, the ceremonies he *did* conduct, they said, were mixed (*mescladas*) with superstition and idolatry. One example noted was the "kissing of the images," in which everyone prostrated him- or herself before all the various images of saints, without appropriate hierarchic distinction between images of the Divine Crucifixion and the Holy Virgin, from the rest of the lesser saints. The mixing and lack of necessary distinction was reported of Canudos's social makeup too: the priests referred to the people variously as fanatics, fools, imbeciles, and perverts.

The priests had no doubt, nevertheless, that Canudos was—though in unruly ways—truly "Catholic." When the priests celebrated Mass it was attended by at least four thousand, including the Counselor himself.[59] The Counselor sat mostly silent and attentive, the priests' document stated, but shook his head in disapproval during their homily when fasting only "in moderation" was recommended. The Capuchins also performed 55 marriages, 102 baptisms, and 400 confessions. Followers of the Counselor eagerly availed themselves of the priests' presence;

FIGURE 2. Flávio de Barros's nineteenth-century photograph of the old Church of Santo António at Canudos at the end of the war. The people depicted in the photograph are either captives being forced to pose or soldiers dressed as jagunços after the conquest. Photograph courtesy of Arquivo Histórico e Institucional do Museu da República, Rio de Janeiro, Brazil.

thus it is unlikely that Antonio Conselheiro himself aspired to the intermediary role of a priest or saint, whatever his followers' hopes.

Nevertheless, on the fourth day of the priests' visit, their rapport with the town abruptly fell apart. On that day they preached on the need for obedience to the republic and the maintenance of public order. France had long been a monarchy but was now a republic, they lectured, and all in France obey its laws. Several villagers erupted in loud retort, accusing the priests of being "masonic priests, protestants and republicans." By the seventh day the accusations turned louder. The survivor Honório Vilanova recounted that "Friar John (one of the priests) tried to count people, to tell the government."[60] Some roared that they had no need of priests for their salvation because they had their Counselor. One encounter especially conveys that confidence: the priests were scheduled to perform Mass in the church, and the Counselor along with many congregants waited until long past the appointed hour. Finally a messenger named Venâncio was sent to inquire after the visiting priests. "The Counselor is waiting for you to give Mass," Venâncio announced. "Go take your Counselor's Mass!" Padre João replied roughly, and then made the sign of the cross and cursed the counselorists—as he now feared for his very life. Venâncio, however, did not did not let that stand, responding, "You, sir, cannot curse me!" The priest said nothing, and Venâncio then expanded, "I curse you too! in the name of the Father, the Son, the Holy Spirit and the Virgin Mary," and traced the sign of the cross in the air before the face of the priest.[61] That was the day the Italians fled, after having been there for only a week. This exchange, wherein a peasant layman traded condemnations and signs of the cross with the Italian Capuchins, suggests the degree to which at least some counselorists had taken ownership of their church. This was a people's church that welcomed priests' help but refused to cower before it.

FRAGMENTS

The priests did not report on what the Counselor actually preached, but hints appear in manuscripts he left behind. Among the most important discoveries after the war were the hand-copied version of the Bible and some of the sermons of the Counselor. What was the Counselor counseling? At least in part his messages were informed by a book he read and copied routinely—the *Missão Abreviada* (Abbreviated Mission), a set of condensed versions of the gospels, reflections on the lives of saints, and ritual instructions drafted by a Portuguese priest, which went through more than a dozen editions between 1859 and 1904.[62] The book was the Counselor's constant companion, according to eyewitness Honório Vilanova, and it seems to have provided some of the more apocalyptic content of the Counselor's pronouncements.[63]

A redacted Bible was another source. Fernando da Rocha Peres traced the likely Bible that served as source for the Canudos Bible, probably copied by the Counselor himself, and by Leão de Natuba, the community scribe.[64] It appears to be a selection from an edition of the Vulgate published in 1857, in Lisbon. The Canudos Bible is abbreviated, including only certain books of the New Testament—the Gospels, Acts, Epistles, and the Apocalypse. What is more, Peres discovered certain apparently deliberate discrepancies between the source Bible and the handwritten copy. For example, at the end of the first chapter of Matthew in the Vulgate, verse 25 reads, "And he knew her not till she brought forth her firstborn son: and he called his name Jesus." The Canudos manuscript, presumably used in collective oral recitation, reads, "And she gave birth to her firstborn and gave the name Jesus." Joseph is absented from the passage. It is unclear what this means, but on the face of it one might surmise that the Virgin Mary is elevated in her central role, authority, and power.

The stories of the Old Testament likely provided a useful narrative frame for the Counselor's sermons. His writings are selective in regard to which stories he used. From the prophets, Jonah and Job are featured, especially in their endurance of suffering and their obedience. Moses and the story of Exodus are prominent, not surprisingly, given that those at Canudos also wandered in the desert, also were under the threat of pharaoh, also saw themselves as long-suffering but somehow chosen by God. In this context, Antonio repeatedly invoked "the people." One sermon describes the building of Solomon's Temple in meticulous detail; again, this must have resonated profoundly when told from scaffolds between the half-finished walls and towers of the new church being raised. In addition to texts and stories paraphrased from the Bible, the Counselor preached on topics he judged most central to the faith: the Ten Commandments, Mass, the cross, confession, the end of man, and religion. The latter he defined as that which "shows us our misery, and points us to its remedy. It teaches us that we cannot gain salvation on our own, but that we can do much to become stronger."[65] In general the sermons emphasize finding peace in suffering and dignity through work. They underscore durable strength in obedience over the weakness of individual desire (*vontade frouxa*).[66] Antonio narrated what seemed the most immediate and impactful stories of the Bible in a discerning way, and with attention to stories' details—the exact number of people conscripted to cut cedar or quarry stone for the building of Solomon's Temple, for example.

How these texts were used in ritual contexts is unclear. Attendance at gatherings was not required, and some men almost never entered the church at all.[67] The Counselor often preached in the evening, after the day's work was done and the new temple filled with rapt listeners. He did not read as he spoke. Often he described visions or dreams, which he narrated in a state of reverie. Thus Eduardo Hoornaert recommends thinking of the community's practice as "oneiric Christianity," which drew from the Bible and mimicked the primitive church but was also open and innovative, pulling visions from *sertanejo* life experience in the arid backlands and from the imposing landscape itself.[68] On occasion a passionate voice spills out from the written sermons and suggests emotional nuance lacking from descriptions of the Prophet's trancelike monotone speaking voice. The written appeals are sometimes punctuated by a heartfelt "Oh!"

or "But ah, how ungrateful are those." Some texts communicate also a visceral, fleshly appeal, not only in the call to endure suffering but in the announcement of Jesus's comfort in the form of his chest, on which Jesus's disciples are described as finding repose.[69]

For the most part the Counselor preached a counter-Reformation form of Catholic orthodoxy in keeping with the late-nineteenth-century ultramontane reform.[70] He emphasized devotion to the Virgin Maria as key intermediary. He spoke of the king's divine right as the earthly emissary of God. Property should be respected; the family is the proper social form, and both God and king are analogous to the father and his children. Enemies of the church include Jews, Freemasons, Protestants, and Republicans. The devil is near and shifty, and one should remain vigilant against him. The key point of departure from this relatively conventional and conservative theology was the Counselor's emphasis on worldly injustice and the fight against slavery. He had preached against slavery for decades, including when it was still in force, until 1888. He credited the monarchy with emancipation, and in particular Princess Isabel.

In a sermon titled "On the Republic," the Counselor said, "Dona Isabel liberated the slaves by doing nothing but following the order of heaven; it was because the time marked by God for the liberation of this people had arrived."[71] Such blessings are the worldly benefit of legitimate power: "All legitimate power is an emanation of the eternal Omnipotence of God, and subject to a divine law, in the temporal as in the spiritual order, so that we obey only God by obeying the papacy, the prince, the father, those who are the true ministers of God." The republic, on the other hand, constitutes illegitimate power, because it is based on "false principle," from which "legitimate consequences cannot be taken." In the sermon, the Counselor focused on civil marriage as his key example: illegitimate, unauthorized marriages will fail even as the republic must fail. But even if they did not fail, they would be wrong: "Even if it [the republic] brings good to the country, it is in itself bad," because it contravenes the foundational order that undergirds all legitimate government, all community, all family. All social life must be convened as ekklesia, the Counselor seemed to believe, publics conforming to a ritual hierarchy that is at once social and natural. "The peace (*sossego*) of a people," he wrote, relies on it. For the Counselor, the notion of a republican state standing outside this monarchic order of reality was as unthinkable as time skidding to a stop: "To negate these truths would be the same as to say that the dawn did not discover a new day."

Striking in the sermon "On the Republic" is the repeated question of what is *legitimate* or what is *authorized*—the words were together invoked no fewer than seven times in only a few pages—used as terms of practice spoken to and by those at Canudos. Reportedly in his sermons he decried even the word "república," as it seemed a conjunction of "public" with the prefix "ré"—in Portuguese a defendant in court—and by implication a public on trial, a form of public that is an accused criminal. Thus, he pronounced, the *republic* was a criminal form of governance on trial.

Additional and more colloquial texts were recovered by soldiers after the firebombing of Canudos. One hut contained a paper fragment with scrawled verses:[72]

Sahiu D. Pedro Segundo	Dom Pedro the Second set forth,
Para o reyno de Lisboa	For Lisbon he was bound,
Acabosse a monarquia	And so the monarchy came to an end
O Brazil ficou atôa!	And Brazil was left aground.
Garantidos pela lei	Backed up by the law,
Aquelles malvados estão	Those evil ones abound,
Nos temos a lei de Deus	We keep the law of God,
Elles tem a lei do *cão*!	They keep the law of the *hound*!

Bem desgraçados são elles
Pra fazerem a eleição
Abatendo a lei de Deus
Suspendendo a lei do *cão*!

Oh wretched ones are they,
When election comes around,
It's down with the law of God
And up with the law of the
hound!

Casamento vão fazendo
Só para o povo illudir
Vão casar o povo todo
No casamento civil!

A mockery they make of
marriage,
They'd have all true
marriages cease
And have us all get married
By a justice of the peace!

D. Sebastião já chegou
E traz muito regimento
Acabendo com o civil
E fazendo o casamento!

Dom Sebastian came
With a mighty regiment
And put an end to these
marryings,
And we were all content

O Anti-Christo nasceu
Para o Brasil governor
Mas ahi está o *Conselheiro*
Para delle nos livrar!

The Anti-Christ was born
That he might govern Brazil,
But here is our Counselor
To save us from this ill!

Visita nos vem fazer
Nosso rei D. Sebastião
Coitado daquelle pobre
Que estiver na lei do *cão*!

Dom Sebastian our King
On a visit to us is bound,
And woe to that poor sinner
then
Who is under the law of the
hound!

The verses reinforce the sacred king Dom Pedro II's link to the sixteenth-century Portuguese King Sebastian who disappeared fighting Muslims in Morocco, but who will one day return. All legitimate kings, the lyric suggests, are part of one body represented by Sebastian, the disappeared meta-king. One stanza likewise points to the emptiness of marriage and, by extension, law, when presided over by a mere civil judge. It points to the ways the verses of everyday folk reproduce in simpler terms the same ideas as the sermons of the Counselor, an organic circuit. Another letter found by a journalist after the war was dated December 3, 1896. Its text hints at families separated by some leaving while others remained and at the concern of the Counselor to persuade the people to stay, or return: "My Counselor is looking for you . . . soon no one will be allowed to enter [the town] with republicans. . . . The Counselor said three times that whoever dies in Belo Monte will be guaranteed salvation. . . . From your Father who will stay here, Bonifácio Manuel João."[73]

In addition to texts, there are a few other material and sonic clues as to the community's practice and theology. After Canudos's fall, in assembling their forensic report, republican soldiers found rosaries made of coconut shells in many households, suggesting the centrality of the rosary in everyday ritual practice. Hundreds of clay saints were recovered by the republican "Commission of Engineers." Like the rosaries, they intimate a richly tactile Catholic practice that sought to bring the saints close in visual and tangible household forms, using whatever materials were at hand.

Music was another crucial part of the sensorium. Even before settling at Canudos, the Counselor and his band would sing as they walked. They were said to be singing as they entered their first violent conflict over the missing wood, at Joazeiro. Within Canudos, the journalist Euclides da Cunha recorded that even during fierce battles, whenever the guns would cease, he could hear singing. In fact the residents of Canudos were immersed in music. "Profane" music was sung and performed, but the liturgical music provided a nearly constant daily vibration.[74] Some songs were litanies or chants (*ladainhas*) in a mix of Portuguese and Latin.[75] All the community gathered to sing at certain junctures, especially in the morning and at dusk, but some women close to the Counselor sang nearly all the time; singing to produce a sonic-sacred space was their role and vocation.[76]

The space of Canudos radiated out from the two churches and plaza, and the experience of time was measured and announced by the bell tolling—which continued right to the end of the war, when Timoteio the ringer, like the tower itself, was felled by cannonball—and by the singing. Very likely the music offended the ears of the visiting priests. The church had initiated attempts to stamp out some Brazilian music, observing the diminution of Gregorian chants and other time-honored genres in favor of more popular songs and melodies. By 1895 this official position was articulated in print, with the proviso that "noisy and profane songs" simply could not express the sense of "sacred words" no matter how well intended their ritual purpose.[77] To Italian ears, we might imagine, Canudos signified once again *excess*, this time an overabundance and lack of control over sacred sounds.

In sum, at least based on the partly recovered written and material record, the Counselor's message could not be construed as counter to the Catholic Church or the authority of priests. To the contrary, he was emphatic on the necessity of confession, of Mass, of sanctioned marriage, and even antipathetic sources concede that he nowhere claimed to be more than human or to exceed the status of layperson. Alexandre Otten summarized the Counselor's theology: "Conselheiro is a simple man of the people. Out of his charisma and his apostolic life were born an eschatological project of communal life, simple but effective, in the mold of the primitive church. He did not try to reorganize sertanejo society as such, since he had no leverage with elites, who thought him ridiculous. His message was directed to the poor. In this way, he achieved an exodus."[78]

Nonetheless, perhaps in consequence of their own prejudices, the visiting Capuchins' report declared that this was an established "politico-religious sect," reaching beyond mere fanaticism and superstition to portend a bona fide schism in the church.[79] Canudos was a veritable "state within the State," governing itself without regard for (republican) law. They judged that in Canudos existed a disturbing disaggregation of religion, the social good, and the dignity of civil power. "There is no rule of law or respect for (state) authority," they wrote, "yet public liberties are constricted (*coarctadas*)." What was needed, they concluded, was a plan to reestablish the proper regard for law, the guaranteed special status of the Catholic faith (*culto*), and the return of the "fora of civilized people."

The report, and in particular the classification of Canudos as a politicoreligious sect, was the critical juncture in helping to spawn tales of a monarchist conspiracy and unleash a total war against Canudos.[80] From it unfolded a weaponized hybrid of churchstateness, only a few years after the constitutional separation of church and state.

SONIC CIVIL RELIGION

Republican forces carried their own ritual repertories and soundscapes with them as they marched toward Canudos. Martin Horcades was a medical student in Salvador when he embarked on July 27, 1897, with a medical corps of twenty-three to support the fourth and final march. His eyewitness dispatches appeared in the newspaper *Diário de Notícias*, and two years after the war's end he published his notes in a single volume. It offers a window into republican religion, and the sounds it produced over and against the practices of the counselorists.

Horcades wrote of taking part in a holy mission, the "sacred cause of the Patria, of Order and of Law," and bearing in their bodies the patria's "living incarnation."[81] Meals were punctuated with loud "Vivas" to the Republic. In Canudos, he wrote, the men would either encounter triumph or the "holocaust of the Republic."[82] Yet even those who fell in civic duty would be made immortals. Euclides da Cunha likewise recounted the journey toward Canudos as formative. He departed on a steamship, the *Espírito Santo*, from Rio. A month later in Cansanção, Bahia, one hundred kilometers from Canudos, Euclides and his companions attended Mass. Kneeling on the rough tile floor, he reported thinking, "Why not satisfy the naïve beliefs of these simple villagers?" and noted Durval's 1889 account of the "laughable" Catholicism of the region.[83]

By August 4, the medical corps neared the theater of war and began to encounter refugees and corpses. Horcades wrote, "Oh Patria, holy, pure and chaste enchantment for those who love you, for those who are not prodigal sons; Patria, where were you that you did not hear the supplications, the desperate woes of your children who suffered for you? Why do you let them be deceived, those who sacrificed so much to save you?!"[84]

The report reads like that of Conrad's narrator Marlow in *The Heart of Darkness* (and indeed, "savage" African figures later)[85] or a tour of the levels of hell. In this spatial schema, the coastal cities like Rio or Salvador are the blessed lands set in chiaroscuro against a dark frontier. On the afternoon of August 6, Horcades saw a decapitated cadaver, the body of Colonel Tamarindo, second in command of the third mission. Then one of their own group of doctors, Joaquim Pedreira, died of fever: "He may have died, but he died covered by the grand banner of yellow and green, gripping the swords of Order and the Law, and crowned by the angel of Charity with the grateful laurels of the Patria."[86]

Euclides da Cunha's notes emphasized the theme of martyrdom for the nation even more forcefully. In his journal we find repeated iterations of the soldier who, in the very act of raising his voice in an impassioned "Viva!" to the Republic, is shot dead. The narratives convey that it was perhaps *because* of this passion for the Republic that the young men were shot, falling "in the moment when his sincere and noble soul worried itself over the eternal existence of the Republic. He died as only the immortals can die."[87] Through the willing sacrifice of young soldiers, the otherwise indifferent cities are "reanimated."[88] Later in his journal, Euclides jotted the words of a telegram sent by General Arthur Oscar de Andrade Guimarães just after the war: "All important ideas have their martyrs; we are elected to a sacrifice . . . to leave to the next generation a strong Republic."[89]

If Canudos was bathed in song, according to da Cunha's and Horcades's reports the republican army vibrated with the sounds of a holy republic. Da Cunha described the immortality of the republic heard in the "sharp, electrifying heroic vibrations" of the marching band's trumpets. *Saudade*—combined sadness, nostalgia, and longing—was countered by the republic's martial sounds, "consoling and strong, vigorously protecting those who suffer pain, pressing them along the straight, noble course of duty."[90] The officers of the republican army routinely arrived at the front accompanied by band music. At the end of the war, there occurred a bizarre scene of republican soldiers dressed as women to parody a casual peacetime "stroll" over and around the dead bodies, and so ridicule the counselorists' attempt at resistance, while the national anthem was repeatedly played in every part of the ruins.[91] The journalist Favila Nunes heard the moaning of the dying replaced by "happy sounds of the hymns of victory."[92] The conquest included visual cues like the raising of the flag over the ruins, but even more important was the sonic eclipse of the songs of Canudos with the trumpets of the republic, ricocheted down roads of burning flesh.

Perhaps one could interpret the soldiers' attempt at humor charitably, as an unthinking eruption of relief after weeks of terror and exhaustion. After all, many of the soldiers were poor conscripts from backgrounds not so unlike their tattered enemies. Perhaps it was the nervous laughter of fear, of life "suspended by chance," an "indefinable gaping," or perhaps laughter to give vent to "a weird sort of success."[93] Perhaps. But as Georges Bataille observed, there is a difference between laughter that bonds two persons, as communication, contagion, even "compenetration," and the laughter of a group toward an object, or the dead, which announces rupture or, in Bataille's idiosyncratic terms, a shift from an erotic to a sacrificial mode.[94] In the case of this early October morning, 1897, the staged, perverse comedy of the bourgeois connubial stroll over cadavers suggests something less like relief or contagion and more like violent excess beyond any reason at all. On this score, Derrida engaged Bataille to consider the difference between lordship and sovereignty.[95] Lordship entails hierarchic order still shot through with reason; it has form and allows for a potential coming to consciousness, as in Hegel's myth-theory of the master and slave. Sovereignty, by contrast, stands outside meaning. Its absolute excess marks the ability to stand outside or over the laws of social life, history, or purpose. In Derrida's reading of Bataille, it is comedy that scores the plane dividing lordship from sovereignty. Sacrifice, for example, is comic in its meaningless surplus. We might say that this macabre comic scene pressed republican sovereignty at the frontier, through its parodic exercise of force: the soldiers in burlesque "stroll" over cadavers; the haws of laughter keep time to trumpet blasts and eager vultures' hisses and grunts. The sounds announce a shift from purposeful conquest to meaningless violence and, within Canudos, from the rule of the Counselor's lordship to one of republican sovereignty, instantiated through sacrificial excess.

A HORDE IS NOT A PEOPLE

The visiting priests described a lack of "civilized people" in Canudos and a state outside the state. Their observation calls for a return again to the question of the people raised in the introduction.

Agamben drew on Walter Benjamin's phrase *das blosse Leben* to describe those with but bare life compared with those with political existence. This cleavage or split, and the capacity to convert human bodies into the People, and vice versa, is crucial to the power exercised by states, as well as to the hierarchy among states.[96] There are manifold reasons for the word's schizophrenic nature. One is the advancement of various interests through the discourse of peoplehood. For example, it may be considered desirable to be "of the people" (Port. *do povo*). Nevertheless, while many anxiously avoid distinction, few aspire to be completely absorbed into "the masses" (Port. *povão*, "big people"), with rare exceptions.[97] To crib from Ian Hacking, the ways we make up people "changes the space of possibility for personhood."[98]

Brazilian sociologist Nelson Werneck Sodré distinguished "the people" (*o povo*) from "the population," "the nation," or "the electorate," with these latter terms denoting bounded, authorized, and politically empowered collectives. The word "people" always stands slightly to the side of power. "People" shifts across time and place, Sodré supposed, but can be comparatively defined: "In all situations, *people* is the conjunction of classes, ranks and social groups committed to objective solutions to the problems of progressivist and revolutionary development, in the area in which they live."[99] Sodré's point is that "the people" is often deployed toward the countering of socioeconomic and political advantage. Everyone thinks they are "of the people," wrote Sodré, but privately each thinks he is *more* "of the people" depending on how humble his social condition.[100] Sodré foregrounded its emancipatory potential, but also the uses of "people" to advance political projects that render it suspect. Conservative thinkers like Edmund Burke, to wit, had been suspicious of the notion of a (French) revolution genuinely "of the people" not least since it seemed too detached from a defined past.[101]

If Agamben and Santner identified the chiasmic split in "people" and scholars from Burke to Sodré noted its divided interests and political uses, Immanuel Wallerstein sought a deeper cause.[102] Peoplehood, he argued, contains within it a strategic ambiguity. It includes within it multiple alleged continuities: physical ("race"), sociopolitical ("nation"), and cultural ("ethnicity"). "The People" draws on all of these resources in order to generate pastness. Peoplehood is a fiction linked to that of pastness, "a mode by which persons are persuaded to act in the present in ways they might not otherwise act," that is, acting on behalf of their own state and class interests.[103] It is only the conjunction of sufficient groupness and sufficient pastness that produces "a people in history." Nonpeoples have no history. Thus Hegel famously left Africa and its peoples outside of historyness.[104] Marx and Engels applied the phrase "people without history." Eric Wolf wrote on how the "people without history" are, often against their will, pulled into capitalist history through their very marginalization.[105] This is by now familiar. Wallerstein's further intervention, though, was to point out that peoplehood is in most cases produced *after* the creation of a given state, even though states work to present themselves as organic growths out of a preexisting peoplehood.[106] States cultivate and promote the idea of "a people" and seek to quicken national sentiment in order to negotiate their place within the basic core-periphery logic of world capitalism. In short, discourses of peoplehood mask, mediate, and modulate structures of race and economy. From this perspective, some, even the majority, *must* be kept outside the bounds of peoplehood.

In the Americas, "the people" carries a territorial seed. Paul Eiss writes that *el pueblo* in Yucatán conveys at once a place, a community, and a political ideal.[107] "El pueblo" can mean a rural village, but it also carries a specific tone of indigeneity for Mayans. Thus "la Virgen del pueblo" points to the saint's multiple embeddings—with a group, with a town, with a class, with a place.[108] In Brazil, *o povo*, like el pueblo, can suggest the strong association of a group with the land. "Povo da terra"—people of the land—was one descriptor applied to those at Canudos. Prior to its 1890s explosion the town of Canudos was a village described as a *povoado*, a small rural settlement of people. The recurring Portuguese word *povo*, people, and phrases *o povo*, the people, and *o povão*, the faceless masses, are in this context worth pausing over. Residents of Canudos clearly understood themselves as a people, constituted as a ritual community with a shared foundation in sacred authority and an organic connection to the land. From the perspective of the republic, however, they were but povão, masses. The povão is made up of the "declassificados"—the de- or unclassified as Laura de Mello e

Souza called them—those faceless numbers who were neither precisely reckoned slaves nor landowners.[109] They represented the uncounted in-betweens resident at Canudos. Yet somehow the Counselor shaped them into an ekklesia.

In his preaching, the Counselor often referred to his congregation as "the people," *o povo*; as when narrating the story of the Exodus, *o povo* as a chosen people.[110] And the Counselor was certainly considered a man "of the people."[111] At Canudos, "o povo" specified a class identity—pride in being a working community of the most poor and humble—a social identity tethered to the land, akin to el pueblo, and a religious identity, as a community chosen by God. The three senses were tightly woven and helped to knit Canudos together.

The people of Canudos were far from faceless. They were individuals, and we know some of their names. Antonio Beato was in charge of the images; Timotinho was the bell ringer; Ana prepared the Counselor's meals. Benta and Caridade administered the Counselor's quarters, called the Sanctuary. José Felix lit candles before prayers and sometimes did divination; Manuel Faustino was a master builder of altars; Leão da Silva from Natuba served as scribe; Antonio Fogueteiro crafted and launched fireworks that accompanied processions and other special occasions.[112] Chico Ema carried out reconnaissance missions in the lands surrounding Canudos.[113] José Bernabé was charged with retrieving the recalcitrant. There were artisans of all kinds—instrument makers, cobblers, masons, blacksmiths. The best fighters, some of them former bandits like Pajeu, Pedrão na Canabrava, José Venâncio, or former slaves like João Grande, were appointed to the Catholic Guard (Guarda Católica) as the defenders of the Counselor and as the administrators of justice, including corporeal punishment. Their general (or "commander of the street," *commandante da praça*) was João Abade, who approved newcomers arriving in the city prior to their being given permission to take up residence. In all, the central military corps included about six hundred.[114] Additional persons were crucial to the rhythms of everyday life such as the schoolteachers Maria Bibiana and Marta Fiqueira, who taught class every day, and Manuel Quadrado the healer, who practiced his craft in a simple health center for medical treatment.[115] Still others were traders or merchants who ensured the flow of needed construction materials and other goods between Canudos and the surrounding world. Antonio Vilanova served in this role as the Counselor's right-hand man, together with his brother Honório. Their storefront balcony, operated by Honório's wife, Teresa Jardelina de Alencar, was a buzzing hive of activity and talk. Other merchants included Marciano de Sergipe, and Macambira. A few, like Jesuino Lima, were expelled when connections with the republic were reported and denounced. Lima got his revenge by guiding and fighting for the republican forces, where he was known as Captain Jagunço.[116] Finally, the town included entertainers, storytellers (*cantadores*), and musicians, like Roman and Chico Ferreira.[117] From these diverse talents emerged a fluid division of labor, mostly democratically and from the bottom up. As Honório Vilanova recalled, "Canudos was large in my time: those who farmed, farmed by the river; those who had cattle, took care of their cattle; those with a wife and children took care of their family; those who liked to pray went to pray; everything got done because everything belonged to all, little and big, according to the rule taught by the Pilgrim."[118]

It was a relatively egalitarian community. Women, especially those without the security of marriage or kin, enjoyed a wider range of freedoms than elsewhere in Bahia—they fought in the wars, they engaged an array of livelihoods, and prostitution, the fate of unmarried women without family in many Bahian towns, was strictly prohibited. Yet Canudos's social differences were still evident in its layout. Traces of class difference shaped neighborhoods. The commercial district of the city was in the plaza of the two churches. That was where the Counselor resided and where the best-built homes were erected, built of brick and roofed with shingles. There were a dozen of these more solid structures, surrounded by what the Capuchins called "the miserable habitations of his fanatic disciples."[119] These occupied four different districts. One of them was called "13th of May," named for the day of the abolition of slavery. Afro-Brazilians' houses were especially clustered there.

HORDE

Da Cunha's classic referred to the counselorists as a horde (*horda*) at least four times. Milton's, Horcades's, Benicio's reports too—nearly everyone applied the word, from Turkic for nomadic tent dwellers.[120] A horde is fickle, mobile, on the frontier, and hard to measure, tax, or conscript. As the opposite of a public composed of citizens, it threatens the "public order" and the "public good."[121] Just as the people must be made through political rituals of legitimation, a horde is also fashioned, by unmaking. It doesn't simply exist. How were the followers of the Counselor fashioned as such? First they were imagined to act less by will than by imitation, the "contagion of fanaticism," and delirium.[122] They were rendered a gang of cast-off fools. Here again we encounter the genre of comedy.

The future police chief Durval encountered the Pilgrim in 1882 and described him and his followers as buffoons: "There was the famous Counselor, a short, dark-skinned mix, with long, black hair and beard, dressed in a blue tunic. . . . This fellow is more ignorant fanatic than anchorite, and his occupation consists of preaching an incomplete morality, teaching prayers, giving banal sermons . . . to a civilized traveler it's a laughable spectacle, especially when he recites Latin that no one understands. The people flow to his rituals *en masse* and blindly obey."[123] Journalist Manoel Benicio similarly depicted Canudos as a comedy of castaways: "cripples, albinos, single women, thieves, the sick, murderers, vagabonds, singers, runaway slaves [*mucambeiros*], the blind, the possessed, the incestuous, the poor, the undeserving rich [*afortunados*], prostitutes, the most repulsive mixture that could possibly agglomerate around religious monomania."[124] The carnivalesque atmosphere of misfits was amplified in Mario Vargas Llosa's novel by the role of an actual traveling circus from which one of the Counselor's closest aids, the scribe Leão de Natuba, defects. In Vargas Llosa's depiction, Leão walks on all fours and flees the troupe and his life as spectacle to the protective side of the Counselor. But the idea of a circus also crept into actual depictions. Young Dr. Horcades began his report on Canudos with a reference to the Roman circus.[125] If Canudos was a circus, the Counselor was the ringmaster. One judge from the town of Monte Santo, Dr. Genes Fontes, was impressed by the "stupendous prestige" he inspired over this funhouse, as a "master of multitudes."[126]

Next, congregants were made a horde by virtue of their skin color, a disquieting mix. Many were former slaves or of mixed race.[127] The percentage of persons of color in Canudos was likely higher than that of the region's population.[128] Not surprisingly, elites judged the town in late-nineteenth-century terms of social Darwinism and racialist criminology. Euclides da Cunha described the people of Canudos as they swung into view:

> The procession came to a halt alongside the tents. . . . And then it was, for the first time, that our men had a chance to see the population of Canudos en masse. Aside from those variations due to the imprint of suffering variously borne, there was a rare and striking uniformity. . . . There were few whites or pure Negroes among them; an unmistakable family likeness in all these faces pointed to the perfect fusion of three races. The legitimate pardo type predominated, a mixture of Kafir, Portuguese and Tapuia Indian—bronzed faces, stiff and straight or curly hair, unshapely torsos. . . . And round about them all were the victors, separate and disparate, proteiform types, the white man, the black man, the cafuso, and the mulatto, with all gradations of coloring. There was a contrast here: the strong and integral race thus reduced, within this square, to these indefinable and pusillanimous mestizos.[129]

Elsewhere Euclides applied euphemisms—"multifarious population" (*população multiforme*) or "unconscious brute mass," or a community with an appearance like "a fetish in flesh and bone . . . calculated to revive the degenerative stigmata of the three races"[130]—but the subtext was always clear. Promiscuity, bastardy, criminals, miscegenation, even the huts of Canudos, skeletal frames packed with soil, were "monstrous."[131]

The baron of Jeremoabo did not bother with euphemisms or misdirection. He specifically situated the Canudos movement in the wake of abolition: "The effects of his propaganda on the servile element were felt even more strongly given the lack of working hands in the wake of abolition."[132] Benicio too described them as generally negros and mestiços.[133] As did the colonel in the national guard, José Américo Camelo de Souza Velho, who wrote in his 1894 letter to the baron that they were all former slaves and criminals.[134] Another letter described them as "people of May 13" (abolition), again suggesting a large number of former slaves. We know, though, that the Counselor also attracted large groups of Amerindians in certain places; at the village of Soure a large number of "indios de Mirandela" listened, armed with bow and arrow.[135] Moreover, among the last 146 survivors of the destruction of Canudos, mostly children, 41 were registered as "white." The town presented a multiracial society joined not only in religious devotion but also by class and common life chances, though it was almost always represented as tied to blackness and miscegenation.[136]

This gives purchase to see how the characterization of the Canudos horde took shape. Canudos became a horde, at least in part, by being racialized as dark-skinned "rabble."[137] The fact of being a mixed population carried entangled religious and political implications. Some argued that not only the race but also the religion of the jagunço backlander was dubiously mixed, "a mixture of Indian animism, African fetishism and Portuguese superstition."[138] The famous Bahian doctor Raimundo Nina Rodrigues, who after the war kept Antonio Conselheiro's head for study, likewise linked racial atavism (*mestiço atavismo*), the contagious masses, fetishistic religion, and bad politics; in this case, the Canudos fetishists' "instinctive need for a king." Even as fetishistic religion needs materials to hold onto, he wrote, monarchists need their king's body. Both fetishists and monarchists were to be understood as incapable of abstract thought or democratic representation.[139] According to Nina Rodrigues's influential diagnosis, then, monarchism was a political version of religious fetishism. Like fetishist religion (his empirical referent was Afro-Brazilian Candomblé), this was a politics befitting a certain stage and destined to be surpassed. Yet he doubted that Afro-Brazilians, or in this case the Canudos counselorists, were mentally equipped to leave either religious fetishism or monarchism behind. The result, in his view, was an episode of anthropological tragedy. Fate, circumstance, and history sentenced Canudos to burn.

In sum, despite occasional valorizations of the frontier mestiços' "robust, organic integrity," Afro-Brazilians, Amerindians, and mixed-race members of the ekklesia were mostly packed into second-order descriptors like the horde.[140] Then this assemblage was rhetorically and "scientifically" yoked to bad religion (fetishism), bad politics (monarchism), and the idea of the primitive. Euclides da Cunha wrote in his diary, "He pulls together the multitude—invested and dominated—not because he dominates them as such, but because they are his complete and *natural* product.[141] It was in their nature to follow, he seemed to propose, because they were people of nature, part of the land itself. The people become "povo da terra," people of the land, as opposed to a people making themselves through their relation to the land (*fazer-se da terra*).[142] Skin color seemed to matter a lot; so did the material form of religious practice. These two factors became durably entwined to recast a people as mere *povão*, a horde of excess declassificados.

There are examples of ones who left the horde and the barbaric state of nature to be converted to the status of citizen, by defection. One former resident of Canudos, Miguel de Aguiar Mattos, was asked to leave the village. He became a known personage of the republican army, a bona fide citizen recognized by the patria. Such rare exceptions were able to join themselves to a different kind of multitude, the redemptive crowd, the vigorous and beatific doppelgänger to the horde's rachitic shape.

THE PHILOSOPHERS' HORDE

The racial horde was more than a late-nineteenth-century echo. Analogous depictions of the fearsome, disposable horde trace a long arc. Sociology had often been mapped onto geography, as the irrational possessed body shifted from the state of nature Hobbes had located in the Americas to racialized representations of certain religions. Especially dangerous were religions leading to possession or the horde's swarming enthusiasm, Kant's feared *Schwärmerei*.[143] In Hegel's writing the swarming horde was depicted above all in the African religion of fetishes, imagined to elevate random objects for veneration, misrecognized as containers of presence. This became standard. "The fetich doctor and fetich belief were a *vis a tergo* with the native horde," read a popular missionary account written at around the same time as the Canudos conflict.[144] Fetishism drew on stereotypes of African and Afro-Brazilian religious practice to critique empty ceremonialism and, in Brazilian republican discourse, to monarchists' alleged lack of the capacity for abstract representation—hence their need to see and touch an actual king's body.

The most popular work on the dangerous force of the crowd at the time of Canudos was Gustave Le Bon's 1895 *Psychologie des foules*.[145] It exerted clear influence on Dr. Nina Rodrigues's evaluation of the Counselor and his community. What was striking in Le Bon's work, and replicated in Brazilian authors from Nina Rodrigues to Euclides da Cunha, was the drawing together of vivid portraits of the blind masses—in Brazil, the *povão*—and bad religion. In Le Bon's scenario, modern humanity, under the force of the crowd, descended the evolutionary ladder to become a nonrational primitive, for which "Ethiopians" and "negroes" played the foil.[146] Socialism and traditional religion were but two versions of the same phenomenon for Le Bon, and in the view of influential Brazilian writers like Nina Rodrigues and da Cunha, the two malign forces were combined at Canudos. The man lost in the crowd, like the primitive, was blindly obedient and incapable of exercising free will. This posed political risks, as Le Bon warned: "In this way the religious spirit replaces at one stroke the slow hereditary accumulation necessary to form the soul of a nation."[147]

This horde, this contagious epidemic of delirium, indexed the lack of a properly bounded self and the lack of a properly circumscribed society capable of forming the people. Whereas for Le Bon, as for Hegel, Africa served as the foil for the politically incapable masses without history, for republican Brazilian writers at the end of the nineteenth century, Canudos served as chronotope of the anticitizen and the ungoverned state, a place and time of a monarchist rabble, or an undifferentiated mob.[148]

SUBLIME CROWD

Among the representations of "the people," the dangerous horde was juxtaposed not only with the rational individual but also with the sublime or redemptive masses, the "crowd of citizens."[149]

The very terms deployed to disparage the "May 13 people"— that is, those slaves freed by abolition on May 13, 1888, and become residents of Canudos—were, in the immediate wake of actual abolition applied in a positive, even utopian sense. In the days after Princess Isabel's signing of the Golden Law, immense crowds packed the streets of the capital—especially Ouvidor Street, where the newspaper officers were quartered, what would later be the site of riots in the wake of the third failed expedition against Canudos. Less than a decade earlier, on the same site of the riots, the crowd was depicted as a signature of the "vast heart of the nation," its "great national soul."[150] Here is the news report from May 15, 1888: "The extraordinary animation of popular festivities continued yesterday. Waves of people flooded Ouvidor St . . . explosively manifesting their vivid contentment and enthusiasm. . . . One noted the fevered eye of each citizen, each a doubling of the great soul of the patria. . . . It's difficult to describe what we saw. So impressive, so gorgeous and majestic was this beautiful image of a people agitated by the fever of patriotism." On May 17 the people continued their jubilation: "It's a delirium, a genuine delirium in which one feels the vertiginous pulse of the heart of the patria . . . no music is more sonorous to the ears of the people . . . than this, released in the divine harmonies of each syllable in that sacrosanct word, Liberty!"

The effervescence continued, as detailed on May 18: "Indescribable is the enormous happiness agitating the masses . . . in the vibrations of this enthusiasm is an expression of unspeakable superhuman grandeur. A single sentiment, a unique passion dominates this wave of people that coils without ceasing, like a giant serpent following wherever this delirious enthusiasm leads." May 20 brought further chronicles of "enchantment," including patriotic "vibrations" of the people with a multitude of arms waving as one single form.

Let us note the terms of this idealized national body of citizens: A frenzy of fevered people was not presented as grotesque, dangerous, or primitive but rather as "most sublime," even holy (*santa*). This feverish mass, this vibrating multitude was "gorgeous" and "majestic." No need for accountable individuals now: rather the masses formed a "single body" with no head, dominated by passionate enthusiasm. This sublime crowd consisted of a doubling, the individual become an expression of the group soul in "collective delirium." Even the trope of the diabolical snake was inverted and made a wonder, the masses of people formed into serpent's coils so formidable that one could not find their end.

Da Cunha described a similarly sublime crowd gathered in Rio to celebrate the fall of Canudos: "The days now were filled with the movements of noisy crowds, storming in the streets and squares, shouting and laughing, weeping and wailing, which was their way of paying solemn tribute to the nation's heroes."[151]

How shall we make sense of the apparent disjuncture between the crowd in the capital as "heart of the nation" and the crowd in Canudos as heart of darkness, an infected organ in need of removal? The descriptions of the crowd, *as* crowd, were the same—delirious, uncontrolled, frenzied, massive, irrational. Nothing changed but the presentation and location of bodies, framed on the one hand as mixed race, degenerate, fetishist, politically retrograde, and on the frontier and on the other hand as patriotic, nationalist, loyal, emotionally robust, forward-looking, racially unmarked, and metropolitan. The horde was on the frontier, ranged around a prophet. The sublime crowd was in the capital, gathered tight at the throne of governance.

In this last section I tried to step back from direct state power—the march of men and cannons to Canudos—to consider indirect techniques of unmaking a people, rendering them expendable excess and legitimately sacrificeable. Foucault argued that the analysis of power never, in effect, liberated itself from focusing on the state and rule of law, never "cut off the head of the king," in order to move from violence toward the capillary analysis of biopower, the internalization of discipline, or the manufacture of categories from madness to the horde.[152] That said, at Canudos, bodily violence *was* central. Churchstateness was enabled to appear, come alive, and take on tangible form through the capacity to extend military force, prodded and buttressed by the church, even to the backlands frontier, to nowhere. Biopolitical methods of unmaking the ekklesia through classifications of deviance were not enough—the horde, the fanatic, the fetishist—because the counselorists occupied their own buffered zone of valued signs, things, sounds, and words. But sharper tools and techniques remained. They focused less on undoing the ideological heart or spirit of the people than on simply aiming for the head.

ACEPHALOUS: THE SPECTACULAR WAR

Vargas Llosa's fictional character Gall is a scientific phrenologist who palpitates the heads of everyone he meets. The character was fictional, but not the type. Republican reporters, doctors, and soldiers were focused on the heads of rebel subjects. Da Cunha noted the "flat" cranium of the backlands jagunço.[153] After his death, the Counselor's head was taken for careful phrenological examination by Nina Rodrigues at the Faculty of Medicine, in Salvador, Bahia. "[His cranium] was really very likely to be degenerated given its mestiço quality," he wrote.[154]

If a few on the expedition dedicated themselves to palpitating the backlanders' crania, republican soldiers devoted themselves to removing them. Manuel Ciríaco described leaving Canudos on September 26, knowing the Counselor to already be dead and the resistance at an end, and seeing soldiers cutting off heads. Survivor José Travessia reported, "After the fighting ended, I returned to find nothing but mountains and mountains of rotting bodies without heads."[155] Honório Vilanova likewise recalled soldiers deforming counselorists' heads. Marciano de Sergipe was a victim of having his eyes dug out. A boy was beheaded. Vilanova recalled that the soldiers decapitated (*degolar*) one of the Counselor's aids, Antônio Beatinho, who led a group of refugees—mostly women and children, and the wounded—to surrender.[156] Ultimately they were all (up to six hundred) executed by having their throats cut or by full beheading, in an area later called the *vale dos degolamentos* (valley of decapitations).[157] This was at least in part to inspire fear among the counselorists, who were reported to fear above all else dying by metal blade instead of by gunshot, in battle. They said that dying by throat-cutting was a dishonorable end and might even prevent the victim from receiving a heavenly reward. Presumably the army

FIGURE 3. Flávio de Barros's photograph of those who surrendered on October 2, 1897, at the end of the war. Originally entitled *400 jagunços prisoneiros*. Most of the prisoners were massacred soon after the photograph was taken, both at the warzone and at a detention camp. Photograph courtesy of Arquivo Histórico e Institucional do Museu da República, Rio de Janeiro, Brazil.

forces made use of such fears. One republican soldier achieved an awe-inspiring reputation to rebels and fame among his peers for his skill, garnering the nickname of "degolador," the throat cutter or beheader.[158] Horcades wrote that he saw almost all survivors killed in this way, "sacrificed" (his term)[159] (fig. 3).

The photographs of Augusto Flávio de Barros became iconic, but this one was most important of all. It's the only image of the Canudos ekklesia in a large group. Probably a skilled amateur, Flávio de Barros was contracted by the army to document the triumph, arriving at Canudos on September 26, 1897, and remaining in camp until October 12. He took seventy-two photographs, none of which appeared to the public until after the war, when they circulated both in studio expositions and sales, as well as in public electric projection shows. Ana Maria Mauad notes that Flávio de Barros was one of a number of intellectuals mobilized to witness, narrate, and help to constitute the "end of the monarchists" as an event.[160] He did his job exceedingly well. The great majority of his photographs were posed shots of the army. As Mauad argues, almost all of them were horizontally configured and focused in sharp definition, visually ratifying the army as a cohesive, well-organized collective and a conscientious, dutiful guarantor of order. But if this particular photograph—depicting the battalion of the police of Pará surrounding surrendered captives—initially communicated such disciplined control, journalists' narratives later transformed it into a testimony to a terrible crime.

There were also instances of the rebels beheading republican soldiers. The leader of the third expedition, General Moreira César, had been known by the nickname "Headcutter" (*Cortecabeça*). As described above, after Moreira César was wounded, his second in command, Colonel Tamarindo, was killed as well. After being buried by his fellow soldiers, Tamarindo was disinterred and decapitated, his headless body hung on an angico tree, ten kilometers from Canudos, dressed in his uniform and gloves.[161] On the afternoon of August 6, Horcades saw Tamarindo's withered frame as the medical corps neared the battle zone. But Tamarindo's fate seems to have been unusual. A few republican heads were set on pikes along the route to Canudos to demoralize arriving reinforcements, but, overall, beheaded republican soldiers were rare. However, a statement from journalist Favila Nunes indicated that rebels sometimes dug up republican soldiers' bodies to cut off their hands and feet.[162]

What could it mean that, at least on occasions when there was opportunity to sculpt the enemy corpse, the jagunços sometimes cut off republican soldiers' hands and feet, while republican soldiers consistently detached the heads of their captive dead and prisoners? One possibility is that the jagunços were acting out biblical texts, passages perhaps communicated to them orally in sermons and teachings from the Counselor. The Hebrew Bible text 2 Samuel 4:12, for example, narrates that "David gave an order to his men, and they killed them. They cut off their hands and feet and hung the bodies by the pool in Hebron. But they took the head of Ish-Bosheth." Interesting here is that Ish-Bosheth was a king and received a king's death, namely beheading. Perhaps the jagunços cut off the head of Colonel Tamarindo because he was the acting commander in chief after the mortal wounding of Moreira César on the third expedition. Rank-and-file soldiers in the biblical tale, by contrast, who served with hands and feet rather than with their heads, were prepared according to their proper station: their hands and feet were removed. Likewise the republican soldiers whom the rebels were able to disinter were disfigured according to their rank, as footmen. For the backlanders, soldiers' hands and feet may have been treated as tools of extending the republic's power to the frontier and into Canudos. To remove them may have been an act of amputating and foreshortening the motile force of the republic.

Or perhaps hands and feet were taken as a mode of posthumously branding republican soldiers as sinners, or even as an attempt to advance their eternal redemption: in the New Testament, Mark 9:43 reads, "If your hand causes you to stumble, cut it off. It is better for you to enter life maimed than with two hands to go into hell, where the fire never goes out." There isn't sufficient evidence in the written record to push any interpretation very far. Beheading and disfiguring were intended as communicative statements that "said" something different for each side. The jagunços treated enemy cadavers in accord with a sacred monarchic world. They did not rob money or remove personal effects from the soldiers. Divinely conferred rank was respected: kings or military leaders were treated one way, basic footmen another. I see the beheading as wielded by the counselorists against Tamarindo as a monarchist performance, a fleshly statement on the rightful hierarchic privilege of a commander. Their necropolis installed the proper church-state order into the very soil. Republicans' beheadings of counselorists, by contrast, were democratic. All were treated the same, all beheaded according to what, following Foucault, we could call "a legal code of pain . . . calculated according to detailed rules."[163]

All were kings, since the king was dead. No *noblesse oblige*—to all the same mortification. In this way, the republican army, too, impressed its political order onto the stacks of the dead.

Beheadings of prisoners were mirrored by the army's defacement of saints. At the end of the war, republican soldiers stationed as reserves in Monte Santo used the points of their sabers to cut off faces in images of Jesus and the saints at the Church of Santa Cruz. The observer Alfredo Silva described this as soldiers' "religious exaggeration,"[164] but to me it seems consistent. They aimed to craft a republican religion properly purified of saints in parallel with a government properly purified of the monarch's face and a frontier purified of rebel kings. If the ideas of fetishism and monarchism were joined in the writings of Dr. Nina Rodrigues, here they were joined in practice, the carving of bayonets.

THE COUNSELOR'S TWO BODIES

Colonel José Américo reported that several of the Counselor's followers—including Macambira, Norberto, and Manuel Franco—spent three days with Antonio's corpse, awaiting its resurrection. When the Pilgrim failed to rise again, his friends crowned him with four images of saints, one on each shoulder, one on his feet, one on his head, and then covered him with a leather shroud. They completed his burial with dirt and flowers. Manuel Franco fled, but Macambira and Norberto refused to leave and were shot or shelled by his side.

Republican forces discovered the Counselor's body eight days later. It was found in the building called the Sanctuary on October 6 at 11:00 a.m. Disinterred by the army's sanitary corps (*Comissão do corpo sanitário*), the corpse was moved to the better light of the church plaza, where it was photographed by Flávio de Barros in three positions (fig. 4).

An affidavit certifying its identity was drawn up and remitted to Minister of War Bittencourt.[165] The medical intern Martins Horcades cleaned and disinfected the body of the Counselor,

FIGURE 4. Flávio de Barros's photograph of Antonio Conselheiro's body on October 6, 1897, prior to the removal of his head. Photograph: Courtesy of Arquivo Histórico e Institucional do Museu da República, Rio de Janeiro, Brazil.

which had begun to putrefy. The army initially reburied him but upon deliberation decided to remove the head.[166] "Since it was a waste of time to exhume the body once more, a knife cleverly wielded at the right point did the trick. . . . After that they took it to the seaboard, where it was greeted by delirious multitudes with carnaval joy."[167] (Note again the sublime crowd juxtaposed with the sick horde.) Major Mirando Curió retained the head of the Counselor for future study. After being paraded on a pike in major cities along the coast, it was given to the medical faculty in Salvador, the capital of Bahia. Dr. Nina Rodrigues tried to determine whether there were cranial anomalies that might account for the Counselor's bizarre, delusional acts. He found none.

The Pilgrim walked on. For some he was not truly dead and would return in bodily form. For others he continued to live as a saint, invisible but vital, approached in pilgrimages to his shrine near Canudos. For still others he became an object of science, a cranium in a storage jar, until the head was consumed by fire in 1906. For many more he became a part of the history of the Brazilian republic—a heritage, a state park, a memorial, and, via Euclides da Cunha's book of 1902, *Rebellion in the Backlands*

(*Os Sertões*), a sacred national text. Still, his body was never fully cannibalized by these motives and movements. If his head was removed, his flesh remained. That place, where many descendants of the counselorists reside, remains as a trace of how a community grew outside of, or at least on the margins of, the republican state. This was less a "public" composed of citizens—recall the Counselor's denial of even the term "republic" based on his neologistic interpretation of it as *ré-publica*, a "defendant" or "criminal public"—than an ekklesia made of songs, stones, and work.

After Canudos the church in Brazil also occupied two bodies. The first, expressed and historically manifested at Canudos, was born of that nowhere place. It included homemade rosaries and clay images of saints. It had hand-copied Bibles and chants and songs in Portuguese and Latin both. Its beloved emissary might be an official priest, but was more often an untrained *beato*, made holy by walking and working the land. It had few official rites or masses but many material exchanges with saints, frequent visits by the dead, and abundant songs and stories. This body of the church was its popular form as constituted over three previous centuries, and it continued to periodically reappear during the twentieth century—in liberation theology, in the "inculturated mass," in the late-twentieth-century drive led by priests to gain legal recognition for Afro-Brazilian and indigenous identities and communities across the region.[168] The other body of the church took the form of the newly ascendant, re-Romanized version of the church, in partnership with the state. In a sense it too was born in Canudos, when the Capuchin priests shook the dust from their shoes and condemned the town to the coming hell.

CONCLUSION: ~~REPUBLICAN~~ LEGAL AFTERLIVES

Euclides da Cuhna, writing in his shorthand notebook en route to Canudos, scratched out "republican" and substituted the word "legal": "The people of Rio de Janeiro are in meeting aware of loss of ~~republican~~ legal weapons to monarchists in the backlands."[169] The moment was just after the disastrous third expedition but before the juggernaut of the triumphant fourth. The strikethrough is a clue, but to what? The fourth expedition shifted from a contest over the nature of churchstateness, and the profile of the nation's peoplehood, to a legal mandate. In keeping with one of law's etymologies, law would now be *laid down*, set and said with authority, even at the frontier. The substituted word "legal" inscribed over "republic" remains as a signature of the shift from politics to the sword. One might say that the blocking out of "republican" indexed the abandonment of the mission to Canudos as political project devoted to recuperating a strayed part of the nation. Thereafter the mission, fueled by "civic energy" back in Rio de Janeiro, was to perform and impose the republic as spectacularly as possible. The strikethrough marks the shift from instrumental lordship to a figure of sovereignty that exceeds any meaning whatsoever.

There had been, and would be, other "legal" decapitations and paraded heads of famous insurgents in the history of Brazil: Zumbi of Palmares, leader of the kingdom of runaway slaves; Tiradentes, the anticolonial rebel; and the notorious outlaw bandit Lampaião from the same region as Antonio. I've never seen a photograph of Nina Rodrigues with the head of the Counselor, but we do have a cheery cliché from the medical faculty of the mummified heads of Lampaião and his wife (fig. 5).

In addition to giving silage for emergent psychiatric and phrenological sciences, it's hard not to see these heads through the genre of performative sacrifice. The journalist Favila Nunes placed Antonio squarely in that role. His corpse's beheading and burial marked "the victory that consolidated the Republic and left a tremendous lesson for the disturbers of order. The Patria's honor was saved."[170]

Martin Horcades's narrative marked this kind of shift in register, from republican politics to violently imposed law. At

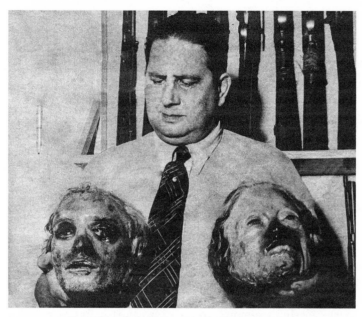

FIGURE 5. Photograph first published in the *Diário de Pernambuco* (April 19, 1959), 14. Severed in 1938, the heads the *cangaçeiro* [bandit] Lampaião and his partner, Maria Bonita, enjoyed a long tour before finally being exhibited at the Nina Rodrigues Institute. The caption in the newspaper reads, "Director of the Nina Rodrigues Institute of Bahia exhibits the heads of Lampaião and Maria Bonita. Completely deformed, these heads cannot serve for research, and should be buried." It appeared as part of a journalistic polemic in 1959 on exotic museum exhibitions of the famous bandits' heads. In an interview published in the magazine *O Cruzeiro* (June 6, 1959), Dr. Estácio de Lima defended their exhibition. He said they served as "inestimable documents of a period of Brazilian criminology" and would show later generations that, far from being a natural-born killer, Lampaião was "the fruit of social, political and economic conditions." He added, "These heads are a lesson for all time teaching that phenomena like banditry cannot and should not be exterminated with arms, but rather with the creation of factors that do not cause their outbreak." (*O Cruzeiro*, consulted at http://www.memoriaviva.com.br /ocruzeiro/, March 20, 2017.)

the end of Horcades's account, the nature of the narrated event morphs from a story of the imperiled republic to the holocaust of Canudos. Following the emotional oath made by President Prudente de Morais on October 7, not to leave a single "stone on stone," in the following days it was burned to the ground.[171] At the end many jagunços were incinerated, dying as they cried "Viva" to the monarchy and to their Counselor, refusing to save themselves with oaths to the republic. Horcades described how, after the last bombs fell and the cannons cooled, the moaning of the dying was replaced by "happy sounds of the hymns of victory." After all, their extermination was "necessary." The national flag was raised "in all the corners of Canudos" as musicians kept playing the glorious hymn. General Arthur Oscar de Andrade Guimarães posted an announcement: "Long live the Republic of the United States of Brazil! The Canudos campaign is ended.... Valiant soldiers! I was proud to command you; the Republic fills you with blessings."[172] Until that point Dr. Horcades still had faith and welcomed those blessings: if the soldiers had incinerated Canudos, it was "to carry out the most sacred of duties, and with the peculiar indifference of the heart that is generous and filled with faith."[173] Though the horror continued, and in spite of the dead bodies everywhere and the huts fogged with putrid fumes, uplifting music announced the end of fighting: bands formed on the main plaza by the churches to play the hymn of the Republic, "sonorous and majestic." The enthusiasm of the troops verged on delirium.[174]

But Horcades's faith was suddenly shaken.[175] As the Flávio de Barros photograph shown in figure 3 shows, some six hundred prisoners had surrendered during the last firebombing and filed out under a white flag, walking skeletons. Instead of being protected, as General de Andrade Guimarães promised, they were executed. They were led out in groups and commanded to shout praises to the republic, "but they said they preferred to die, and shouted vivas to Bom Jesus Conselheiro and Bello Monte." The soldiers cut their throats—the so-called red necktie (*gravata vermelha*)—then piled their bodies on huge fires, sacrificial pyres. There, Horcades wrote, they were "reduced to formless shapes." As though they were not that already. It was as though they had to be killed. They couldn't join the republic or be incorporated into the people. They were the living frontier, the *declassificados* who, by their externality, gave boundaries and anthropological shape to the republic within. Two years later, in 1899, the killing of surrendered prisoners was declared an international war crime in The Hague Conventions. But it was still legally undefined in 1897.

Victory was celebrated, and after the parades for returning soldiers subsided, even the dead of Canudos began to be redeemed. They were recruited into the republic. This should not surprise. In the United States in the same period, by way of comparison, the Lakota people were fashioned as national heritage and western romance concomitantly with their extermination and confinement. Buffalo Bill's Wild West Show employed Sitting Bull in 1885 and Black Elk multiple times thereafter, even before and while the last trace of Lakota sovereignty was erased at the massacre of Ghost Dancers in 1890—another example of uncivil, bad religion. The Lakota people were incorporated into the republic simultaneously as heroic captives and as corpses.

As to Canudos, perhaps a few hundred people had survived, many escaping before the final cataclysm.[176] Nearly all men were killed, but a few women and children were held captive. One landowner wrote the baron to propose the beheading of these remainders as well, since they would otherwise cost the state dearly to maintain.[177] But General de Andrade Guimarães's victory address already tried to humanize the jagunços as "people who had been equally committed to their ideals as the republicans," and some were taken back to Rio. Thus one officer arrived in Rio two weeks after the war's end, on October 26, with a *jagunçinha* ("little ruffian") named Maria in tow.[178]

The photographer Flávio de Barros arrived in Rio's port on the same ship, the *São Salvador*. The president took a launch out in the bay to greet them personally.

The shows in Rio opened a few months later on Christmas Eve.[179] "Curiosity! Amazement!! Horror!!! Wretchedness!!!!" read the announcement for a public, electric projection of Flávio de Barros's photographs of the end of the war, presented on a Molteni machine for a charge of one *mil-reis* (about US$4 today) per person. The advertisements were clear about the main attraction, namely his shot of "THE CADAVER OF THE FANATIC COUNSELOR."[180] Once news of the atrocities circulated, though, newspaper reports began to describe the rebels in mixed terms, not only as fanatics but also as fellow Brazilians and coreligionists. Published reports of eyewitnesses like Horcades generated outrage and posthumous sympathy for the Counselor's followers. The doctor and politician César Zama vehemently defended the counselorists. Politics is also a religion, he wrote under a pseudonym in 1899, and those at Canudos had a "sacred right" to advocate monarchism if they so wished. With that phrase he pulled the counselorists into the national embrace, as members of the people endowed with inalienable rights. Zama accused the republic of barbarism—of being made up of cannibals, who consume their own, and this in a so-called Catholic nation.[181] The statesman Rui Barbosa wrote an imaginative lecture to congress on the obligations placed on him by the victimized dead of Canudos, as their lawyer, again belatedly transforming them into people with legal rights that must be defended even postmortem.[182]

Over time, the counselorists were posthumously incorporated as citizens, even idealized. They were honored as a necessary sacrifice; in their blood the republic gained footing and traction. Their conversion into patrimony began with news reports, outrage at the scandal, and postmortem legal defenses. Initially that shame led to effacement: the town was burned in 1897 and then flooded to create a reservoir in 1962; only during

FIGURE 6. The text on the sign begins: "Massacrá Road: This road that you walk is a sacred road. Antonio Conselheiro and his followers walked it during romarias and processions. An extension of the Road of the Rosário, Massacrá Road ended at the Plaza of Churches." Photograph by Paul Christopher Johnson.

droughts does the water level lower enough to see the ramparts of the Church of the Good Jesus.

Still, over the last half century, effacement has been balanced by other values. The Estrada da Massacrá, the road that entered Belo Monte and where the Counselor walked in ritual processions, was converted into a new currency: "This road is *sacred* ground," a park sign confers (fig. 6).

Finally the fanatics of Belo Monte were admitted to the ranks of the people—but only against their will, as consecrated dead.

Canudos has too easily and often been called a millenarian movement, but such a glamorous gloss does it no service. It was closer to the earth than that. Apocalyptic ideas were mostly marginal

FIGURE 7. House of a jagunço of Canudos. Photograph: Courtesy of Arquivo Histórico e Institucional do Museu da República, Rio de Janeiro, Brazil.

to its workaday routine prior to the wars. Women and men with little to lose came to join an ekklesia on the frontier of a distant and disinterested republican state, and an increasingly Romanized church. For a short time it thrived as a community of acclamation gathered around Antonio, the Bom Jesus. The people crafted sonic, tactile, and visual techniques that made God appear and matter in collective life, outside of a newly armed and purified version of churchstateness. For reasons contingent on local political dynamics rippling in relation to the newborn republic, they were destroyed. Yet Canudos continued to harrow the nation—in projection shows, books, telenovelas, and skulls that still sing in the valley of decapitations.

NOTES

1. Euclides da Cunha, *Rebellion in the Backlands*, trans. Samuel Putnam (Chicago: University of Chicago Press, 1944), 163.

2. The impeachment process may well soon be repeated. The current president, Michel Temer, reels from scandal to scandal, from charges of graft to illegally pushing business deals on behalf of cronies. On May 17, 2017, the newspaper *O Globo* released tapes

of Temer apparently authorizing the payment of "hush money" bribes to Eduardo da Cunha—currently jailed—to buy the latter's silence on Temer's corruption. The problem is that the next in line to the presidency, Speaker of the House Rodrigo Maia, is also under investigation. And so on.

3. Marina Brandão, "No dia do santo casamenteiro, pedidos agora são por emprego," *O Globo*, June 14, 2016, 16. Here and elsewhere, all translations are mine unless otherwise indicated.

4. The idea of stateness as a structural and metaphysical effect, or conjured appearance, is from Mitchell, "The Limits of the State," 94.

5. In a memo sent on August 24, 2016, she asked an evangelical group still supporting her, the Frente de Evangélicos pelo Estado de Direito, to pray for the failure of the "coup."

6. "Foi Deus que fez com que várias pessoas percebessem o que estava acontecendo com o nosso país e criassem coragem para se levantarem e fazerem alguma coisa a respeito."

7. Thaís Reis Oliviera and João Batista Jr., "Janaína Paschoal: 'Não sou a menina pastora e prefiro Pink Floyd,'" *Huffington Post Brasil*, accessed August 31, 2016, http://www.brasilpost.com.br /2016/04/06/janaina-paschal-pink-floyd_n_9626466.html.

8. Senator Magno Malta (PR-ES), for example, invoked God, Solomon, the Bible, and his family.

9. The four-part miniseries *Guerra de Canudos* (1997).

10. From the journalist Euclides da Cunha's field notebook, *Caderneta de campo* (Rio de Janeiro: Fundação Biblioteca Nacional, 2009), 98.

11. Samuel Butler's 1872 novel *Erewhon* explored the key role of religious estrangement in marking the edge of "nowhere," the frontier. In the land of Erewhon, physical sickness is treated as a moral failure demanding imprisonment, while moral flaws like stealing are healed through sympathy and convalescence. No one in Erewhon believes in the public religion with its many gods, elaborate temples, and numerous priests, but everyone is devoted to the publicly shamed and rarely mentioned deity, Ydgrun. Samuel Butler, *Erewhon* (1872; Mineola, NY: Dover, 2002), 87.

12. This was the official tally proposed by the Brazil's corps of engineers in 1897. Some eyewitnesses gauged the number substantially lower. See, inter alia, Henrique Duque Estrada de Macedo Soares, *A Guerra de Canudos* (Rio de Janeiro: Philobiblion, 1985), 46.

13. Euclides da Cunha, *Diário de uma expedição*, ed. Walnice Nogueira Galvão (São Paulo: Companhia das Letras, 2000), 91.

14. "State-informed body" plays on Bourdieu's key phrase "the socially informed body." Bourdieu, *Outline of a Theory of Practice*, 124.

15. Eric Santner, *The Weight of All Flesh: On the Subject Matter of Political Economy* (Oxford: Oxford University Press, 2015), 244.

16. On the origin of *jagunço*, see da Cunha, *Rebellion in the Backlands*, 148. Levine added that the term "probably came from Portuguese Africa, where *zarguncho* (or zagunço) was used for someone uncouth and quarrelsome." Robert M. Levine, *Vale of Tears: Revisiting the Canudos Massacre in Northeast Brazil, 1893–1897* (Berkeley: University of California Press, 1992), 331. The quotation on jagunços and citizens appears in Aristides A. Milton, *A Campanha de Canudos* (Rio de Janeiro: Imprensa Nacional, 1902), 60, 62. Abelardo F. Montenegro wrote that in everyday use "jagunço" refers to "an individual who is habitually surrounded by disorder caused either by himself or others." Abelardo F. Montenegro, *Antônio Conselheiro* (Fortaleza, Ceará: A. Batista Fontenelle, 1954), 30.

17. "Infused" (*erfüllt*) and "spirit of the State" (*Geist des Staates*) are from the vocabulary of Karl Marx, *Zur Judenfrage* (Berlin: Ernst Rowohlt Verlag, 1919), 19; Marx in turn borrowed "spirit of the State" from Georg Wilhelm Friedrich Hegel, *Grundlinien der Philosophie des Rechts* (Berlin: Nicolaischen Buchhandlung, 1821), 299.

18. Consuelo Novais Sampaio, following Calasans, observed three cycles: first, that of eyewitness reports, mostly in books published by journalists who had followed the end of the war; second, a half century dominated by Euclides da Cunha's *Os Sertões*; and the third, a cycle initiated by José Calasans that seeks to revisit Canudos again without the burden of *Os Sertões* and its legacy, and without the ideological weight of the republic. We remain in this "third cycle." Conseulo Novais Sampaio, *Cartas para o barão* (São Paulo:

EdUSP, 1999), 12; José Calasans, "Canudos Não Euclidiano," in *Subsídios para a sua reavaliação histórica* (Rio de Janeiro: Fundação Casa de Rui Barbosa, 1986), 1. On the meanings of this mass of materials on Canudos, this discursive excess, see Adriana Michéle Campos Johnson, *Sentencing Canudos: Subalternity in the Backlands of Brazil* (Pittsburgh: University of Pittsburgh Press, 2010).

19. Adriana Johnson also noted this, distinguishing "crowd" from "public." Johnson, *Sentencing Canudos*, 115.

20. Jan French, *Legalizing Identities: Becoming Black or Indian in Brazil's Northeast* (Chapel Hill: University of North Carolina Press, 2009), 18.

21. Rui Facó provides a broad summary of the social conditions that helped to motivate the movement at Canudos, in *Cangaceiros e fanáticos: Gênese e lutas* (Rio de Janeiro: UFRJ, 2009), 25–47.

22. Durval Vieira de Aguiar, *Descrições práticas da provincia da Bahia* (Rio de Janeiro: Editora Cátedra, 1979), 82. "Moral equivalence" is from Todd Diacon, *Millenarian Vision, Capitalist Reality: Brazil's Contestado Rebellion, 1912–1916* (Durham, NC: Duke University Press, 1991). As he showed, rural peasants' lives were ordered by complex relations of ritual reciprocity with landowners and Catholic saints, and above all through institutions like godparenthood. Patricia R. Pessar's work described how this assemblage still appears in informants' discourse as the *antiga lei* (old law). Its perceived loss is a part of what accounted for the rise of the movement under study, as well as comparable religious movements. Patricia R. Pessar, *From Fanatics to Folk: Brazilian Millenarianism and Popular Culture* (Durham, NC: Duke University Press, 2004).

23. See French, *Legalizing Identities*, 21.

24. Ralph Della Cava, "Brazilian Messianism and National Institutions: A Reappraisal of Canudos and Joaseiro," *Hispanic American Historical Review* 48, no. 3 (1986): 404.

25. Nertan Macedo, *Memorial de Vilanova* (Rio de Janeiro: Edições O Cruzeiro, 1964), 17.

26. S. de Souza Dantas, *Aspectos e contrastes: Ligeiro estudo sobre o estado da Bahia* (Rio de Janeiro: Revista dos Tribunaies, 1922), 144.

27. Sílvio Romero, *Estudos sobre a poesia popular do Brasil* (Petrópolis: Vozes, 1977), 41. Della Cava notes that the *beato*, the wandering lay servant of the church, was a known and respected role, having become a recognized "office" in the northeast through the work of a beloved reformer-priest named Father Ibiapina, whom Antonio may have encountered in the early 1870s. Della Cava, "Brazilian Messianism and National Institutions," 407.

28. Macedo, *Memorial de Vilanova*, 40; Calasans, "Canudos não Euclidiano," 17; Marco Antonio Villa, *Canudos: O povo da terra* (São Paulo: Editora Ática, 1995), 26.

29. Manoel Benicio, *O rei dos jagunços: Chronica historica e de costumes sertanejos sobre os acontecimentos de Canudos* (Rio de Janeiro: Typographia do Jornal do Commercio, 1899), 62; João Evangelista de Monte Marciáno, *Relatório apresentado pelo Revd. Frei João Evangelista de Monte Marciano ao Arcebispado da Bahia sobre Antonio Conselheiro* (Bahia: Typographia do Correio de Noticias, 1895), 4.

30. Da Cunha, *Rebellion in the Backlands*, 129; Benicio, *O rei dos jagunços*, 104.

31. Max Weber, "The Nature of Charismatic Authority and Its Routinization," in *Max Weber on Charisma and Institution Building*, ed. S. N. Eisenstadt, trans. Talcott Parsons (Chicago: University of Chicago Press, 1968), 50.

32. As Levine notes, the charges were absurd and obvious fabrications. Levine, *Vale of Tears*, 137.

33. Waldemar Valente, *Misticismo e região* (Recife: MEC, 1963), 67.

34. Villa, *Canudos*, 25. On the welcome accorded him by local priests, see Della Cava, "Brazilian Messianism and National Institutions," 407; Montenegro, *Antônio Conselheiro*, 31; and Milton, *A Campanha de Canudos*, 10.

35. Benicio summarizes this official correspondence. Benicio, *O rei dos jagunços*, 44–59.

36. Da Cunha, *Rebellion in the Backlands*, 138.

37. Aguiar, *Descrições práticas*, 82–83.

38. Robert M. Levine, "Canudos in the National Context," *The Americas* 48, no. 2 (1991): 211.

39. Facó, *Cangaceiros e fanáticos*, 98.

40. In fact a republican newspaper later accused Princess Isabel and her husband, the Conde d'Eu, of funding monarchist restorationists. Levine, "Canudos in the National Context," 214.

41. The land's title was held by the baroness of São Francisco do Conde. Levine, "Canudos in the National Context," 146; cf. Eurides de Souza dos Santos, *A música de Canudos* (Salvador: Coleção Selo Editorial, n.d.), 22. Montenegro wrote that the land was technically owned by Mariana Fiel de Carvalho but had been abandoned since 1891. Montenegro, *Antônio Conselheiro*, 29.

42. Levine, "Canudos in the National Context," 211.

43. This perspective is forcefully defended by Facó, *Cangaceiros e fanáticos*.

44. Testimony of Francisco Cardoso de Macedo, in Odorico Tavares, *Canudos: Cinqüenta anos depois* (Bahia: Conselho Estadual da Cultura, 1947), 49.

45. Álvaro Dantas de Carvalho and Consuelo Novais Sampaio, "A posição do Barão de Jeremoabo," in *Canudos: Cartas para o barão* (São Paulo: EdUSP, 1999), 18.

46. Sampaio, *Cartas para o barão*, 90–94.

47. Barão de Jeremoabo, *Jornal de Notícias*, Bahia, March 4, 1897. Quoted in ibid., 45.

48. Da Cunha included a concise timeline of the four expeditions, which I follow here. Da Cunha, *Rebellion in the Backlands*, 477–78.

49. Manuel Ciríaco, one of the counselorists interviewed fifty years later by Odorico Tavares, in 1947, refuted the idea of foreign sources of weapons. He offered details on the rebels' practice with the new weapons left behind by Moreira César, including mastering guns that could take the neck off a bottle from a kilometer away. Tavares, *Canudos*, 44.

50. Walnice Nogueira Galvão, ed., *No calor da hora: A guerra de Canudos nos jornais* (São Paulo: Editora Ática, 1994), 16.

51. Reporter Favila Nunes, in *Gazeta de Notícias*, reprinted in ibid., 160. The telegraph line to Monte Santo was laid specifically to cover the war. Nunes reported that the telegraph station was wildly overrun with five to six hundred messages submitted for transmission daily. While some lines were cut, other telegraph lines were laid specifically for communications with, and coverage of, the fourth expedition, such as that from Queimadas to Monte Santos. See Soares, *A guerra de Canudos*, 56. Thus, part of the war was over the insistence upon, or the resistance to, the region's communication links to the coast and capital.

52. Manuel Benício of the *Jornal do Commercio* was forced to leave the front for writing unflattering stories about the army. Euclides da Cunha of the newspaper *Estado de São Paulo*, by contrast, was seen as supportive and given privileged access. See Berthold Zilly, "Flávio de Barros, o ilustre cronista anônimo da Guerra de Canudos," *Estudos avançados* 13, no. 35 (1999): 107.

53. In Walnice Nogueira Galvão and Fernando da Rocha Peres, eds., "Apêndices," in *Breviário de Antonio Conselheiro* (Salvador da Bahia: Universidade Federal da Bahia, 2002), 144.

54. Printed in the *Gazeta de Notícias* on October 28, 1897. In Nogueira Galvão, *No calor da hora*, 211.

55. Macedo, *Memorial de Vilanova*, 41; cf. Tavares, *Canudos*, 40, 48.

56. Macedo, *Memorial de Vilanova*, 69.

57. Eduardo Hoornaert emphasizes the value of family, including fictive kin, which seems to have been part of the social structure at Belo Monte. Eduardo Hoornaert, *Os anjos de Canudos: Uma revisão histórica* (Petrópolis: Vozes, 1997), 49.

58. Ibid., 31.

59. Marciáno, *Relatório*, 5–7.

60. Macedo, *Memorial de Vilanova*, 127.

61. Ibid., 128.

62. Manoel José Gonçalves Couto, *Missão abreviada* (Porto: Typographia de Sebastião José Pereira, 1859).

63. Macedo, *Memorial de Vilanova*, 50; Levine, *Vale of Tears*, 194.

64. Fernando da Rocha Peres, "Fragmentaria," in *Breviário de Antonio Conselheiro*, ed. Walnice Nogueira Galvão and Fernando da Rocha Peres (Salvador da Bahia: Universidade Federal da Bahia, 2002), 25.

65. Ibid., 86.

66. Ibid., 85, 88.

67. As reported by Honório Vilanova, in Macedo, *Memorial de Vilanova*, 39, 68.

68. Hoornaert, *Os anjos*, 54.

69. Walnice Nogueira Galvão and Fernando da Rocha Peres, eds., *Breviário de Antonio Conselheiro* (Salvador da Bahia: Universidade Federal da Bahia, 2002), 77, 84.

70. Here I follow the summary points from the essay by Walnice Nogueira Galvão, "Piedade e paixão," in *Breviário de Antonio Conselheiro*, ed. Walnice Nogueira Galvão and Fernando da Rocha Peres (Salvador da Bahia: Universidade Federal da Bahia, 2002), 15–16.

71. The sermon "Sobre a república" was published in Ataliba Nogueira, ed., *António Conselheiro e Canudos, revisão histórica: A obra manuscrita de António Conselheiro e que pertenceu a Euclides da Cunha* (São Paulo: Companhia Editoria Nacional, 1974), 175–81.

72. English translation by Samuel Putnam from da Cunha, *Rebellion in the Backlands*, 163–64. Da Cunha first recorded the poem in Portuguese in his field notebook. Da Cunha, *Caderneta*, 147–52. In his notebook he recorded fifty-five stanzas but selected just the seven that appear here as representative to reproduce in *Os Sertões* (*Rebellion in the Backlands*).

73. Galvão, *No calor da hora*, 203.

74. Hoornaert, *Os anjos*, 19–23, 36.

75. Benicio, *O rei dos jagunços*, 69.

76. Honório Vilanova's firsthand report, cited in Hoornaert, *Os anjos*, 20.

77. Alexandre Otten, *Só Deus é grande: A mensagem religiosa de Antonio Conselheiro* (São Paulo: Loyola, 1990), 43.

78. Ibid., 383.

79. Marciáno, *Relatório*, 7.

80. See Della Cava, "Brazilian Messianism and National Institutions," 413.

81. Alvim Martins Horcades, *Descrição de uma viagem a Canudos* (Bahia: Typographia Tourinho, 1899), 2.

82. Ibid., 6.

83. Da Cunha, *Caderneta*, 77.

84. Horcades, *Descrição*, 25.

85. In relation to republican atrocities. To be fair, Horcades notes that Menelik II of Ethiopia treated the invading Italians with legal decorum and mercy in comparison with Brazil's treatment of those who surrendered at Canudos. Yet the anecdote's rhetorical work is still predicated on notions of African savagery. Ibid., 105.

86. Ibid., 29, 42–43.

87. Da Cunha, *Caderneta*, 103.

88. Ibid., 75.

89. Ibid., 242.

90. Ibid., 70.

91. According to the report of journalist Favila Nunes, in *Gazeta de Notícias*, reprinted in Galvão, *No calor da hora*, 195–98.

92. Ibid., 207.

93. The phrases are from Georges Bataille, *Guilty*, trans. Bruce Boone (Venice, CA: Lapis, 1988), 90, 103, 95.

94. Ibid., 142. Bataille also took pains to point to the slippage between these modes.

95. Jacques Derrida, *Writing and Difference*, trans. Alan Bass (Chicago: University of Chicago Press, 1978), 255–57.

96. Santner, *The Royal Remains*, 54–56; Agamben, *Homo Sacer*, 177. Agamben works through analogous cleavages in the concept "man." Giorgio Agamben, *The Open: Man and Animal* (Stanford, CA: Stanford University Press, 2004), 16. Hansen and Stepputat address the fragility of the status of "citizen," so easily (often secretly) moved to a place and status without rights. Hansen and Stepputat, "Sovereignty Revisited," 289–315.

97. Like Bataille or Leiris, endlessly on a quest to forfeit the

"self" within an imagined totality (often conjured through occidentalist fantasies of the Other). Most other quests after self-loss in ritual, whether described in terms of Victor Turner's "communitas" or Romain Rolland's "oceanic," figure a temporary state, not a permanent dissolution.

98. Ian Hacking, *Historical Ontology* (Cambridge, MA: Harvard University Press, 2004), 107.

99. Nelson Werneck Sodré, *Quem é o povo no Brasil* (Rio de Janeiro: Editôra Civilização Brasileira, 1962), 14, 22.

100. Ibid., 10.

101. Edmund Burke, *Reflections on the Revolution in France* (London: James Dodsley, 1790).

102. Immanuel Wallerstein, "The Construction of Peoplehood: Racism, Nationalism, Ethnicity," in *Race, Nation, Class: Ambiguous Identities*, ed. Etienne Balibar and Immanuel Wallerstein (London: Verso, 1991), 71–86.

103. Ibid., 78.

104. Hegel, *Philosophy of History*, 58, 59.

105. Eric R. Wolf, *Europe and the People without History* (Berkeley: University of California Press, 1982).

106. Wallerstein, "The Construction of Peoplehood," 81.

107. Paul Eiss, *In the Name of El Pueblo: Place, Community, and the Politics of History in Yucatán* (Durham, NC: Duke University Press, 2010), 7.

108. John F. Collins shows in vivid ethnographic detail how ideas of a distinct Bahian people were shaped through the labor of purification, especially in relation to the proper predications of Afro-Brazilianness, and the high financial stakes involved in persuasively selling a group and its practices as "a people." See his *Revolt of the Saints: Memory and Redemption in the Twilight of Brazilian Racial Democracy* (Durham, NC: Duke University Press, 2015).

109. Mello e Souza, in Hoornaert, *Os anjos*, 14.

110. Nogueira Galvão and Peres, *Breviário*, 94.

111. Otten, *Só Deus é grande*, 383.

112. José Calasans, *Quase biografias de jagunços: O séquito de*

Antonio Conselheiro (Salvador da Bahia: EDUFBA, 2013); Da Cunha, *Caderneta*, 96.

113. Facó, *Cangaceiros*, 111.

114. Soares, *A guerra de Canudos*, 47. Da Cunha also cites some of the key figures reported by Bernabé, a surrendered resident of Canudos, in his notebook (*Caderneta*).

115. Da Cunha, *Caderneta*, 96.

116. Calasans, *Quase biografias*, 61; Horcades, *Descrição*, 98.

117. Benicio, *O rei dos jagunços*, 106, 160.

118. Macedo, *Memorial de Vilanova*, 67.

119. Marciáno, *Relatório*, 4.

120. Horcades, *Descrição*, 98; Milton, *A Campanha de Canudos*, 14, 17.

121. Milton, *A Campanha de Canudos*, 15.

122. Ibid.

123. Aguiar, *Descrições práticas*, 82–83.

124. Benicio, *O rei dos jagunços*, 67.

125. Horcades, *Descrição*, 1.

126. Calasans, "Canudos Não Euclidiano," 12.

127. The key presence of slaves and ex-slaves is productively emphasized in Villa, *Canudos*; Levine, *Vale of Tears*, 159–60; as well as Dale Torsten Graden, *From Slavery to Freedom in Brazil: Bahia, 1835–1900* (Albuquerque: University of New Mexico Press, 2006).

128. The 1872 census records that about 11 percent of those living in the regions the Counselor traversed were slaves. Yara Dulce Baneira de Ataide, "As origens do povo do Bom Jesus Conselheiro," *USP* 20 (1994): 95.

129. Da Cunha, *Rebellion in the Backlands*, 473. He cited the description from his travel diary.

130. Ibid., 149.

131. Ibid., 255.

132. Cited in Villa, *Canudos*, 29.

133. Benicio, *O rei dos jagunços*, 301.

134. "Povo este miserável tudo que foi escravo." Letter of February 28, 1894. In Sampaio, *Cartas para o barão*, 97.

135. Calasans, "Canudos não Euclidiano," 20.

136. Robert M. Levine, "Mud-Hut Jerusalem: Canudos Revisited," in *The Abolition of Slavery and the Aftermath of Emancipation in Brazil* (Durham, NC: Duke University Press, 1988), 183.

137. "Rabble" is the term applied by E. Roquette Pinto, *Seixos rolados*, cited in Gilberto Freyre, *The Masters and the Slaves*, trans. Samuel Putnam (Berkeley: University of California Press, 1986), 68.

138. Montenegro, *Antônio Conselheiro*, 30.

139. Raimundo Nina Rodrigues, *Coletividades anormais* (Brasilia: Edições do Senado Federal, 2006), 47, 51–52.

140. Da Cunha, *Rebellion in the Backlands*, 88.

141. Da Cunha, *Diário*, 90. "Arrasta a multidão, contrata e dominada, não porque a domine, mas porque é o seu produto natural mais completo."

142. Marcia Sá Cavalcante Schuback, *Olho a olho: Ensaios de longe* (Rio de Janeiro: Fundação Biblioteca Nacional, 2011), 50–52.

143. Immanuel Kant, *Observations of the Feeling of the Sublime*, trans. John T. Goldthwait (Berkeley: University of California Press, 1960), 107, 123.

144. Robert Hamill Nassau, *Fetichism in West Africa: Forty Years' Observation of Native Customs and Superstitions* (New York: Negro University Press, 1904), 127.

145. Gustave Le Bon, *Psychologie des foules* (Paris: Félix Alcan, 1895). Le Bon's use of "la foule" and the question of governance seems inspired by Tocqueville: "Je veux imaginer sous quels traits nouveaux le despotisme pourrait se produire dans le monde: je vois une foule innombrable d'hommes semblables et égaux qui tournent sans repos sur eux-mêmes pour se procurer de petits et vulgaires plaisirs." Alexis de Tocqueville, *De la démocratie en Amérique* (Paris: C. Gosselin, 1811), 313. Tocqueville also writes about the "contagion" of the crowd, a theme important to Le Bon.

146. Le Bon, *Psychologie des foules*, 100, 104, 109.

147. Gustave Le Bon, *The Psychology of Peoples* (New York: Macmillan, 1898), 194.

148. Hegel also feared the mob as a threat to the People: "Besides, it is a dangerous and false prejudice, that the People alone

have reason and insight, and know what justice is; for each popular faction may represent itself as the People, and the question as to what constitutes the State is one of advanced science, and not of popular decision." Hegel, *Philosophy of History*, 43.

149. I think of these types as agentive political fictions, or discursive representations, that "act" in consequential ways. Ian Hacking called this "dynamic nominalism." Hacking, *Historical Ontology*, 106.

150. *Gazeta de Notícias*, May 14, 1888. All the quotes that follow are from the same daily, from the week following abolition. Translations mine.

151. Da Cunha, *Rebellion in the Backlands*, 383.

152. Michel Foucault, *History of Sexuality*, trans. Robert Hurley, vol. 1 (New York: Vintage Books, 1990), 89.

153. Da Cunha, *Caderneta*, 87.

154. Rodrigues, *Coletividades anormais*, 90.

155. Quoted in Tavares, *Canudos*, 42.

156. Macedo, *Memorial de Vilanova*, 67, 134, 138, 149.

157. Montenegro, *Antônio Conselheiro*, 40. The eyewitness Horcades estimated the number of prisoners. Horcades, *Descrição*, 89.

158. Montenegro, *Antônio Conselheiro*, 40.

159. Horcades, *Descrição*, 103.

160. Ana Maria Mauad de Sousa Andrade Essus, "O 'olho da história': Análise da imagem fotográfica na construção de uma memoria sobre o conflito de Canudos," *Acervo: Revista do Arquivo Nacional* 6, no. 1–2 (1993): 28.

161. Tavares, *Canudos*, 34.

162. Favila Nunes, in *Gazeta de Notícias*, reprinted in Galvão, *No calor da hora*, 165.

163. Michel Foucault, *Discipline and Punish: The Birth of the Prison*, trans. Alan Sheridan (New York: Pantheon Books, 1977), 34.

164. Report of Alfredo Silva, September 18–19, 1897, cited in da Cunha, *Diário*, 297.

165. Da Cunha, *Rebellion in the Backlands*, 476; Manuel F. Meneses, November 9, 1897, in Sampaio, *Cartas para o barão*, 74.

166. Sampaio, *Cartas para o barão*, 74. The story from the news-

paper *Correio de Noticias*, Bahia, October 23, 1897, read as follows: "The Head of Antonio Conselheiro: Dr. Curio brought the head of Antonio Conselheiro packed in a large box packed with lime, and was escorted from the train station by a soldier. This relic will certainly be submitted to rigorous medico-legal exams, so that science may clarify the reason for the mental aberration that caused so much trouble for Bahia and the entire nation."

167. Da Cunha, *Rebellion in the Backlands*, 476.

168. French, *Legalizing Identities*, 17. On the inculturated mass, see John Burdick, *Blessed Anastácia: Women, Race, and Popular Christianity in Brazil* (New York: Routledge, 1998).

169. The passage in Portuguese reads, "O povo do R.J. reuinido em meeting e ciente do doloroso revés das armas ~~republicanas~~ legais nos sertões da Bahia, tomadas pela caudilhagem monárquica e congregado em torno do governo, aplaudindo a todos os atos de energia cívica que praticar pela desafronta do exército e da Pátria, aguarda ansioso a pronta sufocação da revolta . . ." Da Cunha, *Caderneta*, 243.

170. Favila Nunes, in *Gazeta de Notícias*, reprinted in Nogueira Galvão, *No calor da hora*, 211.

171. President Prudente de Morais's statement of October 7, 1897, in the Palácio do Governo (in Catete), as he received official emissaries from the military forces; as reported in *Jornal do Commercio*, October 8, 1897, p. 1. The full statement was, "Em Canudos não ficará pedra sobre pedra, para que não mais possa reproduzir-se aquella cidadella maldita e este serviço a Nação deve ao heroico e correcto exercito." The report includes a descriptor of the President's disposition as highly emotional ("extremamente emocionado"). The phrasing of not leaving one stone on another is a citation from Jesus, in Luke 21:6.

172. Quoted in Favila Nunes, in *Gaveta de Notícias*, October 28, 1897 (drafted on October 8, 1897), cited in Nogueira Galvão, *No calor da hora*, 207–14.

173. Horcades, *Descrição*, 80.

174. Ibid., 92.

175. Ibid., 113–15.

176. There were 146 captive survivors who were not executed, but others managed to escape Canudos before the roads were closed and the last assault begun. See Levine, *Vale of Tears*, 191.

177. The letter is cited in Johnson, *Sentencing Canudos*, 165.

178. *Jornal do Brasil*, October 27, 1897, 1.

179. Cícero Antônio F. de Almeida, *Canudos: Imagens da guerra* (Rio de Janeiro: Lacerda, 1997).

180. *Jornal do Brasil*, January 29, 1898. The projection show first opened on Christmas Eve 1897, showing from 7:00 to 10:00 p.m. at Rua Gonçalves Dias 46.

181. César "Wolsley" Zama, *Libelo republicano acompanhado de comentários sobre a guerra de Canudos* (Bahia: Diário da Bahia, 1899), 17, 24, 38, 55.

182. Rui Barbosa, "Terminação da guerra de Canudos," in *Obras completas*, vol. 24 (Rio de Janeiro: Ministério da Educação, 1897), 301. Barbosa never actually presented the lecture.

SPIRITUAL JURISDICTIONS

*TREATY PEOPLE AND
THE QUEEN OF CANADA*

Pamela E. Klassen

In the Americas, Canada stands out as a land with a queen, a hereditary leader touched by divinity. By contrast, the proudly republican nations to the south invest their political leaders with the power of the people—common, democratic, meritocratic. In Brazil, the road to Canudos—a Christian utopia led by a nineteenth-century prophet seeking to restore royal rule—now leads to a flooded site of salvation and slaughter. The state memorializes the road as sacred ground, but the reservoirs of the modern Brazilian republic drowned the remains of the Canudos church years ago. In Canada, the churchstateness of the Crown remains above water, at the heart of the ekklesia that constitutes the people.

Canada, compared to the republican tradition of the United States, does not have such doggedly articulated legal and popular traditions of the separation of church and state, as exemplified by American debates over whether the people, gathered as a death-qualifying jury, may hold the lives of the convicted in their hands at the same time that they also hold Bibles.[1] Though Canadians rarely ever pledge allegiance to anything in everyday life, the government reminds them: "We do not swear allegiance to a piece of cloth (office), a document (a constitution) or a political entity. Rather we swear allegiance to a person who embodies all these as well as our collective values as a people."[2] But even if the people pledge allegiance to Her Majesty and not to a flag, Canada has its Canudos too—communities of resistance pressured to live by collective values that they do not necessarily share. Across Canada, Indigenous nations have been removed from their lands—their sacred ground—to make way for hydroelectric dams and reservoirs that empower and water people far away.[3] As the ancestors and homelands of the Cree, Ojibwe, and other Indigenous nations were sunk beneath waters of progress in the Americas, however, they have resisted—at James Bay, at Standing Rock—being deluged by new peoples, new powers, or visions of new worlds.

"We are all treaty people." So said the Right Honourable Adrienne Clarkson in a lecture in 2007, breathing new life into an old idea.[4] Not just any lecturer, Clarkson had recently ended her term as Governor General of Canada, representing Queen Elizabeth II, the "Queen of Canada" and "Head of the Commonwealth, Defender of the Faith."[5] The Governor General is a node of power where the people and the Crown cross, thus bearing the most ceremonial, political, and even spiritual authority in the Canadian system of parliamentary democracy. As representatives of the Queen of Canada, governors general are sometimes dismissed as figureheads, but they nevertheless have significant authority that rests on centuries of royal tradition and raw political power. For example, at the opening of a session of parliament the Governor General ascends to an elaborately carved wooden chair to deliver the "Speech from the Throne" on behalf of the government in power, but in extraordinary circumstances she can also prematurely dissolve a session of parliament and request that government to step down. As embodied representatives of the Crown, governors general have also been the preferred audience of Indigenous peoples when they petition the government to honor the treaties that made the very idea of Canada possible. Addressing the Crown on a nation-to-nation footing, and not as Canadians, Indigenous nations have had high expectations that governors general will uphold the "sacred promises" recorded in the treaties, despite repeated evidence of their inability or unwillingness to do so.[6]

The concept of treaty people clarifies the materiality and deep history of ekklesia in its "New World" formations. To be a "treaty people," in Clarkson's view, means that the "two sides," Indigenous and British/Canadian, that negotiated the treaties had both agreed to abide by their terms. Now used widely by those arguing that Canada must live up to its treaty relationships with Indigenous peoples, the idea of being treaty people has become embedded in the curriculum of provincial schools through class projects, in museum exhibits, and in the rhythms of state calendars, such as in Treaties Recognition Week. In this twenty-first-century public remembering of the treaties, however, the ongoing influence of churchstateness is rarely acknowledged; the protocols and ceremonies required to animate the treaties are similarly often overlooked.

In the Americas, new ekklesia came into being through the colonial attempt to eradicate or assimilate Indigenous peoples and force them from their homelands. Long before the kings and queens of Europe dispatched their representatives across the ocean, Indigenous nations had their own words, that were neither Greek nor English, to name the collectivities that gave them legal and ceremonial foundation on the land. In diverse languages, they understood themselves as the "People." For example, across what is now considered the border between Canada and the United States, the Anishinaabeg, a word that translates as "the people," continue to live in what is now called Ontario, Manitoba, and Minnesota. The Niitsitapa—"the real people"— also known as the Blackfoot Confederacy, live today in what is called Alberta and Montana. And in what is now northern Quebec, the Cree recently renamed their territory as Eeyou Istchee, or "the People's Land," after fighting off the latest threat of being flooded out by a hydroelectric project.[7] As an oft-repeated phrase insists, "since time immemorial" diverse Indigenous nations have organized themselves quite literally as peoples with laws and ceremonies shaped by the understanding that "the Great Spirit has planted us on this ground where we are."[8]

To assert their jurisdiction over these Indigenous lands, spirits, and peoples, colonial settlers had to define their own ways of structuring religious and political authority—church-stateness—over and against those articulated and embodied by Indigenous nations and alliances. Sometimes this meant advocating for the separation of church and state as a sign of enlightened governance; at the very same time this could also mean combining forces between church and state to declare Indigenous peoples savage, uncivilized, and ignorant of the laws of property. Either way, colonial understandings of Indigenous spiritual jurisdiction—ways of speaking the law rooted in sacred authority derived from a relationship to land and place—were often unenlightened, mistaken, or willfully uncomprehending.

Many theorists have convincingly argued that all political power is also sacramental power, as we discuss in our introduction to this volume. In this essay, I approach this argument through the lens of material religion, focusing on the question of spiritual jurisdiction by paying attention to the explicit language of sacredness and spirituality used in reference to the treaties, as well as to the material protocols associated with Crown-based symbols of treaty people.[9] I consider two examples that were both made in the name of the Crown, albeit more than 250 years apart: first, King George III's Royal Proclamation of 1763, which designated lands west of the Appalachians and east of the Spanish territory as unceded Indigenous territory, and second, Queen Elizabeth II's silver "ring of reconciliation," crafted in recognition of Indigenous peoples and gifted by Prince William to the people of British Columbia during a royal visit in 2016. As reminders of nation-to-nation relationships that were produced by the British and the Canadian Crown, these artifacts tell a complex story of the possibilities and failures of the meanings of treaty people. I follow these Crown-based protocols in their materiality and textuality, asking where they are housed, what they symbolize, how they have been forgotten and remembered, and how protocols of spiritual jurisdiction and rituals of public memory shape their current uses.

Indigenous and non-Indigenous scholars who work collaboratively with Indigenous elders have developed innovative methods for thinking with material culture about the origin stories of the Americas. For example, historian Heidi Bohaker analyzed Anishinaabeg doodem signatures—clan symbols—on treaty documents to discern Indigenous kinship and political alliances. Anthropologist Richard Daly worked ethnographically to document and deploy the role of oral history and the material culture of storytelling in Gitksan and Witsuwit'en legal claims.[10] Anishinaabe scholar Alan Ojiig Corbiere has traced the provenance and continued care of treaty medals by Anishinaabeg families to show the ongoing significance of the medals as markers of treaty obligations.[11] Corbiere and Bohaker, together with Ruth Phillips and others, have designed a collaborative digital database to gather together material culture such as wampum strings, with archival texts, such as letters, to make more widely accessible treaty histories that include Indigenous perspectives.[12] Even in this digital realm, however, elders exert spiritual jurisdiction by deeming some "heritage items" too sacred for the broad distribution of an online database. Understanding treaties as living promises made with the backing of the Crown, Indigenous peoples counted on their treaty partners to keep the pledges that they made in the name of their monarch and their God.[13] As material objects made in recognition of the protocols and promises of treaty, the Royal Proclamation and the ring of reconciliation carry with them memory and obligation.

King George III of England issued a 1763 Royal Proclamation regarding the territories he "acquired" by defeating France in what is variously called the Seven Years' War or the French and Indian Wars. Most importantly for Indigenous peoples, he acknowledged that they collectively owned their lands that they had not ceded by treaty. Though the king likely did not imagine the long legal life that his proclamation would have, it continues to be cited by some, but not all, Indigenous legal scholars as a "foundational document" for ensuring their territorial rights. Not considered by these scholars to be a form of law truly "indigenous" to the land, the Royal Proclamation is nevertheless a key part of the corpus of "Aboriginal law" that emerged in relation to the establishment of Canada.[14] After 250 years of obscurity as a material object, but some renown as a royal edict, an eighteenth-century printed broadsheet of the Royal Proclamation has now gone on tour as a heritage artifact. Recently installed at Winnipeg's Canadian Museum of Human Rights within an exhibit called "Protecting Rights in Canada," the proclamation received visitors while enshrined in a museum under the sacred guise of human rights.[15]

The ring of reconciliation is a more recent attempt to make a material reminder of treaty promises and shared jurisdiction. In 2016 Prince William, the Duke of Cambridge, added a silver engraved ring to a Canadian version of a British symbol of the Crown's authority, the "Black Rod." In London, the Black Rod is both a man and a wooden staff that together represent the authority of the sovereign and the limits to her authority in the parliamentary democracy elected by the people. The British Columbia version of the Black Rod, gifted by Queen Elizabeth II in 2012, is a short staff encircled with three silver rings that symbolize the overlapping jurisdictions of the Crown, the federal government, and the province. In a province with very few treaties between Indigenous nations and the Crown, largely because the British Columbian leaders persistently considered Indigenous sovereignty irrelevant to their ownership of the land, the new silver ring of reconciliation added to the Black Rod was meant to become a new symbolic marker of Indigenous jurisdiction.[16] Both in its performance and in its significance, however, the ritual of the ring of reconciliation was a contested and multivocal way of saying the law.

The ongoing significance of the Crown and its embodied representatives—in this case the Duke and Duchess of Cambridge and their two small children—for interactions between Canada and Indigenous nations was on full display during their 2016 royal visit. The royal couple visited both the Heiltsuk and Haida peoples, two nations with strongly articulated positions on their ongoing sovereignty, who have not signed historic treaties with the Crown. In the case of the Haida nation, however, the prince visited a people that had recently negotiated a "Reconciliation Protocol" with his grandmother, Queen Elizabeth II, as the signatory for Canada. The written version of the protocol states that "the Haida Nation and British Columbia hold differing views with regard to sovereignty, title, ownership and jurisdiction over Haida Gwaii."[17] Layered on top of the Kunst'aa guu-Kunst'aayah Reconciliation Protocol, the silver ring of reconciliation may be more than just artful decoration.[18]

The ritual of the ring of reconciliation came almost one year after the publication of the Final Report of the Truth and Reconciliation Commission of Canada (TRC), which told the history and stories of survivors of one of the most devastating forms of churchstateness in Canada: state-funded and church-run residential schools for Indigenous children, which operated from the mid-nineteenth century until well into the latter half of the twentieth. Sites where Indigenous children were forcibly stripped of their languages, families, and homelands, as well as sexually and physically abused, the residential school system was described by the TRC as a form of "cultural genocide." In their report, the commissioners of the TRC listed ninety-four calls to action that included everything from addressing inequities in Indigenous educational and health-care funding to calling for schools and universities to teach about Indigenous spirituality alongside comparative religion.[19]

The TRC also echoed the 1996 Royal Commission on Aboriginal Peoples, so christened in the name of Her Majesty, by calling for a "new Royal Proclamation":

> We call upon the Government of Canada, on behalf of all Canadians, to jointly develop with Aboriginal peoples a Royal Proclamation of Reconciliation to be issued by the Crown. The proclamation would build on the *Royal Proclamation* of 1763 and the *Treaty of Niagara* of 1764, and reaffirm the nation-to-nation relationship between Aboriginal peoples and the Crown.[20]

What is the power of the Crown in an age of nation-to-nation reconciliation? Some may hope that the ritual protocols of royal visits and material symbols of royal proclamations serve as effective reminders of the Crown-infused relationships of treaty that undergird the making of Canada. Others contend that they are mere performance: "affective refoundings of the settler state" that fail to carry with them treaty promises and obligations.[21] Either way, if the "true spirit" vested in the principle of treaty people is ever to be realized, the texts of the treaties will have to be animated by the protocols and symbols not only of the Queen and her bodies, but also by those elders who have preserved the knowledge of the treaties in their languages, their ceremonies, and their stories of jurisdiction.

POWERS OF JURISDICTION

The history of treaty making reveals how what we are calling churchstateness in the Americas is made from the enmeshment *and* the contest of rival religiopolitical sovereignties. As negotiations between Indigenous leaders and representatives of the Crown—including lieutenant governors and missionaries—treaties were conversations held in multiple languages and paced with the rhythms of ceremonies such as smudging and pipe smoking. Many of what are called the "numbered treaties" were negotiated in the nineteenth century, ranging across northern Ontario to the Rocky Mountains and northward. They were negotiated with reference to the spiritual jurisdiction of the "Creator" and of the "Great White Mother," or Queen Victoria (1819–1901). The Queen's negotiators wrote down the treaties in English, driven by a fixation on recording what the Indigenous leaders had supposedly agreed to "cede and surrender" to the Crown; the printed words of the treaties gave little attention to the wider multilingual and ceremonial context of treaty. These monological treaty accounts had devastating consequences for the people's land. Without the interpretations of the elders preserved in oral history and ceremony, the treaties were read by the Canadian state as land surrenders that placed Indigenous nations under Canadian jurisdiction and not as agreements to share the land in a multijurisdictional frame.[22]

The spiritual jurisdiction of the Crown that undergirded the treaties is deeply connected to the problem of the king's two bodies. The king—who for most of the nineteenth and twentieth centuries in Canada was actually two queens—is at once a living, breathing human being and an embodiment of immortal sovereign power. With echoes of Jesus Christ as the incarnation of the omnipotent God in human flesh, the doubled-bodied Crown is backed by ekklesia, in which her power is rooted in both divine sanction and her relationship to the people. But her body is dispersed through material culture and law as well. When her authority is marked in distant Canadian jurisdictions, it is at once spiritual and material, sovereign and shimmering. On paper money and silver coins, her image guarantees the currency; on acts of Parliament and legal rulings, her name secures the law.[23]

Introducing the concept of spiritual jurisdiction requires me to define my terms. The colonial provenance and violent effects of "religion" as a category in the Americas have been well documented; these effects are part of the reason why "religious" authority is so rarely referred to in Indigenous discussions of law, sovereignty, and ceremony.[24] In this literature, spirituality is a much-preferred term to designate power that exceeds human intention or control and flows from divinity, ancestors, or creation. "Spirituality" also has a complicated colonial history, however, as an English word emerging from a Christian vocabulary in which political authority is legitimated by divine favor or connection.[25] For example, in the British parliamentary system, the Church of England bishops and archbishops sit as "Lords Spiritual" in the British House of Lords. (By contrast, Jewish Rabbis began sitting as "Lords Temporal" in 1988.)

In turn, "jurisdiction," literally "saying the law," has both a pragmatic and a metadiscursive sense. In the first sense, jurisdiction is law used to assert authority over—and responsibility for—land and people. At a broader level, jurisdiction is "law about law," or deliberation about the grounding and limits of specific legal authority, as in deliberations about whether a particular court of law actually has the jurisdiction to adjudicate a particular claim.[26] The literature on the question of jurisdiction is large and growing, but one perspective is particularly helpful for my argument here. Justin Richland, a lawyer and anthropologist who has worked with the Hopi for many years in both capacities, argues that jurisdiction is a concept that reveals the ongoing practices of and conflicts over Hopi sovereignty in the United States. As a way of speaking the law that also continually establishes *and* limits the power of the law, jurisdiction is the ongoing practice of Hopi tradition in Richland's analysis. As the Hopi Tribal Court makes decisions about which disputes it can resolve and which ones need to return to village and clan bodies for resolution, jurisdiction as tradition becomes the "potentializing limit on Hopi sovereignty."[27] Jurisdiction, then, is the process by which people as collectives make possible *and* circumscribe political power. In a similar way, the queen, and by extension, the governor general, also have this "potentializing limit." They perform and embody the Crown in such a way that names and enacts its authority in a constitutional monarchy at the same time that they acknowledge and perform the limits of royal power in a parliamentary democracy.

Understanding jurisdiction as tradition in this way, Richland responds critically to the theoretical literature on sovereignty, which considers the authorizing processes of state power as always grounded in political theology. For Richland this focus on theologically derived authority misses the more everyday deliberative practices of jurisdiction: "The capacity of tradition to serve as such a potentializing limit to Hopi sovereignty is its unique power, and it affords unique insight to scholars, like myself, who are interested in discerning the contours of sovereign power less in the censer smoke of its theological origins and more in the pragmatics of everyday life."[28] As I hope to show here, however, the censer smoke, the pipe smoke, and the invocations of the spiritual are central to the pragmatics of power for all treaty people. If we want to understand the significance of jurisdiction for the ongoing contests over sovereignty in the Americas, we must consider both its pragmatic and its spiritual forms; we must consider churchstateness and its limits.

Bringing together two freighted terms into the concept of spiritual jurisdiction, I signal a way of claiming power over and responsibility for a territory and its people by saying the law while undergirded by the divine authority of a God or Creator. Spiritual jurisdiction is a phrase that I first came across as a term used to describe a colonial Anglican bishop's authority over his far-flung Northwest Coast diocese.[29] The bishop's spiritual jurisdiction referred to his responsibility for and oversight of the parishes and people under his care and territorial authority. A queen's spiritual jurisdiction would be similar but multiplied across vast spaces and several realms—she needs more than two bodies to honor her responsibilities and thus delegates them to governors general and lieutenant governors around the world. A very literal version of what Michel Foucault called "pastoral power," the queen's spiritual jurisdiction is often considered to be not quite *real*, whether by republicans who recoil at the thought of "fetishistic" monarchists or when contrasted with the on-the-ground power of the prime minister. Though Foucault acknowledged the reality of pastoral power, he nevertheless insisted that until the eighteenth century it was quite distinct from "political power." Their specific differences, he insisted, "remained as an absolutely typical feature of the Christian West."[30] But when the "Christian West" sought to encompass the New World as its own, its kings and ministers used pastoral power to achieve their political, territorial ends. Along with violence and epidemics of disease, colonial nations claimed land with a "power of jurisdiction" that was sacramental and civilizing, bringing chosen people into their communion and expelling all others.[31]

Not only Anglican bishops have thought with the concept of spiritual jurisdiction. James Sákéj Youngblood Henderson uses a similar term in his analysis of the ongoing political significance of treaties for Indigenous nations. According to Henderson, "Treaties are consensual manifestations of the right of self-determination. In general or specific terms, Aboriginal peoples' treaties constitute an elaboration of the arrangements relating to the political, economic, social, cultural, or spiritual rights and jurisdictions of the Indigenous peoples concerned."[32] Treaties negotiated between colonial representatives and Indigenous leaders were a powerful motor of colonial dispossession, divvying up land and creating borders according to colonial mapping. At the same time, as Henderson and others have shown, Indigenous peoples consider treaties to be ongoing, spiritually charged promises that provide grounds for challenging that same colonial dispossession.[33] Even the Royal Commission on Aboriginal Peoples declared it so in 1996: "Historical treaties were meant by all parties to be sacred and enduring and to be spiritual as well as legal undertakings."[34] Put even more strongly: "Treaties are sacred and spiritual covenants that cannot be repudiated."[35] Treaties emerged from the meeting of both Indigenous and Christian spiritual jurisdictions, an ambiguously powerful mix of ceremony, negotiation, and legally binding promise.

Throughout the Americas, with varying concepts of political authority in play and diverse languages for naming this power, colonial occupiers thought they were claiming Indigenous territories, while Indigenous peoples thought they were sharing the land, or even just renting out the topsoil. Generated by face-to-face conversations, ceremonies, and efforts of translation between diplomatic representatives on both sides, the treaties agreed to between the British Crown and Indigenous allied nations were rooted in a metaphysical blend of spiritual and political power materialized in symbols, rituals, and stories.[36] For Henderson, achieving spiritual jurisdiction, or the authority to have responsibility for a people and the land, has required appropriate use of protocol, through networks of what he calls "Indigenous diplomacy," a historical and present-day network of Indigenous representatives who have long articulated Indigenous sovereignty. Working toward goals such as the 2007 United Nations Declaration of the Rights of Indigenous Peoples, Indigenous diplomats embarked on broad-based political mobilization rooted in shared convictions about the significance of protocol: "Through our various international ceremonies and diplomacy, we learned to unite by respecting our diversity."[37] It would follow, in this view, that if treaties are spiritual covenants, then Canadian diplomats must also be aware of their protocols in ongoing negotiations of spiritual jurisdiction with their Indigenous treaty partners.

Indigenous understandings of spiritual jurisdiction actively shaped politics long before the advent of colonialism. As Leanne Simpson has written of the precolonial "One Dish" or Gdoo-naaganinaa treaty between the Anishinaabeg and the Haudenosaunee: "For the Nishnaabeg people, Gdoo-naaganinaa . . . gives us an ancient template for realizing separate jurisdictions within a shared territory. It outlines the 'rights' and 'responsibilities' of both parties in the ongoing relationship, and it clearly demonstrates that our ancestors did not intend for our nations to be subsumed by the British crown or the Canadian state when they negotiated those original treaties."[38] Agreeing about overlapping jurisdiction was thus a way to map relationships in shared space by way of promises that were "sacred, made in the presence of the spiritual world and solemnized in ceremony."[39] Recognizing that spiritual jurisdiction was in play for both Indigenous peoples and the Crown opens up a new space for thinking through what it means to be a treaty people. As George Erasmus wrote in 1989, as national chief of the Assembly of First Nations, the treaties are "sacred documents" that express principles of "shared jurisdiction."[40]

Key to all Canadian protocol is the underlying authority of the Crown. Compared to other Commonwealth settler colonial nations such as Australia, and in contrast to Brazil and the United States, Canada has fewer avid republicans who seek to end the role of the monarchy. Those who publicly defend the Crown and the Crown's representatives in Canada—the governor general and the provincial lieutenant governors—are not legion, but they are prolific and articulate. For the most part Anglo-Canadian men, these writers often turn to the language of spirituality to make their claims. David Johnston, a recent Canadian Governor General, quoted Canadian novelist Robertson Davies to argue that the Crown is the "consecrated spirit of Canada."[41] Canadian senate committee clerk Paul Benoit described the governor general as acting with "liturgical authority" that is at once "sublime"—a secular form of spiritual power—while also drawing from a combination of Indigenous and Christian "spirituality."[42] Embodying such diverse forms of spiritual jurisdiction would have to mean that the governor general embodies the persistence of competing and overlapping sovereignties. This is partly why the Crown and its representatives in Canada remain so central to the question of church, state, and treaty peoples.

Theories of the Crown distinguish between the "dignified Crown," denoting the "largely ceremonial" role of the queen and the "efficient Crown," meaning the queen's delegation of her powers to ministers elected by the people.[43] Though her ceremonial role is predominantly "passive" and symbolic, it is nonetheless considered to be powerful in its ability to induce loyalty and undergird the state's political legitimacy.[44] Nathan Tidridge, an astute thinker about the ongoing meaning of the Crown for Indigenous-settler relations, qualifies this "passivity" when it comes to treaties: "The Monarch detailed in the treaties is an active one, a figure in direct relationship with the Indigenous population who has a duty to ensure that the Canadian government lives up to its obligations."[45] By this reading, the Queen and her heirs have a duty to uphold the promises made between treaty peoples.

For Tidridge, the queen has this duty in part because of her spiritual jurisdiction: "The Canadian Crown benefits from the mystique and historic prestige of an ancient hereditary monarchy, while making it thoroughly indigenous through the local representatives of the Sovereign."[46] Tidridge's use of the language of indigeneity to describe the mystique of a Crown implanted on new land is a curious erasure of local forms of ancient power. Describing the *Canadian* Crown as benefitting from its links to an "ancient hereditary monarchy," however, is the key to the duty it has to protect the treaties. It was in part through its lineage of hereditary chieftainship—and hence its ancestors— that the Crown could enter into treaty relations with Indigenous nations. Treaties were based in what Heidi Bohaker has called a "political geometry" of kinship and alliance, whereby promises are rooted in relationships understood within metaphors of family and clan, and including both ancestors and future generations.[47] The Crown, as a hereditary chieftainship that could pass to either man or woman, claims sanction from God and ritual protection through ceremonies of the Church of England, the state, and the Commonwealth.

THE QUEEN'S SACRED PROMISES

Thinking about spiritual jurisdiction in Canada reveals a different perspective on "the royal remains," or what Eric Santner refers to as what is left of the "King's body" in the transition from monarchical to postmonarchical, republican nations. When Santner writes of a postmonarchical nation, he means one in which the "place of the royal personage has been emptied and the principle of sovereignty relocated in the will, life, and fate of the 'People.'"[48] Put another way, these are people governed by presidents and not ruled by princes. Drawing heavily from Ernst Kantorowicz's *The King's Two Bodies*, Santner traces the "ongoing exchanges of properties between Church and State" that first legitimated the power of the king. With the shift to democratic governance, the exchange of properties between church and state comes to legitimate sovereignty of the "people," or the demos, as the embodiment of the nation-state. Something of the royal remains, Santner argues, when a state shifts from rooting itself not in the "representational corporeality" of the king but in the crafting of laws that will apply to the "soil of a particular territory."[49]

The twinned power of church and state does not disappear in a postmonarchical setting. As Santner argues, "There is more political theology in everyday life than we might have ever thought though it is surely much more difficult to identify in the absence of the body of a royal personage where it could be focused and dramaturgically elaborated."[50] In a republic, the dramaturgy of a presidential inauguration, a courtroom ritual, or even a state-sponsored and church-sanctioned massacre, as at Canudos, feeds this political theology. But what about a constitutional monarchy in which the Crown is still alive and well and the queen's authority is dramaturgically performed by the representatives of not just one but many "peoples"?

In Canada, the royal remains in the soil, in the Crown, and in the people. The Queen's face is etched on the coins that jingle in pockets, her portrait gazes out over students in school lobbies, and her coat of arms is carved into the speaker's chairs that sit in legislatures across the nation.[51] The Queen also remains in the nation-to-nation relations between the Canadian nation and Indigenous nations, carrying with her the power of a mother who holds a bundle of sacred promises about how to share land—namely treaties—handed down to her via her grandfathers and her great-great-grandmother, Queen Victoria. As a hereditary chief herself, she embodies and enacts ritual proximity through which her ceremonial gestures—or those of her regents, such as the governor general—collapse time, place, and even spiritual traditions. A metaphysical being unto herself, the Queen—as the Crown who is also a great-grandmother—guarantees treaty rights while also embodying the fragility of Canadian, and even US, claims to territorial sovereignty.

The history of treaty making with Indigenous peoples in what is now called Canada and the United States is most often a history of treaty breaking, through which the peoples and governments of both colonial nations have sought to dispossess, assimilate, and violently eliminate the Haudenosaunee, Anishinaabeg, Cree, and many other Indigenous nations.[52] The promises made with wampum belts, communion silver, peace pipes, and paper proclamations, however, have not disappeared, and neither have the peoples who care for them. The history of British colonial treaty making with Indigenous peoples in North America goes back more than three centuries and carries with it a rich material culture that evidences the importance of ceremony and symbol for these political negotiations. At the center of these rituals and symbols was the conviction that treaty promises were sacred. Indigenous peoples invoked the Creator as their witness in treaty conversations, while the "treaty commissioners who represented the British Crown demonstrated a great reverence for their Queen who was head of state and church."[53] For example, the late-seventeenth-century Silver Covenant Chain was a network of alliances between the Haudenosaunee (Iroquois) and the English, symbolized by a wampum belt—beads made of purple and white shells that Haudenosaunee artisans strung together in a pattern of figures linking arms. The "silver" of the wampum referred to its ability to be regularly polished, not literally, but through acts of remembrance on the part of the Haudenosaunee, the Anishinaabeg, and the British. Such memorial acts were to recall the "the sacred and binding agreement" that treaties embody.[54]

For its part, the Crown gifted silver in the form of communion sets and treaty medals. For example, in the wake of a visit by four Mohawk "Kings" in 1710, Queen Anne (1665–1714) bestowed a set of communion silver on the Mohawks of what is now called upstate New York. Furnishing the Mohawks with both silver and missionaries, she also financed the building of a royal chapel—a church built in the name of the Crown in recognition of the Mohawk nation. By the end of the century, in the violence of the American Revolution, the Mohawks were driven from their land. In recognition of their loyalty to the British, the Governor General of Quebec granted them land on Anishinaabeg territory in what became Upper Canada; they brought with them their silver communion sets and rebuilt their royal chapels. Now divided between two Mohawk royal chapels, at Tyendinaga and Six Nations, the silver communion sets are still cared for by the communities as "bearers of memory and reminders of obligation."[55]

On both sides of what is now the Canada-US border in the area of Lake Ontario, Haudenosaunee and Anishinaabeg nations have long held ceremonies to honor the treaties. They bring out wampum belts for public remembering and public reading and display and polish the treaty medals that they received in treaty negotiations. By contrast, the gifts of peace pipes and wampum belts that British and Canadian officials received from Indigenous peoples during treaty negotiations were not housed in Houses of Parliament, where they could be cared for with protocol. Instead, these material reminders of treaty promises often retreated into the attic trunks of the descendants of politicians or into the hands of collectors. Some wampum belts, treaty medals, and peace pipes found their way to museums via the custodianship of colonial officials, missionaries, a few Indigenous collectors, and even a governor general.[56]

On the settler side, treaties are most often remembered—and forgotten—by books and documents that, until recently, were rarely accorded ceremonial respect. Treaty documents, when not ignored, were more likely to have been viewed by lawyers and politicians as vessels of law rather than occasions for protocol and relationship. Similarly, while the documents inaugurating US sovereignty such as the Declaration of Independence and the Constitution have long been enshrined behind bulletproof glass in the rotunda of the National Archives building in Washington, DC, it was only recently that US treaties with Native American nations were encased in glass for an exhibition across the mall at the National Museum of the American Indian.[57]

Provoked by centuries of Indigenous petitions to the Crown about land claims and abrogated treaties, lawyers have turned primarily to the print culture of treaties to sort out the ongoing question of Indigenous jurisdiction in a settler-colonial nation. Severing the pipes and the medals from the printed versions of the agreements, however, allows for colonial amnesia about how both parties saw these promises as sacred. Forgetting and misrecognizing this sacredness—in part through the separation of church and state—was central to the assertion of colonial power over and against Indigenous sovereignty.

As the descendants of European immigrants sought to claim ever more ownership of the lands that they called Canada and the United States of America, they did not remember Indigenous understandings of the sacred promises. They worked tirelessly to rename and restory the land, often with Christian names in play, from Sault Ste. Marie in northern Ontario to St. Augustine in what is now Florida.[58] Even in the wake of American constitutional efforts to separate church and state, the orienting power of colonial law and its "ceremonies of possession" remained rooted in spiritual jurisdiction watered by deep wells of Christian imagination.[59] To take seriously the concept of the sacred as many Indigenous theorists have articulated it requires rethinking the foundational power of churchstateness for treaty making and for all treaty people.

FINDING THE ROYAL PROCLAMATION

For a fundamental document that Canadian Supreme Court justices have called the "Magna Carta" of Indigenous peoples, that helped to instigate the American Revolution, and that is deployed to secure Indigenous sovereignty today, an actual paper copy of the Royal Proclamation is hard to find.[60] The Magna Carta tours the great libraries and museums of the world; the Declaration of Independence is an object of pilgrimage. For such an important document in the history of Indigenous nations, Canada, the United States, and Great Britain, the Royal Proclamation has had a comparatively modest shelf life. When I did find one in the Rare Books Library of McGill University, it was a very curious artifact indeed.

It was thanks to a graduate student in my book history and print culture seminar that I first thought to go looking for the proclamation in the first place. After a class in which we had discussed how Indigenous peoples have cited the Royal Proclamation to challenge or refuse Canadian sovereignty for more than two centuries, one of my students asked a great question: where is the Royal Proclamation today? She was underwhelmed to discover that historic copies of the proclamation were only available in two places in Canada: Library and Archives Canada and the McGill University Rare Book Library.[61] With a trip planned to Montreal in a few weeks' time, I promised the class that I would pay a visit to the Royal Proclamation in the flesh.

I arrived on the fourth floor of Rare Books and Special Collections at McLennan Library at McGill University together with companions who shared my excitement about coming face to face with a powerful Canadian relic.[62] The librarian had kindly readied the Royal Proclamation for our visit, and as the trolley rolled toward us, we prepared ourselves to gaze at a royal document with the aura of the king still residing in the paper and ink. While I expected, in my naïveté, a scroll with a royal seal and the signature of the king himself, what faced us was a faded, mass-produced printed copy of the document, about two feet by one and a half feet, enclosed in a faux wooden frame and covered in Plexiglas. There was no remnant of the king in the form of his autograph, but there was a sketch of his profile drawn in pencil onto the Plexiglas, in which he sported a wig and a medal bearing the insignia of the Order of the Garter. It was a decidedly bizarre object that at once glorified and trivialized the King and his Proclamation. This mix of pomp and kitsch, I would discover, fits well with the historical trajectories of how both the King and the Proclamation have been remembered (fig. 8).

The librarians could not say for sure who had framed the Proclamation in this unusual way or who had drawn the pencil portrait of the King over top of his words. They did know that the proclamation arrived at McGill in 1965 together with the Canadiana collection of Lawrence Lande (1906–98), a collector from Ottawa. I later found that the pencil portrait is modeled after a 1762 portrait of the King by artist Allan Ramsay.[63] A side view of King George III depicts him with his hand over his heart, his tricorne hat (perhaps made of Canadian beaver) lodged under his arm. King George wears a large medal depicting the Order of the Garter insignia, announcing *"Honi Soit Qui Mal Y Pense,"* over his left breast. Ramsay's 1762 portrait of King George had many admirers over the years, who drew stylized black-and-white versions of it long before the pencil sketcher applied another version on the Plexiglas cover of the Royal Proclamation found in the Lande collection.

What does the material form of the Royal Proclamation matter? For it to be a foundational text for treaties, revolutions, and the establishment of empires, does it need to actually exist somewhere as a tangible thing? Is the curious document carefully preserved in its cheap frame in McGill's library just one version of a mass-produced claim to power, whose jurisdictional

FIGURE 8. The Royal Proclamation (1763). Courtesy of Rare Books and Special Collections, McGill University Library.

effectiveness is due more to later legal citations than to its material form? The answer to these questions depends on who is doing the remembering.

The performative and ritual aspects of law are always key to its binding authority; this is especially true in the case of the laws connecting treaty people.[64] For many Indigenous peoples, the Royal Proclamation was not a unilateral declaration of the king's authority. Instead, they read the printed materiality of the Royal Proclamation alongside the protocols and material forms of the 1764 Treaty of Niagara. As John Borrows insists, to understand the significance of the Royal Proclamation for Indigenous peoples requires going beyond the text to consider the roles of gift giving, wampum, and oral storytelling in later treaty negotiations, especially those at Niagara in 1764.[65] Together, the Royal Proclamation and the Treaty of Niagara were considered "a treaty of peace and friendship," according to Borrows, and not a sovereign assertion of Crown title to all land.[66] Many Indigenous peoples held their own copies of the proclamation, which was widely distributed by colonial officials.[67] From sea to sea, and from 1763 until today, they have cited it in their petitions to colonial authorities.[68] For example, from the nineteenth century onward, Nisga'a petitions and protests of white settlement in what is now northern British Columbia named the Royal Proclamation as one source of their "Charter of Rights."[69]

Two and a half centuries after the issuing of the Royal Proclamation, the Anishinaabeg and Haudenosaunee nations marked the 250th anniversary not of the Royal Proclamation but of the Treaty of Niagara by displaying wampum and holding lectures.[70] The government of Canada, by contrast, largely ignored the anniversaries of both the Royal Proclamation and the Treaty of Niagara, choosing instead to focus considerable resources and media on the two hundredth anniversary of the War of 1812, in which the British held off the American incursion and made a foray to burn down the first White House in the process. Despite this amnesia on the part of the Canadian government, the king's Royal Proclamation remains a site of memory in which churchstateness endures and adapts.

CHRISTIAN MAJESTIES

Considering the circumstances of the Royal Proclamation's origins crystallizes its churchstateness most clearly. In the case of the Spanish, Portuguese, French, and British colonizers, spiritual jurisdiction looked a lot like churchstateness: they asserted ownership of the New World by embedding laws into the land that were rooted in the power of a monarch sanctioned by a Christian God. The precursor to these laws, fifteenth-century papal declarations that comprised the doctrine of discovery, were a "conspicuously theological" legal assertion of European sovereignty, premised on the idea that "conquest and subjugation were . . . permissible in the interest of spreading Christianity."[71] This "conquest" depended on symbolic gestures, such as planting flags and burying coins, as well as on physical occupation of the land by settlers who were not always united in their task; they often struggled among themselves over questions of jurisdiction and property holding, fighting both for and against the power of kings.[72]

The Royal Proclamation emerged out of one of the many violent rejections of a king's sovereignty that brought Canada into being. Still referred to by some Quebecois as "The Conquest," the end of the Seven Years' War in 1760 came when the British king, known as "His Britannic Majesty," conquered the French king, known as "His most Christian Majesty." As the Articles of the Capitulation of Montreal from 1760 show, however, both the British and the French were well aware of another source of political power and sovereignty active their conflict: the Indigenous allies who had fought on both sides in the war.[73] Article 40 guaranteed that the British would not "molest" the "Indian allies of his most Christian Majesty" and that they would be "maintained in the lands they inhabit, if they chuse to remain there."[74]

The Indigenous allies were guaranteed, along with French Catholics, "liberty of religion, and [that they] shall keep their missionaries."[75] Since the Articles of Capitulation were agreed to between the British and French kings, the perspective of the Indian allies is harder to trace, but there is no doubt that for them, liberty of religion would have included a much broader compass of protocols, practices, and convictions.[76] Liberty of religion was not guaranteed to the African and Indigenous slaves—the "negroes and panis of both sexes"—they were to "remain, in their quality of slaves, in the possession of the French and Canadians to whom they belong."[77] In the era of the Royal Proclamation, a document now celebrated as a beacon of human rights, the king sanctioned both religious liberty and the continued enslavement of African and Indigenous people.[78]

Three years after the Acts of Capitulation, the British, French, Spanish and Portuguese Kings all agreed to the Treaty of Paris (1763), which spelled out in great detail what the British had won and the others had lost in their royal and Christian fight for North America. The language of the treaty was one of peace, friendship, and an all-encompassing Christian monarchy, whether Protestant or Catholic: "There shall be a Christian, universal, and perpetual peace, as well by sea as by land, and a sincere and constant friendship shall be re-established between their Britannick, Most Christian [French], Catholick [Spanish], and Most Faithful [Portuguese] Majesties, and between their heirs and successors, kingdoms, dominions, provinces, countries, subjects, and vassals, of what quality or condition soever they be, without exception of places or persons."[79] The Treaty of Paris was written in the wake of a hundred years' worth of earlier treaties between European nations, such as the Treaties of Westphalia and of Utrecht. These treaties, understood by many historians and political theorists to have established and guaranteed innovative rights of religious freedom and toleration, also provided one half of the model for the treaties negotiated with Indigenous nations across the Atlantic Ocean. The other half of the model came from Indigenous protocols and perspectives on spiritual jurisdiction.

The Royal Proclamation was a direct result of the awareness on the part of King George III's counsellors that Indigenous allies would not—and did not—accept incursions on their sovereignty. As Colin Calloway has shown, the Royal Proclamation was written and declared rather quickly, as British administrators sought to respond to coordinated Indigenous attacks, such as those led by Pontiac, an Ottawa chief, against settlers who were advancing on Indigenous territories with no treaties in place. Advised by his privy council, many of whom were Knights of the Order of the Garter, King George tried to fend off this settler land rush to avoid a full-scale war with his Indigenous allies. He ended up picking another fight with the American colonists: the US Declaration of Independence singled out the Royal Proclamation as an illegitimate royal decree that helped to instigate the American Revolution.[80]

A vehicle for the King to shore up his jurisdictional power against the land-hungry colonists, the Royal Proclamation unequivocally stated the rights of "Indians" to their land, unmolested, in a rather long-winded sentence:

> And whereas it is just and reasonable, and essential to our Interest, and the Security of our Colonies, that the several Nations or Tribes of Indians with whom We are connected, and who live under our Protection, should not be molested or disturbed in the Possession of such Parts of Our Dominions and Territories as, not having been ceded to or purchased by Us, are reserved to them, or any of them, as their Hunting Grounds—We do therefore, with the Advice of our Privy Council, declare it to be our Royal Will and Pleasure, that no Governor or Commander in Chief in any of our Colonies of Quebec, East Florida or West Florida, do presume, upon any Pretence whatever, to grant Warrants of Survey, or pass any Patents for Lands beyond the Bounds of their respective Governments as described in their Commissions: as also that no Governor or Commander in Chief in any of our other Colonies or Plantations in America do presume for the present, and until our further Pleasure be known, to grant Warrants of Survey, or pass Patents for any Lands beyond the Heads or Sources of any of the Rivers which fall into the Atlantic Ocean from the West and North West, or upon any Lands whatever, which, not having been ceded to or purchased by Us as aforesaid, are reserved to the said Indians, or any of them.[81]

Acknowledging that Indigenous Nations west of the Appalachians and all the way south to Florida had not ceded their land, the king exercised royal sleight of hand by also declaring this land to be part of "our Dominion." He placed the Crown in the role of "protector" of Indigenous rights and declared that Indigenous peoples could only sell their land directly to the Crown.

As Grand Chief Edward John would tell Prince William more than 250 years later during the ritual of the ring of reconciliation, the idea of Crown land was a unilateral declaration of royal ownership. The proclamation was a metaphysical assertion of spiritual jurisdiction by way of pen and paper, written in the voice of the king's royal "We":

> And whereas great Frauds and Abuses have been committed in purchasing Lands of the Indians, to the great Prejudice of our Interests and to the great Dissatisfaction of the said Indians: In order, therefore, to prevent such Irregularities for the future, and to the end that the Indians may be convinced of our Justice and determined Resolution to remove all reasonable Cause of Discontent, We do, with the Advice of our Privy Council strictly enjoin and require that no private Person do presume to make any purchase from the said Indians of any Lands reserved to the said Indians, within those parts of our Colonies where, We have thought proper to allow Settlement: but that if at any Time any of the Said Indians should be inclined to dispose of the said Lands, the same shall be Purchased only for Us, in our Name, at some public Meeting or Assembly of the said Indians.[82]

By outlawing the private exchange or purchase of Indigenous lands, the king recognized in some way that Indigenous peoples held their land collectively, and that settlement that ignored such traditions of landholding and jurisdiction would not stand the test of time.

The colonists, eager to move westward, were outraged that a king across the ocean proclaimed his jurisdiction over vast swaths of land thousands of miles away from him. Though schoolchildren are more likely to hear a story about Bostonians livid about taxes on their tea as the spark that ignited the American Revolution, many historians point to anger over the Royal Proclamation for its curtailing of westward settlement as a powerful instigator. As Colin Calloway put it, the revolution was perhaps less of a struggle against royal tyranny and more of a "struggle about Indian land and who was to get it."[83] The people, of course, remained divided about just how this struggle should be resolved.

Writing a new people and nation into being through dissolving their allegiance to King George III, the signers of the Declaration of Independence cast the king as a tyrant who urged the "inhabitants of our frontiers, the merciless Indian Savages," to unjust warfare. Aggrieved by the king's "absolute Despotism" and his "unwarrantable jurisdiction," the signers wrote "in the Name, and by Authority of the good People of these Colonies." The good people gave themselves a new warrant of jurisdiction, both temporal and spiritual:

> As Free and Independent States, they have full Power to levy War, conclude Peace, contract Alliances, establish Commerce, and to do all other Acts and Things which Independent States may of right do. And for the support of this Declaration, with a firm reliance on the protection of divine Providence, we mutually pledge to each other our Lives, our Fortunes and our sacred Honor.[84]

Rooting their sacred honor in divine providence, they justified their seizure of Indigenous land.

As the nascent Americans pilloried King George III as a tyrant and a thief, however, many who were loyal to him pledged their allegiance in body and spirit. White soldiers, settlers, and slaveholders, along with slaves, freed blacks, and Indigenous allies moved north to Canada as "United Empire Loyalists."[85] Many of their descendants, including some Indigenous people, still claim, mark, and memorialize the label of "UEL" today.[86] So

while the Royal Proclamation set into motion a counterasser-
tion against the king's sovereignty in the guise of the American
Revolution, it also incited a renewed metaphysical commitment
to the Crown for those who went north.

The Articles of Capitulation and the Royal Proclamation
were both documents that attempted to name and order the
complex interrelationships between Indigenous models of spiritual and territorial jurisdiction and those of the British. As John
Borrows has written, "The Proclamation illustrates the British
government's attempt to exercise sovereignty over First Nations
while simultaneously trying to convince First Nations that they
would remain separate from European settlers and have their
jurisdiction preserved."[87] Knowing well that the proclamation
was a document that could cut both ways, many Indigenous nations made use of it as a guarantor of their rights as a people.[88]
The Royal Proclamation, then, could be understood not only as
a king's decree but also as an agreement that was supposed to
have constituted treaty peoples through a sacred promise.

The significance of the Royal Proclamation for Indigenous
sovereignty—whether it helps to "reconcile" competing Indigenous and Canadian rights or just keeps on trumping Indigenous
sovereignty in practice—remains a fraught question within Indigenous communities and within Canadian jurisprudence.[89]
As Alan Ojiig Corbiere, Bne Doodeman, and Mchigiing Njibaa
write:

> The Royal Proclamation has been called the magna carta of In-
> dian rights and Aboriginal title. However, it was not made *for* the
> Anishinaabeg (Ojibwe, Odaawaa, Potowatomi, Nipissing, Mis-
> sissauga, Algonquin, Saulteux and Toughkawmiwans) nor the
> Haudenosaunee, nor any other nations (Menominee, Sauk, Fox,
> Cree, Sioux, Ho-Chunk), it was made for the settlers and colonial
> officials. It is a legal document designed as a foundation on which
> the British could commence dispossessing Native American na-
> tions of their land.[90]

British and Canadian treaty makers oscillated between recognizing Indigenous spiritual jurisdiction and obliterating it,
while also depending on an equivocation between democratic
and monarchical power.

Where the colonial British, French, and Portuguese depended on divinely authorized monarchs to claim territory as
Christians, Indigenous leaders vested their territorial claims in
the Creator, or the Great Spirit, who had gifted them the land
in their care.[91] They said as much every time they negotiated
a treaty with the colonial representatives of a king or a queen,
and then again every time they sought to hold those representatives to the promises they had made. According to James Sákéj
Youngblood Henderson, "the word 'spirit' in the Aboriginal legal tradition [is used] to mean the power to transcend any established human convention or order."[92] Calling people to responsibility, a spiritual perspective required people to think of
the consequences of their actions both for their ancestors and
for future generations.

Treaties, for many Indigenous nations, were a form of adoption into an Indigenous framework of kinship much broader
than the nuclear, or even extended, family, which stretched into
the past and future. As lawyer and scholar Harold Johnson has
argued, in his nation's territory in the western prairies, Treaty
No. 6 signaled the Cree adoption of Queen Victoria and those
loyal to her, such that "she and her children received the right
to occupy this territory alongside my family."[93] The treaty was
agreed to through ceremony and bound its members "as long as
the Sun shines, the Grass grows and the River flows." Pledging
oneself to treaty with the sun as a witness was not a mere metaphor, according to Johnson:

> We understand that there are spiritual aspects to the sun, the
> grass, and the river (water), and if promises are made that invoke
> these spirits, then the maker of the promise and all his descen-
> dants are bound by that promise. A promise made to their spirits

cannot be broken. If a mere human tries to break such a sacred promise, those spiritual forces will interfere to ensure the promise is kept.[94]

Metaphors and convictions about kinship and spirit oriented treaty relations, with the land and sky as witnesses.

Concepts of the spiritual and the sacred also oriented Canadian and American claims to authority. US Supreme Court Justice John Marshall, a key figure in the jurisprudence of Native American tribal rights in US law, was also a noted land speculator who depended on both the doctrine of discovery and the Royal Proclamation to argue for limiting "tribal" sovereignty.[95] In an 1823 decision on a land title case from Illinois, *Johnson v. M'Intosh*, Marshall showed his understanding of both treaties and the Royal Proclamation for the question of Indigenous sovereignty: "It is not unworthy of remark, that the usual mode adopted by the Indians for granting lands to individuals, has been to reserve them in a treaty, or to grant them under the sanction of the commissioners with whom the treaty was negotiated. The practice, in such case, to grant to the crown, for the use of the individual, is some evidence of a general understanding that the validity even of such a grant depended on its receiving the royal sanction."[96] Adding the papal doctrine of discovery to the Anglican power of the Royal Proclamation, Marshall concocted some history that would have devastating consequences that he would come to regret, as it led quickly to the Indian Removal Act of 1830:

On the discovery of this immense continent, the great nations of Europe were eager to appropriate to themselves so much of it as they could respectively acquire. Its vast extent offered and [sic] ample field to the ambition and enterprise of all; and the character and religion of its inhabitants afforded an apology for considering them as a people over whom the superior genius of Europe might claim an ascendency. The potentates of the old world found no difficulty in convincing themselves that they made ample compensation to the inhabitants of the new, by bestowing on them civilization and Christianity, in exchange for unlimited independence.[97]

Qualifying his grand historical narrative, Marshall stated the contradiction at the heart of the Crown's honor: "Thus has our whole country been granted by the crown while in the occupation of the Indians." As Winnifred Sullivan has written, Marshall's "legal words" were an act "of breathtaking originary violence."[98] At once diagnosing and enacting the potential for sorcery in "treaty metaphysics," Marshall's use of the discovery doctrine and the Royal Proclamation was quickly adapted by the State of Georgia as a "legal mechanism" for forcing the Cherokees off their land and onto the Trail of Tears.[99]

That words can do such violence has everything to do with the metaphysics of written law. Borrows explains the time-traveling shell game on which Canadian legal jurisdiction is based: "Parliament's authority is placed before a treaty's power even though the Crown's authority chronologically follows pre-existing Indigenous legal orders. Questionable jurisdictional claims reverse time's linear order in the law's metaphysics."[100] Textuality and print culture ennobled by a biblical sensibility were central to the legitimacy of the Royal Proclamation's "questionable" claims: if it was not in writing, it did not matter. For Borrows, these jurisdictional claims are metaphysical in a specific sense:

> The Crown acts as if rights flow from its own *a priori* authority whereas Indigenous peoples on Canada's prairies regarded another pre-existing force as being the source of law—Creator. Both rest on foundational arguments though their polarities are reversed. I have been arguing that both views are metaphysical. They depend on presuppositions rooted in abstract concepts related to knowledge, causation, identity, time, and space.[101]

Claiming the precedence of Crown jurisdiction with the help of the doctrine of discovery, Canadian and US treaty metaphysics have written over the history and legal traditions of Indigenous peoples, covering the memory—and monetary—value of wampum shells with ink and paper.[102]

The colonization of the Americas—the creation of the New World—was dependent on a collaboration of church and state through joint ventures premised on ritual familiarity between the two. Colonization drew legal legitimation from sacramental forms heavily redolent of Christian material forms and "spaces of representation."[103] When it came to land, the Crown considered itself to be the protector of the church. For example, when the United Empire Loyalists moved northward after the American Revolution, the British sought to "settle" the land in part through a system of "clergy reserves." An extensive patchwork of surveyed land that was given to the Church of England in Upper Canada, the clergy reserves were a mechanism by which the Crown subsidized the Church of England in the colonies. The church could build on, sell, rent, or otherwise use this land to ensure its flourishing: "In 1791, the British Parliament, far from seizing old church lands or recognizing a North American tendency favouring the separation of church and state, called for the setting aside of fresh lands in Canada, 'to this Maintenance and Support of a Protestant Clergy . . . and to no other Use or Purpose whatever.'"[104] Clergy reserves represented the conviction that the state needed to make special dispensation for specifically Christian lands as a way of supporting the Church of England as the moral foundation of colonial settlement. In the Upper Canada scheme of clergy reserves, Roman Catholics, Jews, Indigenous peoples, and any other religious or spiritual groupings beyond Anglo-Protestants were nowhere on the map.

Amounting to the establishment of the Church of England, clergy reserves incensed other Christians and drew protest from Indigenous peoples, despite efforts to take "special care to assure that the Reserves as material objects did not cause grievances

that would complicate their already controversial 'spiritual' purposes."[105] Even settlers opposed to the clergy reserves and calling
for the separation of church and state, however, could turn on a
dime when it came to accepting state funding.[106] The Methodist
Episcopal and Wesleyan Churches, both strongly committed to
the separation of church and state and vehement opponents of
the clergy reserves, wavered—and capitulated—when promised
a different kind of churchstateness. They quieted their resistance to the fusion of church and state when they accepted state
monies for their missions to the "Indians."[107]

The Anglican elite known as the "Family Compact"—a kind
of fictive kinship clan of the wealthy—strongly resisted the disestablishment of the clergy reserves, but to no avail. By the mid-
nineteenth century the government distributed the reserves to
a broader set of Protestant churches and families, and in 1859
the government of John A. Macdonald, soon to be Canada's first
prime minister and patron of the Indian Act, "voted the clergy
reserves out of existence, with the proceeds to be applied to
municipalities."[108] So a plan made to ensure space for particular
kinds of Christianity, on land that the Crown had committed
to sharing with Indigenous peoples through treaties, ended up
building the cities of the future.

HER MAJESTY'S INDIAN ACT

For Indigenous peoples, the Christian privilege of churchstateness embodied in the clergy reserves was nothing compared to
that of the Indian Act. A set of laws first enacted in 1876, the
Indian Act was a way of saying—or shouting—the law with no
desire for relationship or conversation. It was legislated from
Ottawa without protocols of negotiating with Indigenous
peoples on their territory, and with the goal of legislating out
of existence the people it designated as "Indians."[109] The Indian
Act differs from the Royal Proclamation in that no one—to my
knowledge—has considered it to be a document that holds pub-

lic memory from which reconciliation on a nation-to-nation basis could be reaffirmed. It is a set of colonial laws, still in existence, that has defined Indigenous peoples as "Indians" in accordance with Christian, racialized, and sexist assumptions. At the same time, however, the Indian Act is very much like the Royal Proclamation, in that it establishes the sovereignty of Canada though the body of the Crown.[110]

The current version of the Indian Act, amended in 1985, starts by defining a "band" as "a body of Indians for whose use and benefit in common, lands, the legal title to which is vested in Her Majesty, have been set apart [and] for whose use and benefit in common, moneys are held by Her Majesty."[111] The Queen may hold some of the money of the Indians on her person or in her crown, but most of it was held in institutions within her realm, including banks, universities, and Crown corporations that have never given it back.[112] In the same way that the existence of Canada has depended on the Crown to vouchsafe the treaties that made it possible, it has also depended on the Crown to turn its treaty partners into wards of the state and to claim vast reaches of territory and resources.

The ambiguities of and amendments to the Indian Act provide some of the most revealing examples of the combined force of church and state in the face of continued and creative Indigenous resistance to colonial law. For example, in nineteenth-century courts there was ongoing confusion about the admissibility of evidence from Indigenous witnesses, because of lack of clarity about both their citizenship and their religion. Presumed to be "non-Christian" and therefore unable to swear an oath, Indigenous witnesses were often deemed untrustworthy in a court of law. In practice, some judges exercised creative reinterpretation by expanding their definition of what counted as an oath to a "supreme being" to include deities besides the Christian God.[113] Nevertheless, Christianity was the religion that provided the grounds for reliability as a witness.

The most direct example of how churchstateness shaped

the Indian Act comes with the laws surrounding ceremony. Missionaries, Indian agents, and lawmakers allied in the late nineteenth century to outlaw Indigenous ceremonies, especially the potlatch and sun dance. Casting these ceremonies as heathenism, and as threatening to both the economic and political systems of Canada, the Indian Act sought to destroy Indigenous sovereignty in part through denial of "religion" as an operative concept for Indigenous peoples. In addition to outlawing ceremonies, Indian Act policies had the effect of suppressing Indigenous languages and destroying generations of family relationships through enforced residential schooling and imposed norms of patriarchal Christian marriage and inheritance.[114] When Indigenous peoples call for the honoring of the treaties, they often insist on the termination of the Indian Act. Though the Indian Act seeks to confine them as a "people" with "status" within its regulations, Indigenous nations have continued to proclaim their own jurisdiction and peoplehood outside of its terms.[115]

STICKS OF SOVEREIGNTY: THE BLACK ROD AND THE RING
OF RECONCILIATION

Queen Elizabeth II has yet to declare a new Royal Proclamation, but in 2016 she did send her grandson on a royal visit that included a new ritual of reconciliation. Amid the pageantry and photo ops of a 2016 royal visit to British Columbia, the very popular Duke and Duchess of Cambridge—or William and Kate—participated in an unusual ritual that was meant to join the wider Canadian project of reconciliation with Indigenous peoples. Prince William, in a gesture of repair, slipped a silver "ring of reconciliation" onto a black wooden rod in recognition of relations among the Crown, Canada, British Columbia, and Indigenous nations.

The Black Rod—which in the legislature of the United Kingdom is referred to with no definite article and refers to both a wooden stick and the man who carries the stick in service of the monarch—is a highly ornate door knocker. Clad in precious metals and encrusted with jewels and a "gold sovereign coin," the Black Rod carries with it the shimmer of sovereignty.[116] Shiny things, whether glittering crowns, treaty medals, or rings of reconciliation, help perpetuate sovereignties and bring new ones into being, while distracting the eye from the fragility of their founding. As Mohawk anthropologist Audra Simpson writes, "This youth and fragility is dealt with in law and managed through decisions on indigeneity, and this sustains the settlers' condition of being, because to live fully aware of the youth and fragility of settler nation-status might very well incite a moral panic."[117] The ring of reconciliation, as a brand-new addition to a Black Rod made a few years earlier, but of very old design, served to underscore this instability.

The British Columbia version of the Black Rod takes its place among many such sticks of sovereignty found across the Commonwealth—the countries founded by the British Empire that maintain a relationship with the Crown. About three and a half feet long and topped with an ornately carved, diamond-embedded silver crown, this Black Rod was a gift that William's grandmother, Queen Elizabeth II, had given to the legislature of British Columbia in 2012, the year of her Diamond Jubilee. Four years later, the ring of reconciliation was added, joining three other silver rings that represented the overlapping settler jurisdictions of the Crown, Canada, and British Columbia. The Queen's grandson, representing the Crown in the flesh, had traveled from England to the Pacific coast with his kin to add one more silver ring in recognition of the jurisdiction of the Indigenous peoples of British Columbia.

The various versions of Black Rods used at Houses of Parliaments in London and around the Commonwealth all trace back to a fourteenth-century story about King Edward III (1312–77). Seeking to keep a close watch on his most intimate circle of advisors, the knights of the Order of the Garter, the king selected one of them to serve as a "Gentleman Usher" who carried a "Black Rod" to mark his authority. Over time, the Black Rod became both a person and an object that asserted the monarch's sovereignty, while acknowledging the authority of Parliament as a house for the representatives of the people. As a space where the king or queen was not permitted to set foot, the House of Parliament was the space of the demos, not the divinely sanctioned monarch. The Black Rod, as both door-knocker and emblem, was a tool of churchstateness that allowed for communication between the Crown and the People, while also representing the "potentializing limits" of royal jurisdiction.

Today, in the Parliament at Westminster, Black Rod is a tool used by its bearer, in the service of the Queen, to knock on the door of the House of Commons to call the representatives of the people to proceed to the House of Lords to hear the Queen's speech at the opening of Parliament. Dressed in his elaborate uniform, Black Rod (in human form) knocks three times with Black Rod (in wooden form), only to have the members of Parliament open the door and then, in a gesture of their authority, slam it in his face. The MPs then open the door again and make their way to the speech.[118] At once a royal summons and a marker of the division of powers between a monarch and the elected representatives of the people, Black Rod is a phallic and sonic reminder of how the British version of a constitutional monarchy is a democracy that draws on the power of God, the Crown, and the people.

The meanings of Black Rod have changed since the fourteenth century, and the stick itself has spawned replicas holding their own royal power across the Commonwealth. Compared to the current Black Rod at Westminster, which was made in 1873, the British Columbia version is quite new. Crafted in 2012 of "wood from seven trees indigenous to British Columbia," this Black Rod is adorned at the top by a silver replica of the crown of King Edward III.[119] Just below the crown, a jade carving depicting a man, woman, and child encircles the rod, carved by

Tsimshian carver Clifford Bolton. At the bottom it is, like most Black Rods, embedded with a gold coin depicting the mythical Saint George slaying the dragon on one side and the historical Queen Victoria on the other. At the base of the original rod gifted by the Queen in 2012 were three silver rings, representing the authority of the Crown, the nation-state of Canada, and the province of British Columbia.

Echoing the Order of the Garter medal worn by King George III in the pencil portrait on McGill University's copy of the Royal Proclamation, the first ring is engraved with the order's motto: "*Honi Soit Qui Mal y Pense*," or "shame on him who thinks badly of it." The origins of this motto are connected to several myths, including one in which the king was said to have preserved the honor of a lady who lost her garter while dancing. Over time, however, the shame came to refer to those who doubted that God favoured the monarch's right to rule. Under Henry VIII, the Order of the Garter became a solely male club by which the king favored those loyal to him: "While the garter was the most glittering prize of his reign, it was a manifestation of achieved favor; to a remarkable extent, it went to the male companionship of the Privy Chamber."[120] Elizabeth I, Henry's daughter, adeptly used the Order of the Garter and its motto and insignia to support her rule as a queen in a male-dominated world. And then in 1987, Queen Elizabeth II changed the rules of the order to once again allow women be invited to join.[121] Whether marking male chivalry, a woman's right to rule, or divinely sanctioned sovereignty, the motto of "*Honi Soit Qui Mal y Pense*" is firmly tied to the Order of the Garter as the most intimate circle of the monarch's advisors, as well as to Saint George the dragon slayer and patron saint of England. One can find the motto inscribed in chairs, medals, and papers across the Commonwealth, and even on the speaker's chair in Quebec's National Assembly.

The second ring bears the motto of Canada: "*a Mari usque ad Mare*" or "from sea to sea," a reference to Psalm 72:8. Starkly proclaiming its colonial and missionary aspirations, the full verse reads, in the King James Version: "He shall have dominion also from sea to sea, and from the river unto the ends of the earth. They that dwell in the wilderness shall bow before him; and his enemies shall lick the dust."[122] This verse also inspired the name that won out at the Confederation of Canada in 1867: the "Dominion of Canada," though there was stiff competition from those who preferred the "Kingdom of Canada."[123] When the Dominion of Canada came into existence in 1867, many Canadians would have caught the full scriptural allusions; from sea to sea, vanquished enemies were left licking the dust.

The third ring is inscribed with the motto of British Columbia: "*Splendor Sine Occasu*," translated as both "splendour without diminishment" and "splendour without sunset."[124] The second translation, when paired with the province's flag, is a boldly imperial claim. The turn of phrase is attributed to imperial official Sir George Macartney, who remarked that after its years of colonial expansion, British imperialism had achieved truly global reach, becoming a "vast empire on which the sun never sets and whose bounds nature has not yet ascertained."[125]

The new fourth ring takes an abrupt about-face and aims to symbolize reconciliation after centuries of British and Canadian imperialism. Etched with two eagle feathers framing the words "*Lets'e Mot*, meaning 'one mind' in the Halq'emeylem language" of Coast Salish nations, the ring is engraved with a canoe opposite the words.[126] Gifted by Prince William after the release of the Truth and Reconciliation Commission's final report, the ring of reconciliation could be a response to the injustice of residential schools. The ring might also be a gesture to include—up to a point—Indigenous nations in the shared jurisdictions of the Crown and federal and provincial governments.

The meaning of the Black Rod, a traditional symbol of royal power and its limits, was tested and contested by the very ritual of reconciliation. Prince William's gesture of reconciliation was witnessed by three representatives of sovereignties that orbit or nest within each other's power: the Governor General of

Canada, David Johnston; premier of British Columbia Christy Clark; and Grand Chief Edward John, a hereditary chief of the Tl'azt'en nation and leader of the First Nations Summit.[127] In the days before the ritual, the Duke and Duchess of Cambridge had traveled to several Indigenous nations, including to Bella Bella and Haida Gwaii, where they were told through words, rituals, and even T-shirts of Indigenous peoples' staunch opposition to the latest attempts of federal and provincial governments to hand over their territory to pipelines, dams, and other threats to creation.[128]

The Honorable Stephen Point, a former British Columbia lieutenant governor from the Stó:lō nation, opened the ritual by saying a prayer and blessing the ring with cedar.[129] Grand Chief Edward John then addressed the gathering. Describing how the British created what became British Columbia in an imperial process which "unilaterally took all Indigenous lands on behalf of the Crown, and called it Crown land," the grand chief laid plain the power of empire with the prince as his witness.[130] As Prince William slipped the silver ring onto the Black Rod in the ritual of reconciliation, he had just been told, once more, of the devastating effects upon Indigenous peoples of his ancestors' imperial dreams and desires. The heir to the British throne listened to the hereditary chief use the phrase "cultural genocide" to describe the British and Canadian approach to Indigenous peoples, as exemplified in the system of residential schools and in the concept of Crown land. Participating in a long tradition of rituals at once performative and political, Prince William did what many of his royal ancestors have done for more than 150 years: performed the authority of the Crown while listening to Indigenous people voice their clear opposition to British and Canadian colonization of their land.[131]

The ring of reconciliation instigated a ritual that briefly drew the eyes of the world, which for some viewers was largely because of the duchess's stunning red dress paired with the Queen's shimmering diamond maple leaf brooch.[132] The grand chief's words, however, also materialized the vulnerability and unevenness of colonial power. Canadian jurisdiction is an amalgam of spiritual and political claims rooted in the past and requiring intermittent revitalization through ritual, which depends on the Crown—the head of state and of the Church of England—for its metaphysical being.

For a ritual that sought to reconcile contested sovereignties by acknowledging overlapping jurisdictions, the Black Rod ceremony was not a complete success. Grand Chief Edward John had stepped in at the last minute after Grand Chief Stewart Phillip of the Union of British Columbia Indian Chiefs announced that he could no longer participate, as "the chiefs-in-assembly felt it would not be appropriate for me to participate in a 'reconciliation' ceremony at this time." Citing the lack of action of the current Canadian government to fulfil its promises to a new nation-to-nation relationship, he stated: "The suffering in our communities is too great. I apologize for any inconvenience we may have caused with our decision. We do not mean any disrespect. It is a matter of principle."[133] Shunning a ritual embedded in six hundred years of English/British hereditary power, Grand Chief Phillip had his critics among other Indigenous leaders. He decided, nevertheless, that this was a ritual of reconciliation in which he could not participate as a representative of his own house, and of his own people.

The success and failure of the ring of reconciliation as a ritual innovation reveals how material objects that are subject to elaborate state protocol are vehicles for exposing the ragged edges of sovereignty, at the same time that they enable the acknowledgment of overlapping jurisdictions. Like most Indigenous people in the Pacific Northwest, Grand Chief Phillip considered his people and their allies to have remained fully sovereign over much of the territory that is now called British Columbia, as they never ceded their land through treaties. Problems of "jurisdiction," as Shiri Pasternak writes, are conflicts "over the inauguration of law—or the authority to have authority—and the specific forms of struggle that arise when competing forms of law are asserted over a common space."[134] As a concept, jurisdiction may precede the sovereign state—people can claim it locally or broadly, and even in overlapping and shared ways.[135] In the Americas, treaties or the lack of them both point to ongoing reality of multijurisdictional sovereignties.

Overlapping jurisdictions are found everywhere, but not all kinds of jurisdiction are given the privilege to overlap. In Canada, for example, a municipality can have jurisdiction over its building codes or bicycle paths, while a province has jurisdiction over such areas as education, highways, and health care. The provincial and federal governments have shared jurisdiction over such areas as agriculture and immigration. In honor of this shared jurisdiction, each province also has its own representative of the Crown in the person of the lieutenant governor, who watches over the shaping of new laws. On its own, the Canadian federal government has jurisdiction over a range of spheres, including the military, the money, and, still today, the amending and enforcing of the "Indian Act." But when jurisdiction is claimed in such a way that sharing or overlapping is no longer possible, plural jurisdictions become much more ontologically challenging.

One of the strongest critiques that some Indigenous peoples launch against "reconciliation" as a mode of engagement between Indigenous nations and the Canadian state is that it does not go far enough in questioning the grounding of Canadian sovereignty—the inauguration of law, including the Indian Act, that made Canada.[136] Without such questioning, Indigenous sovereignty—which remains a strongly argued and lived form of spiritual-political organization for many—could easily be reduced to "limited forms of self-government that are nested within the status quo, such as gaining municipal powers only, or becoming another order of government within Canada."[137] A ritual of reconciliation that added to the Black Rod a fourth ring underneath a trio of nested jurisdictions—Crown, Canada, British Columbia—may well suggest a politics of absorption and assimilation rather than the recognition of a political geometry of overlapping jurisdictions.

TREATY METAPHYSICS

For many years, Canadian law downplayed or ignored the treaties—or even tried to argue that the treaties established the full sovereignty of the Crown and the "extinguishment" of Indigenous title.[138] In 1982, however, when Canada "repatriated" its constitution from Britain, the treaties took on new significance. Section 35 of the 1982 Constitution Act recognizes and affirms the "existing aboriginal and treaty rights of the aboriginal peoples of Canada."[139] In the wake of Section 35, Indigenous peoples grew even more persistent in their call to honor the treaties, in both legal and ceremonial genres. Calls from Canadian and Indigenous scholars such as Jeremy Webber and John Borrows for "agonistic constitutionalism" and "jurisdictional spaces" where Indigenous and Canadian sovereignties can coexist have contributed to new ways of saying the law.[140] Webber, Borrows, and others theorize a more frayed view of competing sovereignties, with threads coming loose. Most interestingly for the question of in *what* and in *whom* spiritual jurisdiction lies, the resurgence of Indigenous law has raised robust challenges to Canadian sovereignty by reassessing the historical sources and material culture of treaty negotiations.[141]

The resurgence of Indigenous law points to the metaphysics of treaty making, to use John Borrows' term, both by calling out the spiritual underpinnings of Canadian law and by arguing that treaty making was more than a process of writing down an agreement between Indigenous leaders and the Crown.[142] Even before the ink was dry on many nineteenth- and early-twentieth-century treaties, it had become clear to Indigenous peoples that the promises made on paper were not a pathway to shared care of the land and its peoples. The creation of the Indian Act in 1876, the imposition of the reserve system, and the institution of residential schools—the church-state system of violent assimilation that sought to break the bonds between children, their families, their language, and their land—showed that instead of serving as promises, the relationships established through treaties with the Crown had become threats to Indigenous flourishing and survival.

To counter this treaty breaking, Indigenous people have preserved and sustained the oral history and material culture of treaty conversations. Both academic scholars and Indigenous elders have shown that conventional text-centric methods for discerning historical and legal evidence are not up to the challenge of understanding the full significance of treaties. As Bob Beal has argued, Indigenous people "regarded the treaty relationships as living things that needed regular nourishment, not as static entities set in pieces of paper."[143] Methodological questions about memory and material culture, then, are deeply implicated in any consideration of church, state, and spiritual jurisdiction. As John Borrows writes,

> Alongside Indigenous spiritual forms treaties were influenced by biblical language and metaphors. Missionaries, priests, and Indigenous spiritual leaders played a vital role in securing agreements. However, our society has largely moved on in its deference to these sources when giving treaties meaning. While Indigenous spiritual teachings with legal dimensions might find a small place in treaty interpretation in the present day, it would be very unusual to regard the Bible as possessing this authority in today's courtrooms. Religious and spiritual metaphysics have been replaced with other sanctified "secular" texts. Constitutions are set apart for the guidance of society in an era when we largely pretend there are no foundational metaphysical commitments concerning life's order and meaning.[144]

As Winnifred Sullivan shows in the next chapter, the obsessive effort to expunge the Christian holy book from the deliberation of the people in the death penalty jury room has depended on a conviction that church and state must be cleanly separated—a conviction that in her reading always remains unrealized. Churchstateness can never be fully disentangled in part because all Crowns and all constitutions rest on foundational claims that are themselves profoundly theological-political.[145] But perhaps an agonistic relationship that respects and works through multiple jurisdictions can at once recognize the spiritual and material as "potentializing limits," to use Justin Richland's words, with a sense of humility that rests on more than one, profoundly Christian, version of churchstateness.

MATERIALIZING SPIRITUAL JURISDICTION

Making an inquiry into church and state requires thinking about much more than how the state legislates the formal role of Christianity in a polity. Such an inquiry has to include questions of how a state materializes the church in its rituals, on its money, and most importantly for Indigenous people, on the land itself. In Canada, official ritual protocol, whether royal visits or state funerals, has turned repeatedly to Christian traditions and symbols that may be opaque, or even outdated, to many, but persist nevertheless. Even contemporary projects of urban planning and resource extraction continue to reinscribe churchstateness in ways that privilege Christianity or destroy Indigenous spirituality, such as a city government that preserves churches as sites of local heritage, or Crown corporations that destroy ecosystems, lifeways, and spiritual sites to build dams, pipelines, and ski resorts on Indigenous land.[146] Remembering the past or obliterating potential futures, the power of the Crown is ongoing.

The portrait of King George III that decorates McGill's copy of the Royal Proclamation also found its way onto some of the treaty medals distributed by kings and queens to Indigenous leaders to mark the signing of treaties. Modelled on medals for bravery in war, such as those that King George III gave out to Indigenous allies who fought for the British in the war against the Americans in 1812, treaty medals were considered by Indigenous leaders to be important markers of treaty relationships; some men even requested to be buried with their medals.[147] When they were sent medals of shoddy workmanship, from which the silver rubbed off when polished, they insisted that new medals of better quality silver be sent in their place. Their concerns were not about the monetary but the memorial value of the medals.[148]

This memorial value still holds, as a new display at the Manitoba Museum shows. When curator Maureen Matthews was readying some nineteenth-century treaty medals for an exhibit called "We Are All Treaty People," she consulted with the Treaty Relations Commission and with elders from the Assembly of Manitoba Chiefs. As the medals represented treaty negotiations, the elders recommended that peace pipes also be displayed, in recognition of the pipes that would have been smoked at treaty. As Nancy Louis of the Samson Cree Nation explained to the Royal Commission on Aboriginal Peoples, "We have an agreement as treaty Indians and we believe that these treaties cannot be broken or changed or negotiated because a sacred pipe was used when the treaties were signed and sealed."[149] But to display peace pipes, themselves a living pathway of the spirit, required some special custodial preparation.

To keep the pipes alive, they needed to be touched, and even smoked. The museum, together with elders, brought the pipes to an Indigenous school in southern Manitoba, where they were laid out on blankets and touched by the children, teenagers, and adults of the community. Returned to the museum, the pipes joined the treaty medals: "In every case, the Treaty medals or documents signifying Royal contractual obligations have been matched with pipes and pipe bags signifying the First Nations' commitment to the Treaty as a sacred undertaking meant to last forever."[150] Feasted outside the museum and honored within, the pipes now exhibit their spiritual jurisdiction in the museum cases where they reside.[151]

On my visit to the McGill library in 2016, I was lucky to get a chance to see the Royal Proclamation in its curious frame with the portrait of King George and his medal. A few weeks later it was going to be removed from the frame to travel to Winnipeg for an exhibit called "Protecting Rights in Canada" at the Canadian Museum of Human Rights, down the street from the Manitoba Museum. Looking decidedly less kitschy outside of its Plexiglas frame, and ensconced behind glass, the Royal Proclamation was credited in the museum label with marking "an important first step in recognizing Aboriginal rights," as well as bringing British common law to Canada, or law based not on writing but "on customs." In this display, the Royal Proclamation was placed next to a treaty medal, but no sacred pipes hung nearby. The proclamation was not given context by juxtaposing it with the "customs" and laws of Indigenous peoples by which they received it. Instead, its meaning was largely framed by other pieces of paper, including an early treaty document and the original 1982 Canadian constitution, spattered with rain when Queen Elizabeth II signed it in person on Parliament Hill in Ottawa.[152] The present-day usefulness of the proclamation as a document of display depends largely on the other materializations of power by which it is understood.

The British and Canadian signatories of the treaties would have recognized the Indigenous view of treaties as articulations of shared spiritual jurisdiction. These men sat together around council fires, exchanging wampum at Niagara to solemnize their agreements.[153] They shared sacred pipes in the prairies. On treaty payment days, government officials regularly gifted silver treaty medals in recognition of the treaties and in memory of the loyalty of Indigenous men during the war of 1812.[154] But with time, these Canadian markers of remembrance died out. As more settlers arrived, building churches and city halls on the streets of their towns, they did so largely in ignorance or disavowal of the treaties. The spiritual significance of the treaties became superfluous, or irrelevant, for the settler view of how land was owned. The sacred pipes given to representatives of the Crown at treaty signings ended up in museums, or lost altogether.

But spiritual jurisdiction is a persistent concept. Indigenous diplomacy has kept it alive in ceremony and argument, with the Crown as a binding idea. As James Sákéj Youngblood Henderson argues, "The Supreme Court of Canada has acknowledged that Indigenous treaties are sacred. Failure to respect the status and significance of treaties would be inconsistent with the Crown's constitutional fiduciary obligations—as well as with the principles of good faith, honour of the Crown, and trust that are associated with such obligations and with the process of treaty making itself."[155] At the same time, any honor inhering in the Crown comes from churchstateness, a double-edged power that may constitute treaty people at the same time that it can destroy them.

Making plain how promises made by the Canadian Crown were rooted in churchstateness opens up a perspective on how spirituality and the sacred continue to be framing language for contests over land, water, and people in the Americas. The explicit goal of separating church and state in the Americas often had the effect of giving a latent but still usable power to Christianity as the template for religion writ large. Colonial secular ways of constituting the nation put Christianity in the sphere of religion and the state in the sphere of politics and effectively pushed Indigenous spiritual jurisdiction into the realm of savagery and superstition.[156] The piling up of legal decisions, laws, and bylaws gradually secularized jurisdiction by rooting it in law that was hedged by time, revolutions, and disestablishment; the very notion of the separation of church and state has enabled settler-colonial nations to forget or obscure the Christian underpinnings of their claim to sovereignty in the name of the Crown. But churchstateness remains.

Settler-colonial nations had to rely on rituals and stories, often legitimated in the name of a Christian God, to materialize their power. They could not depend only on the will of the people who voted or on acts of violence to claim the land in an effective way. Both the church, by which I mean Catholic and Protestant ecclesiastical assemblies, and the state, by which I mean, in this case, the Dominion of Canada, have materialized their power through labor-intensive rituals, sedimented laws and regulations, and acts of force over bodies and on land. Despite this ongoing history of churchstateness, the fact of spiritual jurisdiction does not sit comfortably within a body politic that understands itself as secular.

In Canada and the United States, secular politics arose largely through battles in which people of conviction sought to separate the powers of church and state and thereby came to define the "religious" as opposed to the "secular" through a Christian lens.[157] Fighting against clerical arrogance and privilege in such realms as education, land tenure, and women's reproductive rights, self-declared atheists and secularists, and even many Christians, embraced the separation of church and state based on profound dedication to what the early twentieth-century literary critic Van Wyck Brooks called the "critical, disruptive spirit."[158] Especially when churches espoused a missionary zeal to impose their theologies on the life or body of another, for a citizen to ask the state for protection made considerable sense. But not all inhabitants could count on the state to protect them.

The interaction between discourses of secularism and those of church and state are difficult to untangle. As Leigh Schmidt writes in his historical study of atheism in the United States, "Church-state jurisprudence is ever-evolving and necessarily unsettled, always awaiting the next spate of litigation over state-funded chaplaincies, faith-based initiatives, or reproductive rights to sort through the nation's religious-political entanglements."[159] Inquiring into the question of church and state in the Americas, however, must set both Christianity and secularism within wider metaphysical and spiritual discourses, including those of Indigenous peoples.[160]

The separation of church and state in the Americas was not only about battling clerical arrogance and domination. Disentangling the church from the state was also an attempt to forget the metaphysical underpinnings of colonial domination in the doctrine of discovery and the spiritual jurisdiction of the Crown. No matter how many Bibles are removed from the jury room, shearing off divine authority from political legitimacy will not be achieved in North America, as continued ceremonies of possession within protocols of inaugurations and oath takings reveal. But the very idea that the separation of church and state could be achieved, whether in the guise of religious freedom or freedom from religion, perpetuates a perverse amnesia about the foundations of colonial power in both Canada and the United States.

As materializations of spiritual jurisdiction, the Royal Proclamation and the ring of reconciliation demonstrate the changing conditions of mutual recognition between the state and the church. They both embody the tight connection of ekklesia, through which the inauguration of colonial law by way of Christian authority makes one people at the expense of another. Over the course of the nineteenth century, the colonial government moved away from nation-to-nation relations established in treaties and toward a policy of assimilation and destruction of Indigenous spiritual jurisdiction, through the Indian Act and residential schools. These nineteenth- and early-twentieth-century examples of state recognition of the "specialness" of (some) Christian churches and clergy may seem evidence of a long-gone era, when politicians could openly claim that Canada was a Christian nation. But the effects of the twinned power of church and state continue to be felt. Even the Truth and Reconciliation Commission's very focus on churches—and its framing concept of reconciliation—makes space for new forms of churchstateness to emerge.[161]

As the Anglican, Presbyterian, and United Churches (but not the Roman Catholic Church) apologized to Indigenous peoples for their roles in the residential schools and the wider church-state project of Indigenous dispossession and assimilation, the Canadian state followed in their wake. From sea to sea, however, these apologies have not stopped the spilling of diesel fuel from American tugboats in Pacific waters close to Bella Bella or the plan of a Crown corporation to flood Inuit land in Labrador to build a hydroelectric dam or the Supreme Court case in which the British Columbia government insists that it has the right to zone a ski resort on a mountain that the Ktunaxa First Nation considers to be the sacred home of the Grizzly Bear Spirit.[162]

In light of ongoing colonialism, some Indigenous scholars suggest that for Indigenous nations, recognition by the state is best met with refusal. Glenn Coulthard, political theorist and member of the Yellowknives Dene Nation, argues that recognition in multicultural states, as it has been elaborated in the work of Charles Taylor and others, assumes the legitimacy of the state's sovereignty. In a settler-colonial context, state sovereignty was achieved through colonizers taking Indigenous land by the authority of their own law, backed up by the Christian God. To then seek recognition under the laws of the Canadian state is to perpetuate "colonial relations of power . . . through the asymmetrical exchange of mediated forms of state recognition and accommodation."[163] Refusing recognition under the terms of the colonial state, I argue, is also an insistence that spiritual jurisdiction inaugurates both Indigenous and settler law.[164]

Considering the lingering effects of state recognition of the Christian church at a time when Indigenous legal traditions are newly resurgent complicates the comparative axis of the dominant transatlantic frame of thinking about church and state. Bringing both Canada and Indigenous nations into this comparative frame acknowledges the historical legacies and enduring reality of Indigenous legal traditions for the "Atlantic-" and Christian-focused narrative of religion and law—or church and state—in northern America. The long afterlives of the joining together and putting asunder of church and state remain in the

Black Rod with its new ring and in the museum exhibition of the Royal Proclamation. These are ritual displays that are more than merely performative of power.

The shimmer of sovereignty remains a pressing concern for Indigenous nations. The gold, silver, and diamonds used to make the markers of sovereignty—treaty medals, the ring of reconciliation, the Queen's maple leaf brooch, her golden crowns, and the Black Rod itself—come from the earth. The profit-seeking miners and mining companies that have flocked to Indigenous territories since the beginning of colonialism have come in search of gold and silver, and now they look for diamonds and bitumen. Though mining companies now have a "duty to consult" Indigenous nations before opening their mines, the basic calculus of who profits from digging and blasting this shiny matter from the ground still benefits the mining companies much more than Indigenous peoples. And the process of extraction continues to pollute the land and waters of Indigenous homelands—and those of all treaty people. Whether the resurgence of spiritual jurisdiction, inseparable from the revival of Indigenous law, can carry forth the sacred promises of the Royal Proclamation and treaties remains to be seen. As Grand Chief Phillip stated clearly, it will require much more than rings of reconciliation for treaty peoples to remember and to live out such promises through respecting and caring for the land and each other. But as the encounter between Prince William and Grand Chief John suggests, silver rings that say the law in many tongues are a shimmering reminder of the antiquity and the urgency of the challenge.

NOTES

1. Benjamin L. Berger, *Law's Religion: Religious Difference and the Claims of Constitutionalism* (Toronto: University of Toronto Press, 2015).

2. "The Monarch," Government of Canada, http://canada.pch .gc.ca/eng/1444999464289/1444999464291?=undefined&wbdisable =true.

3. Caroline Desbiens, *Power from the North: Territory, Identity, and the Culture of Hydroelectricity in Quebec* (Vancouver: University of British Columbia Press, 2013).

4. J. R. Miller, *Compact, Contract, Covenant: Aboriginal Treaty-Making in Canada* (Toronto: University of Toronto Press, 2009), 345.

5. "The Crown," Government of Canada, http://canada.pch.gc .ca/eng/1444999462589/1444999462592.

6. Jill Carter, "Discarding Sympathy, Disrupting Catharsis: The Mortification of Indigenous Flesh as Survivance-Intervention," *Theatre Journal* 67, no. 3 (2015): 413–32; Aldridge, *Keeping Promises*.

7. Desbiens, *Power from the North*.

8. Walter Hildebrandt, Dorothy First Rider, and Sarah Carter, *The True Spirit and Original Intent of Treaty 7* (Montreal: McGill-Queen's University Press, 1996), 301.

9. Matthew Engelke, "Material Religion," in *The Cambridge Companion to Religious Studies*, ed. Robert A. Orsi (Cambridge: Cambridge University Press, 2012), 209–29.

10. Bohaker, "Reading Anishinaabe Identities: Meaning and Metaphor in Nindoodem Pictographs," *Ethnohistory* 57, no. 1 (January 1, 2010): 11–33; Richard Daly, *Our Box Was Full: An Ethnography for the Delgamuukw Plaintiffs* (Vancouver: University of British Columbia Press, 2004).

11. Alan Ojiig Corbiere, "Treaty Medals," paper presented at Metals and Memory, Toronto, 2016.

12. Heidi Bohaker, Alan Ojiig Corbiere, and Ruth B. Phillips, "Wampum Unites Us: Digital Access, Interdisciplinarity and Indigenous Knowledge—Situating the GRASAC Knowledge Sharing Database," in *Museum as Process: Translating Local and Global Knowledges*, ed. Raymond Silverman (New York: Routledge, 2015), 45–66.

13. Harold Johnson, *Two Families: Treaties and Government* (Saskatoon: Purich Publishing, 2007).

14. John Borrows, "Wampum at Niagara: The Royal Proclamation, Canadian Legal History, and Self-Government," in *Aboriginal and Treaty Rights in Canada: Essays on Law, Equality, and Respect for Difference* (Vancouver: University of British Columbia Press, 1997), 155–72. For an alternate perspective see Keith Jamieson, "The Haundenosaunee / Six Nations and the Royal Proclamation of 1763," *ActiveHistory.ca*, October 2, 2013, http://activehistory.ca/2013/10/the-haundenosauneesix-nations-and-the-royal-proclamation-of-1763/. See also Janice Makokis, "Envisioning an Indigenous Jurisdictional Process: A Nehiyaw (Cree) Law Approach" *LawNow Magazine*, March, 2017, accessed March 20, 2017, http://www.lawnow.org/envisioning-an-indigenous-jurisdictional-process-a-nehiyaw-cree-law-approach/print/.

15. Canadian Museum of Human Rights, "Canada's Magna Carta: Meaning and Misconceptions," August 14, 2015, https://humanrights.ca/newsbg-magnacarta-meaning-misconceptions.

16. Cole Harris, *Making Native Space: Colonialism, Resistance, and Reserves in British Columbia* (Vancouver: University of British Columbia Press, 2002).

17. Jeremy Webber, "We Are Still in the Age of Encounter: Section 35 and a Canada beyond Sovereignty," in *From Recognition to Reconciliation: Essays on the Constitutional Entrenchment of Aboriginal and Treaty Rights*, ed. Patrick Macklem and Douglas Sanderson (Toronto: University of Toronto Press, 2016), 75.

18. "Council of the Haida Nation—Agreements," accessed October 30, 2016, http://www.haidanation.ca/Pages/Agreements/agreements.html.

19. Truth and Reconciliation Commission of Canada, *The Final Report of the Truth and Reconciliation Commission of Canada*, vol. 5, *Canada's Residential Schools: The Legacy* (Montreal: McGill-Queen's University Press, 2015), 277–96.

20. Ibid., 284.

21. Penelope Edmonds, *Settler Colonialism and (Re)conciliation: Frontier Violence, Affective Performances, and Imaginative Refoundings* (Hampshire: Palgrave Macmillan, 2016), 2.

22. See Hildebrandt, Rider, and Carter, *The True Spirit and Original Intent of Treaty 7*; Lauren A. Benton, *Law and Colonial Cultures: Legal Regimes in World History, 1400–1900* (New York: Cambridge University Press, 2002); John Borrows, *Canada's Indigenous Constitution* (Toronto: University of Toronto Press, 2010).

23. I am grateful to Benjamin Berger for helping me to think this through. Mariana Valverde, "'The Honour of the Crown Is at Stake': Aboriginal Land Claims Litigation and the Epistemology of Sovereignty," *UC Irvine Law Review* 1, no. 3 (2011): 957–74; Mariana Valverde, "The Crown in a Multicultural Age: The Changing Epistemology of (Post)colonial Sovereignty," *Social & Legal Studies* 21, no. 1 (2012): 3–21; Ernst H. Kantorowicz, *The King's Two Bodies: A Study in Mediaeval Political Theology* (Princeton, NJ: Princeton University Press, 1957).

24. Jonathan Z. Smith, *Relating Religion: Essays in the Study of Religion* (Chicago: University of Chicago Press, 2004); Talal Asad, *Genealogies of Religion: Discipline and Reasons of Power in Christianity and Islam* (Baltimore: Johns Hopkins University Press, 1993); Vine Deloria Jr., *For This Land: Writings on Religion in America* (New York: Routledge, 1998).

25. Meaghan Weatherdon and Pamela E. Klassen, "The Study of Indigenous Religions in North America," in *Oxford Handbook of the Anthropology of Religion*, eds. Simon Coleman and Joel Robbins, (Oxford: Oxford University Press, forthcoming).

26. Justin Richland, "Jurisdiction: Grounding Law in Language," *Annual Review of Anthropology* 42 (2013): 209–26; Mariana Valverde, *Chronotopes of Law: Jurisdiction, Scale and Governance* (London: Routledge, 2015).

27. Justin B. Richland, "Hopi Tradition as Jurisdiction: On the Potentializing Limits of Hopi Sovereignty," *Law & Social Inquiry* 36, no. 1 (2011): 201–34.

28. Ibid., 209.

29. Pamela E. Klassen, *The Story of Radio Mind: A Missionary's Journey on Indigenous Land* (Chicago: University of Chicago Press, forthcoming).

30. Foucault, *Security, Territory, Population*, 154.

31. Ibid., 153.

32. James (Sákéj) Youngblood Henderson, *Indigenous Diplomacy and the Rights of Peoples: Achieving UN Recognition* (Vancouver: University of British Columbia Press, 2008), 97.

33. The literature on treaties is large and growing. Two helpful places to begin are Johnson, *Two Families*; and Michael Asch, *On Being Here to Stay: Treaties and Aboriginal Rights in Canada* (Toronto: University of Toronto Press, 2014).

34. "Royal Commission on Aboriginal Peoples—Final Report," vol. 2, "Restructuring the Relationship," accessed October 22, 2016, https://archive.org/stream/RoyalCommissionOnAboriginal Peoples-FinalReport-Vo1.2-Restructuring/RoyalCommissionOn AboriginalPeoples-FinalReport-Vo1.2_djvu.txt.

35. Henderson, *Indigenous Diplomacy and the Rights of Peoples*, 97. See also Harold Cardinal, *The Rebirth of Canada's Indians* (Edmonton: Hurtig, 1977).

36. My wording here is inspired by John Borrows, *Drawing Out Law: A Spirit's Guide* (Toronto: University of Toronto Press, 2010); John Borrows, "Origin Stories & the Law: Treaty Metaphysics in Canada and New Zealand," n.d.

37. Henderson, *Indigenous Diplomacy and the Rights of Peoples*, 42.

38. Leanne Simpson, "Looking after Gdoo-Naaganinaa: Precolonial Nishnaabeg Diplomatic and Treaty Relationships," *Wicazo Sa Review* 23, no. 2 (2008): 38.

39. Ibid., 29.

40. Georges Erasmus, introduction to *Drum Beat: Anger and Renewal in Indian Country*, ed. Boyce Richardson (Toronto: Summerhill Press, 1989), 2, 13.

41. Quoted in Nathan Tidridge, *Canada's Constitutional Monarchy: An Introduction to Our Form of Government* (Hamilton: Dundurn, 2011), 81.

42. Paul Benoit, "State Ceremonial: The Constitutional Monarch's Liturgical Authority," in *The Evolving Canadian Crown*, ed.

Jennifer Smith and D. Michael Jackson (Montreal: McGill-Queen's University Press, 2012), 119–38.

43. Nathan Tidridge, *The Queen at the Council Fire: The Treaty of Niagara, Reconciliation, and the Dignified Crown in Canada* (Hamilton: Dundurn, 2015), 18.

44. Ibid., 17.

45. Ibid., 18.

46. Tidridge, *Canada's Constitutional Monarchy*, 79–80.

47. Heidi Bohaker, "Reading Anishinaabe Identities: Meaning and Metaphor in Nindoodem Pictographs," *Ethnohistory* 57, no. 1 (2010): 11–33. See also Johnson, *Two Families*.

48. Santner, *The Royal Remains*, 50.

49. Ibid., 51.

50. Ibid., 46–47.

51. Klassen, "Fantasies of Sovereignty."

52. Suzan Shown Harjo, *Nation to Nation: Treaties between the United States & American Indian Nations* (Washington, DC: Smithsonian Books, 2014); Patrick Macklem and Douglas Sanderson, *From Recognition to Reconciliation: Essays on the Constitutional Entrenchment of Aboriginal and Treaty Rights* (Toronto: University of Toronto Press, 2016).

53. David Arnot, "The Honour of the First Nations—The Honour of the Crown: The Unique Relationship of First Nations with the Crown," in *The Evolving Canadian Crown*, ed. Jennifer Smith and D. Michael Jackson (Montreal: McGill-Queen's University Press, 2012), 160.

54. Rick Monture, *We Share Our Matters: Two Centuries of Writing and Resistance at Six Nations of the Grand River* (Winnipeg: University of Manitoba Press, 2014), 14.

55. Elizabeth Elbourne, "Managing Alliance, Negotiating Christianity: Haudenosaunee Uses of Anglicanism in Northeastern North America, 1760s–1830s," in *Mixed Blessings: Indigenous Encounters with Christianity in Canada*, ed. Tolly Bradford and Chelsea Horton (Vancouver: University of British Columbia Press, 2016), 51.

56. Michelle A. Hamilton, *Collections and Objections: Aboriginal*

Material Culture in Southern Ontario, 1791–1914 (Montreal: McGill-Queens University Press, 2012); Arni Brownstone, "Mysteries of the Sculptural Narrative Pipes from Manitoulin Island," *American Indian Art* 36, no. 3 (2011): 54–84.

57. Harjo, *Nation to Nation*.

58. O'Brien, *Firsting and Lasting*.

59. Patricia Seed, *Ceremonies of Possession in Europe's Conquest of the New World, 1492–1640* (Cambridge: Cambridge University Press, 1995).

60. Indigenous Foundations, University of British Columbia, "Royal Proclamation, 1763," Indigenous Foundations UBC, accessed October 18, 2016, http://indigenousfoundations.arts.ubc.ca/home/government-policy/royal-proclamation-1763.html.

61. I am very grateful to Ashley Morford, a PhD student of English and Indigenous literatures, for her question.

62. I thank my daughter, Magdalene, a history student, and my colleague, Benjamin Berger, a scholar of Canadian law and religion, for visiting the Royal Proclamation with me, and for helping me to reflect on it afterward.

63. Allan Ramsay, *Portrait of King George III in Profile*, c. 1762, http://www.historicalportraits.com/Gallery.asp?Page=Item&ItemID=1170&Desc=Portrait-of-King-George-III-in-profile-(1738-1820-%7C-Studio-of-Allan-Ramsay.

64. Pamela E. Klassen, "God Keep Our Land: The Legal Ritual of the McKenna-McBride Royal Commission, 1913–1916," in *Religion and the Exercise of Public Authority*, ed. Benjamin L. Berger and Richard Moon (Oxford: Hart, 2016), 79–93.

65. Borrows, "Wampum at Niagara."

66. Ibid.

67. Colin G. Calloway, *The Scratch of a Pen: 1763 and the Transformation of North America* (New York: Oxford University Press, 2006).

68. Hamar Foster and Benjamin L. Berger, "From Humble Prayers to Legal Demands: The Cowichan Petition of 1909 and the British Columbia Indian Land Question," in *The Grand Experiment:*

Law and Legal Culture in British Settler Societies, ed. A. R. Buck, Benjamin L. Berger, and Hamar Foster, 240–67 (Vancouver: University of British Columbia Press, 2008); Aldridge, *Keeping Promises*; James (Sákéj)Youngblood Henderson, *The Mikmaw Concordat* (Halifax: Fernwood, 1997).

69. See Klassen, *The Story of Radio Mind*.

70. See Chiefs of Ontario, "250th Anniversary of the Treaty of Niagara," Chiefs of Ontario website, accessed April 24, 2017, http://www.chiefs-of-ontario.org/node/920.

71. Jennifer Reid, "The Doctrine of Discovery and Canadian Law," *Canadian Journal of Native Studies* 30, no. 2 (2010): 336, 338.

72. Ibid., 339.

73. Colin G. Calloway, *The American Revolution in Indian Country: Crisis and Diversity in Native American Communities* (Cambridge: Cambridge University Press, 1995).

74. W. P. M. Kennedy, *Documents of the Canadian Constitution, 1759–1915* (Toronto: Oxford University Press, 1963).

75. Ibid., 12; See also Berger, *Law's Religion*.

76. Borrows, "Wampum at Niagara"; Aldridge, *Keeping Promises*.

77. Kennedy, *Documents of the Canadian Constitution*, 13.

78. Maya Jasanoff, *Liberty's Exiles: American Loyalists in the Revolutionary World* (New York: Knopf Doubleday, 2012).

79. Kennedy, *Documents of the Canadian Constitution*, 14.

80. Calloway, *The American Revolution in Indian Country*; Reid, "The Doctrine of Discovery and Canadian Law."

81. Indigenous Foundations, University of British Columbia, "Royal Proclamation, 1763."

82. Ibid.

83. Calloway, *The American Revolution in Indian Country*, 23.

84. "Declaration of Independence: A Transcription," America's Founding Documents, National Archives, November 1, 2015, https://www.archives.gov/founding-docs/declaration-transcript.

85. Jasanoff, *Liberty's Exiles*.

86. Hamilton, *Collections and Objections*; Monture, *We Share Our Matters*.

87. Borrows, "Wampum at Niagara."

88. J. K. Flyaway et al., "Indian Protest against White Settlers Coming in to the Aiyansh Valley, Naas River, British Columbia," May 17, 1910; Foster and Berger, "From Humble Prayers to Legal Demands." Similar to Winnifred Sullivan's discussion in this volume of the political power of the "eirobiblical," in which African-Americans cited biblical passages to make space for their freedom, the more than 250 years of Indigenous citations of the Royal Proclamation were a kind of serious play, see M. Cooper Harriss, "On the Eirobiblical," *Biblical Interpretation* 21, no. 4–5 (2013): 469–93.

89. Borrows, "Wampum at Niagara"; Brian Slattery, "The Royal Proclamation of 1763 and the Aboriginal Constitution," in *Keeping Promises: The Royal Proclamation of 1763, Aboriginal Rights, and Treaties in Canada*, ed. Jim Aldridge and Terry Fenge (Montreal: McGill-Queen's University Press, 2015), 14–32.

90. Alan Ojiig Corbiere, Mchigiing Njibaa, and Bne Doodeman, "Parchment, Wampum, Letters and Symbols: Expanding the Parameters of the Royal Proclamation Commemoration," *ActiveHistory.ca*, October 2, 2013, http://activehistory.ca/2013/10/parchment-wampum-letters-and-symbols-expanding-the-parameters-of-the-royal-proclamation-commemoration/.

91. Cardinal, *The Rebirth of Canada's Indians*.

92. Henderson, *Indigenous Diplomacy and the Rights of Peoples*, 98.

93. Johnson, *Two Families*, 29.

94. Ibid.

95. Colin G. Calloway, "The Proclamation of 1763: Indian Country Origins and American Impacts," in *Keeping Promises: The Royal Proclamation of 1763, Aboriginal Rights, and Treaties in Canada*, ed. Jim Aldridge and Terry Fenge (Montreal: McGill-Queen's University Press, 2015), 48.

96. 21 US 543 (1823); Lindsay G. Robertson, "The Judicial Conquest of Native America: The Story of Johnson v. M'Intosh," in *Indian Law Stories*, ed. Carole Goldberg, Kevin Washburn, and Philip Frickey (New York: Foundation Press, 2011), 29–60.

97. 21 US 543 (1823); see also Lindsay G. Robertson, *Conquest by Law: How the Discovery of America Dispossessed Indigenous Peoples of Their Lands* (Oxford: Oxford University Press, 2005).

98. Winnifred Fallers Sullivan, personal communication, 2016.

99. Borrows, "Origin Stories & the Law"; Robertson, "The Judicial Conquest of Native America," 54.

100. Borrows, "Origin Stories & the Law."

101. Ibid, 9.

102. Marc Shell, *Wampum and the Origins of American Money* (Urbana: University of Illinois Press, 2013).

103. Santner, *The Royal Remains*, xii.

104. Alan Wilson, *The Clergy Reserves of Upper Canada*, Canadian Historical Association Booklets 23 (Ottawa: Canadian Historical Association, 1969), 21.

105. Ibid, 21.

106. Marguerite Van Die, "Religion and Law in British North America, 1800–1867," in *The Cambridge History of Religions in America*, ed. Stephen J. Stein (Cambridge: Cambridge University Press, 2012), 2:717–45.

107. Ibid.

108. Ibid, 52.

109. Cardinal, *The Rebirth of Canada's Indians*.

110. John Borrows, "Unextinguished: Rights and the Indian Act," *University of New Brunswick Law Journal* 67 (2016): 3.

111. Indian Act, RSC, 1985, c 1–5, s. 2. Available at http://laws-lois .justice.gc.ca/eng/acts/I-5/page-1.html.

112. Monture, *We Share Our Matters*; Daniel Coleman, "Imposing subCitizenship: Canadian White Civility and the Two Row Wampum of the Six Nations," in *Narratives of Citizenship: Indigenous and Diasporic Peoples Unsettle the Nation-State*, ed. Aloys N. M. Fleischmann, Nancy Van Styvendale, and Cody McCarroll (Edmonton: University of Alberta Press, 2011), 177–211.

113. Sidney L. Harring, *White Man's Law: Native People in Nineteenth-Century Canadian Jurisprudence* (Toronto: University of Toronto Press, 1998), 101–2.

114. John S. Milloy, *A National Crime: The Canadian Government and the Residential School System, 1879 to 1986* (Winnipeg: University of Manitoba Press, 1999).

115. Audra Simpson, "Subjects of Sovereignty: Indigeneity, the Revenue Rule, and Juridics of Failed Consent," *Law and Contemporary Problems* 71, no. 3 (2008): 191; Audra Simpson, *Mohawk Interruptus: Political Life across the Borders of Settler States* (Durham, NC: Duke University Press, 2014).

116. I draw the term "shimmer" from my own mishearing of Jill Carter's discussion of the "chimera" of sovereignty; I am grateful to Professor Carter for our ongoing conversations. Jill Carter, personal communication with author, September 23, 2016; Legislative Assembly of the Province of British Columbia, "The Black Rod Fact Sheet," July 13, 2015, https://www.leg.bc.ca/learn-about-us /learning-resources.

117. Simpson, "Subjects of Sovereignty," 214.

118. David Leakey, "Black Rod: Today's Role in Parliament— with a Glance back to 1348," lecture presented at the Open Lecture, UK Parliament, London, England, October 8, 2014, https://www .parliament.uk/get-involved/education-programmes/universities -programme/university-teaching-resources/black-rod-todays-role -in-parliament—with-a-glance-back-to-1348/.

119. Legislative Assembly of the Province of British Columbia, "The Black Rod Fact Sheet."

120. Raymond B. Waddington, "Elizabeth I and the Order of the Garter," *Sixteenth Century Journal* 24, no. 1 (1993): 100.

121. Waddington, "Elizabeth I and the Order of the Garter."

122. H. V. Nelles, *A Little History of Canada* (Toronto: Oxford University Press, 2004). I am grateful to Heidi Bohaker for her suggestion to revisit the biblical reference.

123. John Skirving Ewart, *The Kingdom of Canada: Imperial Federation, the Colonial Conferences, the Alaska Boundary and Other Essays* (Toronto: Morang, 1908).

124. Legislative Assembly of the Province of British Columbia, "The Black Rod Fact Sheet."

125. Quoted in Norval Morris and David Rothman, *The Oxford History of the British Empire*, vol. 2, *The Eighteenth Century* (Oxford: Oxford University Press, 1998), 8.

126. Kamloops This Week, "Chief Gottfriedson Witnesses Reconciliation Ceremony with Prince William," *Kamloops This Week*, September 27, 2016, http://www.kamloopsthisweek.com /chief-gottfriedson-witnesses-reconciliation-ceremony-with -prince-william/. Across Canada, there have been several Indigenous lieutenant governors. To date, there have been no Indigenous governors-general, but the current minister of justice ("appointed at Her Majesty's Pleasure") is Jody Wilson-Raybould, a former regional chief of the British Columbia Assembly of First Nations, of Kwakwaka'wakw descent. "The Honorable Jody Wilson-Raybould MP," Government of Canada, https://www.canada.ca/en /government/ministers/jody-wilson-raybould.html.

127. CPAC, "CPAC Special: 2016 Royal Tour—B.C. Black Rod Ceremony," *CPAC*, 2016, http://www.cpac.ca/en/programs/cpac-special/.

128. Mike Laanela, "B.C.'s Grand Chief Stewart Phillip Won't Attend Royal Ceremony with Prince William," *CBC News*, September 26, 2016, http://www.cbc.ca/news/canada/british-columbia /royal-visit-black-rod-stewart-phillip-1.3778997.

129. I am grateful to Delaine Friedrich, JD, of the British Columbia Assembly of First Nations, for this information.

130. Mike Laanela, "Black Rod Ceremony Comes with Lesson in Colonialism, Cultural Genocide for Prince William," *CBC News*, September 27, 2016, http://www.cbc.ca/news/canada/british -columbia/royal-visit-black-rod-prince-william-1.3780573; CPAC, "CPAC Special: 2016 Royal Tour—B.C. Black Rod Ceremony."

131. Ian Walter Radforth, *Royal Spectacle: The 1860 Visit of the Prince of Wales to Canada and the United States* (Toronto: University of Toronto Press, 2004).

132. Victoria Murphy, "Kate Middleton Dazzles in Scarlet Dress for Reception on Canadian Royal Tour," *Mirror*, September 27, 2016, http://www.mirror.co.uk/news/uk-news/kate-middleton-dazzles -scarlet-cocktail-8920911.

133. Laanela, "B.C.'s Grand Chief Stewart Phillip Won't Attend Royal Ceremony with Prince William."

134. Shiri Pasternak, "Jurisdiction and Settler Colonialism: Where Do Laws Meet?" *Canadian Journal of Law and Society / La Revue Canadienne Droit et Société* 29, no. 2 (2014): 146.

135. Ibid., 149.

136. Coulthard, *Red Skin, White Masks*.

137. Victoria Freeman, "In Defence of Reconciliation Discourse and Negotiations across the Indigenous/Non-Indigenous Divide," *Canadian Journal of Law and Jurisprudence* 27 (2014): 217.

138. Miller, *Compact, Contract, Covenant*; Borrows, "Unextinguished."

139. For a broad discussion of the significance of Section 35, see Macklem and Sanderson, *From Recognition to Reconciliation*.

140. Webber, "We Are Still in the Age of Encounter," 63–64; John Borrows, "Legislation and Indigenous Self-Determination in Canada and the United States," in *From Recognition to Reconciliation: Essays on the Constitutional Entrenchment of Aboriginal and Treaty Rights*, ed. Patrick Macklem and Douglas Sanderson (Toronto: University of Toronto Press, 2016), 482.

141. John Borrows, *Recovering Canada: The Resurgence of Indigenous Law* (Toronto: University of Toronto Press, 2002).

142. Borrows, "Origin Stories & the Law."

143. Bob Beal, "An Indian Chief, an English Tourist, A Doctor, A Reverend, and a Member of Parliament: The Journeys of Pasqua's Pictographs and the Meaning of Treaty Four," *Canadian Journal of Native Studies* 27, no. 1 (2007): 113. See also Borrows, *Canada's Indigenous Constitution*.

144. Borrows, "Origin Stories & the Law."

145. Robert J. Miller, "American Indians, the Doctrine of Discovery, and Manifest Destiny," *Wyoming Law Review* 11, no. 2 (2011): 329–49.

146. Justin Brake, "'We . . . Do Not Recognize Your Authority at Muskrat Falls': Land Protectors," *TheIndependent.ca*, October 7, 2016, accessed November 1, 2016, http://theindependent.ca/2016

/10/07/we-do-not-recognize-your-authority-at-muskrat-falls-land
-protectors/.

147. Provincial Archives of Saskatchewan, "King George III
Medal," Provincial Archives of Saskatchewan, 2011, http://www
.saskarchives.com/node/218; Corbiere, "Treaty Medals."

148. Corbiere, "Treaty Medals."

149. Nancy Samson, cited in "Royal Commission on Aboriginal
Peoples—Final Report," vol. 2, "Restructuring the Relationship."

150. Maureen Matthews, "We Are All Treaty People," Manitoba
Museum, 2014, https://manitobamuseum.ca/main/we-are-all
-treaty-people/.

151. Maureen Matthews, personal communication with author,
2016.

152. Canadian Museum of Human Rights, "Canada's Magna
Carta." I am very grateful to Vicki Sharp for taking photographs of
this display for me, on which I base my analysis.

153. Borrows, "Wampum at Niagara."

154. Hamilton, Collections and Objections.

155. Henderson, Indigenous Diplomacy and the Rights of
Peoples, 97.

156. Smith, Relating Religion; Asad, Genealogies of Religion.

157. Janet R. Jakobsen and Ann Pellegrini, Secularisms (Durham,
NC: Duke University Press, 2008); Sullivan, The Impossibility of
Religious Freedom.

158. Van Wyck Brooks, cited in Leigh Eric Schmidt, Village Atheists: How America's Unbelievers Made Their Way in a Godly Nation
(Princeton, NJ: Princeton University Press, 2016), 1–2.

159. Ibid., 19; Berger, Law's Religion.

160. Jonathon S. Kahn and Vincent W. Lloyd, eds., Race and Secularism in America (New York: Columbia University Press, 2016).

161. Jeff Corntassel, Chaw-win-is, and T'lakwadzi, "Indigenous
Storytelling, Truth-Telling, and Community Approaches to Recon-
ciliation," English Studies in Canada 35, no. 1 (2009): 137–59; Lynne
Bell, "Buffalo Boy Testifies: Decolonising Visual Testimony in a
Colonial-Settler Society," in Decolonising Testimony: On the Possi-

bilities and Limits of Witnessing, ed. Rosanne Kennedy, Lynne Bell, and Julia Emberley, *Humanities Research*, vol. 15, no. 3 (Canberra: Australian National University Press, 2009), 81–96.

162. "Fisheries and Justice Ministers Head to B.C. Diesel Spill Site to Talk to Heiltsuk First Nation," *CBC News*, accessed November 1, 2016, http://www.cbc.ca/news/canada/british-columbia/bella -bella-diesel-oil-leaking-nathan-stewart-tugboat-accident-heiltsuk -1.3828347; "What's Happening in Muskrat Falls? Here's a Primer," *CBC News*, accessed November 1, 2016, http://www.cbc.ca/news /indigenous/muskrat-falls-what-you-need-to-know-1.3822898; Brake, "'We . . . Do Not Recognize Your Authority at Muskrat Falls'"; *Ktunaxa Nation v. British Columbia* (British Columbia Court of Appeal).

163. Coulthard, *Red Skin, White Masks*.

164. Tisa Joy Wenger, *We Have a Religion: The 1920s Pueblo Indian Dance Controversy and American Religious Freedom* (Chapel Hill: University of North Carolina Press, 2009); Michael D. McNally, "Native American Religious Freedom beyond the First Amendment," in *After Pluralism: Reimagining Religious Engagement*, ed. Courtney Bender and Pamela E. Klassen (New York: Columbia University Press, 2010), 226–51.

BANNING BIBLES

DEATH-QUALIFYING A JURY

Winnifred Fallers Sullivan

The American Civil Liberties Union has for years been able to fund its entire operations largely from the donations of individual members whose expressed highest priority is ridding the American landscape of Ten Commandments monuments. These libertarians are not alone. Banning Bibles and biblical material has come to stand in, in a number of public settings, for what is perceived by many to be the ongoing and necessary task of separating church and state in the United States. While histories of the public display of Bibles, public scriptural citation, and various public pictorial representations of figures from the Bible reveal a widely varied range of motives and contexts over the course of American history, the meaning of their continued presence in various domains of US public life has become increasingly consolidated and suspect, with those for and against ranged predictably along the spectrum of the culture wars. Many US Americans apparently have come to assign a singular valence to their presence. This essay will consider the ongoing effort to ban Bibles and biblical citation from the capital jury trial, particularly at the penalty phase, arguing that this effort mistakenly focuses the attention of courts, and of First Amendment jurisprudence more broadly, on the wrong object.

What could be understood to be religious about the administration of the death penalty in the United States is more complex and more troubling, revealing a disturbing absence at the very the heart of American democratic "churchstateness," as we are calling it in this volume. Banning Bibles, I argue, is of one with a larger effort to constitute the people, that is, to separate *the* people from the rest. It is of one with an effort across a number of domains to ensure that *the* people today are understood in law properly to be free of the wrong kind of religion, summoning their moral authority alone, without support, to act to purify the ekklesia.

Extending Ernst Kantorowicz's reflections on the political effectiveness of the metaphor of the king's two bodies into the democratic present, Eric Santner has given attention now in a couple of works to what he sees as the material remainder of those bodies when sovereignty is transferred to the people.[1] What results, he says, is a "surplus of immanence," a surplus requiring "a new liturgy meant to consolidate the consistency of the people as uncontested bearer of the principle of sovereignty."[2] In *The Royal Remains*, Santner traced out a new political theology that emerged with this displacement. European postrevolutionary modernity, visible in art, in literature, in psychoanalysis, and in the economy, among other places, reflected, he suggested, the anxious vacuum epitomized in the bleak black upper half of Jacques-Louis David's painting *The Death of Marat*.[3] In his subsequent work, *The Weight of All Flesh*, Santner describes late capitalism as a time when "life as a whole becomes business, busy-ness," the busyness necessary to secure the flesh of the people as sovereign and to fill the Davidian void.[4]

The premise of the present volume builds on the work of Santner and others to argue that the religious work needed to constitute the people as sovereign is performed in distinctive ways in the New World. Lacking the structuring power of a very specific European lineage from the divine right of kings to the welfare state, locating sovereignty, indeed locating the people, in the countries of North and South America, has been an anxious and always unfinished business, one haunted, among other things, by the bodies of those unwillingly conscripted and the persistent presence of other sacralities, both domestic and foreign. The church-state regimes of the New World display, one might say, signs of apparent arrested development in comparison with those of Europe.[5] We argue that without either a proper state or a proper church, the distribution of political theological tasks, indeed even the identification of tasks, became singularly difficult in the Americas.

In the United States, one of the places in which the predicament of "we the people" is arguably most laid bare is in the administration of the death penalty—and particularly in the work of the death penalty jury. There is an extensive and distinguished literature concerning the political history of "the people" in the United States as well as of the changing understandings of the jury in its role as avatar of the people.[6] This essay seeks not so much to add to that literature as to seek to understand how religious disestablishmentarianism—American style—inflects and reveals the political-theological limits of the concept in the current situation of the criminal jury in the penalty phase of the capital trial. A great deal also has been written about the death penalty in the United States. This essay relies on that interesting and important work while reflecting on the particular way in which US church-state exceptionalism is evident in what David Garland, echoing Kenneth Stampp's work on slavery, calls "the peculiar institution,"[7] particularly in the role of the jury. Taken together with the sheer brute facts of massive incarceration, the punitiveness and violence of the US penal system is distinctive.[8] It has also been shockingly racialized from the beginning.[9] Yet to say that the persistence of the death penalty in the United States is best understood only as a continuation of slavery is too simple.

What is religious, then, about this very American institution? How is the Constitution understood to structure the political theology of the death penalty? Trial by jury is guaranteed by Article 3 Section 2 of the US Constitution and by the Sixth Amendment.[10] The jury is understood to be a distinctively democratic institution protecting the people from the tyranny of government. The secrecy of their deliberations has been understood to ensure their independence.[11] Paradoxically perhaps, today's jury is understood at once to provide a democratic safety valve while also being seen historically to be a continuation of the medieval ordeal, an essentially inscrutable mechanism for determining guilt in the face of the inevitable indeterminacy of evidence.[12] It is an institution both transparent to the people and yet oddly unknowable, placing an enormous weight on each juror individually. Today, in US death penalty cases, each death-qualified juror is explicitly understood to be required to make an independent moral decision about each death-eligible defendant without the guidance of legal mandates with respect to types of offenses or motivations.[13]

Among other jury-room strictures, extraneous material may not be consulted. The jury may not do its own research on the internet, for example. Such extraneous material increasingly includes Bibles and biblical language. Reading the words that judges and law professors use to explain why Bibles and biblical language must be banned from the capital courtroom and jury room, one encounters an object with an unexpectedly lively agency and force. Bibles and biblical language are imagined by these guardians of the law to be irresistibly dogmatic and transparently instructive. How do they make such a determination? And will banning the Bible from the courtroom and the jury room make it secular? What would that mean exactly?

Consider the 2005 en banc decision in *People v. Harlan*.[14] The issue before the Colorado Supreme Court in *Harlan* was whether evidence that a jury had discussed passages from Leviticus and Romans during their deliberations in the penalty phase of a capital murder trial supported a finding that the sentence was "imposed under the influence of passion or prejudice or any other arbitrary factor," the standard set by the Colorado legislature for impeaching a jury decision.[15] The Colorado Supreme Court affirmed the trial court's order to vacate on a finding that discussion of scripture in the jury room constituted jury misconduct under the Colorado rules of evidence.[16]

The majority opinion in *Harlan*, citing the "Papal Edition" of the "Holy Bible," explained why discussion of the passages from Leviticus and Romans in the jury room threatened the constitutionality of the jury's work.[17] Oddly choosing to marshal the authority of Catholic biblical scholars included in a Catholic study edition of the Bible for ordinary churchgoers, although no evidence was offered that any of the jurors were Catholic, the court pronounced as to the force and significance of the cited passages for Colorado jurors:

> The Bible and other religious documents are considered codes of law by many in the contemporary communities from which Colorado jurors are drawn. The book of Leviticus is one of the first five books of the Old Testament, which are considered the books of law, and it contains "ritual laws prescribed for the priests" and is "almost entirely legislative in character." Holy Bible (Papal Edition), "Introduction to the Books of the Old Testament" at xiii. Romans is contained in the New Testament and may be characterized as "a powerful exposition of the doctrine of the supremacy of Christ and of faith in him as the source of salvation." Id., "Introduction to the Books of the New Testament" at xxxix.[18]

Usually precluded by law from inquiring into the mental processes of actual jurors, courts considering the possible prejudicial effect of extraneous material are reduced to speculating how a "typical juror"—a typical Colorado juror, in this case, whose religious attitudes are somehow known to the judges—would be influenced by this material. The *Harlan* court engaged in its own biblical exegesis in support of its view of the text:

> The Leviticus text is written in the first person voice of God and commands death as the punishment for murder. The Romans text instructs human beings to obey the civil government. Here,

the State of Colorado was seeking the death penalty. If the jury was unable to reach a unanimous verdict of death, the trial court would have been required to impose a life sentence without the possibility of parole.[19]

Then, in a highly speculative move, the court concluded, "Drawn from an array of typical jurors in Colorado, at least one juror in this case could have been influenced by these authoritative passages to vote for the death penalty when he or she may otherwise have voted for a life sentence."[20] How do the judges know this?[21] The *Harlan* court apparently does not even need to argue that the possibility that a juror might take the scriptural passages in precisely the way that the court does is sufficient evidence of "passion or prejudice." They write as if the facts speak for themselves. It is self-evident to the court that the biblical text is likely to have the force of law for at least one juror. It is further self-evident that any influence from the biblical text would ipso facto result in irrational decision making produced by "passion or prejudice."

Having banned the biblical text itself as dangerously authoritarian, the Colorado Supreme Court then went on to insist that religion did indeed have a place in the jury's work—just not that place:

> We do not hold that an individual juror may not rely on and discuss with the other jurors during deliberation his or her religious upbringing, education, and beliefs in making the extremely difficult "reasoned judgment" and "moral decision" he or she is called upon to make. . . . We expect jurors to bring their backgrounds and beliefs to bear on their deliberations but to give ultimate consideration only to the facts admitted and the law as instructed. The judicial system works very hard to emphasize the rarified, solemn and sequestered nature of jury deliberations; jurors must deliberate in that atmosphere without the aid or distraction of extraneous texts that could prejudicially influence the verdict.[22]

"Rarified, solemn and sequestered" deliberation, according to the Colorado Supreme Court, demands that the juror rely on and discuss with other jurors her "religious upbringing, education, and beliefs" while not referring in any specific way to the Bible itself, giving "ultimate consideration" only to the law and the facts. The death penalty jury is thus asked to thread a very fine needle in making what is for most of them a very difficult decision.[23] The members are each asked to make an individualized moral decision about whether the defendant deserves to live or die, relying on and even discussing their "religious upbringing, education or beliefs" but in an acultural manner, without any textual specificity. It is difficult to see how such a conversation could happen in an effective way and how banning the Bible enables more rational legal decision making.

Struggling to identify exactly what it is about introducing the actual written biblical text as opposed to the moral opinions of the possibly already Bible-saturated minds of the jurors, the *Harlan* Court opined:

> The written word persuasively conveys the authentic ring of reliable authority in a way the recollected spoken word does not. Some jurors may view biblical texts like the Leviticus passage at issue here as a factual representation of God's will. The text may also be viewed as a legal instruction, issuing from God, requiring a particular and mandatory punishment for murder. Such a "fact" is not one presented in evidence in this case and such a "legal instruction" is not the law of the state or part of the court's instructions.[24]

Strangely anxious themselves about the power and authority of the written word, the justices of the Colorado court strain to purify the jury room of such power. The jurors must be religious in a very precise way, one independent from God, in order to qualify themselves constitutionally to render the verdict.

The dissent in *Harlan* begged to differ about the task before the court and about the majority's evidentiary conclusions. Justice Rice wrote that, given the fact that at the hearing in the trial court on the motion to vacate jurors had testified that they were not influenced by the biblical passages, it was not necessary to use the typical juror test. The court could rely on the juror's own words. Furthermore, after a detailed and informed consideration of the relevant scriptural passages and their range of meanings, Rice wrote that

> the majority puts death penalty jurors in an impossible bind; jurors are instructed to make the ultimate decision about life or death based on their individual moral assessment—so long as their individual moral assessments are made from memory. This holding is demeaning to all jurors, but especially the jurors in this case, because it assumes that jurors cannot be trusted to think for themselves or follow the law in the face of written, but not spoken, religious passages.
>
> My experience with jurors leads me to emphatically reject the majority's way of thinking. Jurors chosen to serve in death penalty cases are selected for their ability, stated under oath, to uphold the law, apply the law to the facts, and to make reasoned judgments based upon their respective backgrounds and beliefs. To presume that jurors who have a religious background cannot distinguish between the written biblical passages referenced here and the written jury instructions—a presumption that must be made in order to find prejudice in this case is to underestimate their intelligence and to belittle their participation in our legal system.[25]

Law professors commenting on this case and others like it tend toward the view of the majority in *Harlan*. There is, to them, something transparently, irresistibly forceful about the written words of scripture—something forbidden.

Jurors in the penalty phase of a capital case, as in other cases, may not do research of their own on matters related to the case, and what is termed "extraneous material" is always excluded from the jury room. In death penalty cases, special rules have developed in many states to define extraneous material specifically to include Bibles, both physical Bibles and most spoken biblical citation by lawyers, judges, and jurors. Jurors are expected to keep scripture to themselves. Increasingly anxious about the presence of scriptural references in final arguments as well as in the jury room, state supreme courts across the country have limited, sometimes entirely excluded, the Bible from the capital courtroom and the jury room.[26] Decisions, as is repeatedly said, are to be made only on the facts presented during the trial and the law as delivered to jurors by the judge in his instructions. The law provides no specific guidance on when death is appropriate, only requiring the jurors to weigh aggravating and mitigating circumstances.[27] The juror is required by law to exercise independent moral reasoning with respect to a particular individual defendant, considered alone. Courts acknowledge, even explicitly expect, that such moral reasoning is appropriately exercised with reference to the juror's particular religious and moral formation—but she must do so without explicit oral reference to scripture in the jury room, written or spoken.

The jury room in the penalty phase of a capital case is thus a place of deliberate secular lawlessness, where those to be sacrificed are examined and chosen. Hedged about with post-*Furman* super-process[28] in the administration of the death penalty trial up until the jury retires to consider its verdict in the penalty phase, what happens in the jury room is secret and deliberately unstructured, by design. Justice Kennedy wrote recently, "The jury is a tangible implementation of the principle that the law comes from the people."[29] But we know little about how the people make that law. Indeed we seem not to want to know. What little we do know about what happens in these jury rooms we know from voluntary post-trial interviews by reporters and researchers and by social scientific reconstruction. We know from these accounts that in the penalty phase jurors discuss the evidence offered by the prosecutor and the defense about the defendant's past, present, and future, his motivation, his intent, and his capacity. But it is less clear how they come to the decision. Particularly in the penalty phase, when the jury decides life or death, it is not always clear what they are expected to ascertain. Is it the defendant's capacity for remorse? For redemption? For being one of the people? His ability to perform the social contract? As Scott Sundby shows in his remarkable book describing the decision-making of a jury in one case, *A Life and Death Decision*, one effect of the evacuation of guidelines from the death penalty jury room is to throw each juror back on her own theory of free will and determinism, with the result often being determined by the particular mix of jurors in a particular case.[30]

While political observers as early as Thomas Jefferson and Alexis de Tocqueville have seen the jury as a valuable and distinctively American democratic institution, and the role of the jury has been extensively debated since, this essay argues that today the members of the jury in the penalty phase of a capital case have acquired a new role; one might say that they have become quintessentially the people in the sense articulated by Eric Santner, tasked with embodying sovereignty in all its ambiguity. Sundby comments that "the effect of allowing great leeway in presenting mitigating and aggravating evidence to the capital jury is essentially to put the defendant's entire life on trial."[31] In religious terms, the jurors are adrift, in the religious no-man's land created by constitutional disestablishment—a small ekklesia—a churchstateness—required to improvise with a man's life at stake just when the structuring textual logic and ritual of an actual church and state might be most useful to the juror, to the defendant, and to the people.[32]

THE DEATH PENALTY IN THE UNITED STATES

Following the 1972 US Supreme Court decision in *Furman v. Georgia* holding that administration of the death penalty in the states was unconstitutionally arbitrary, an elaborate set of regulations and protocols developed to underwrite its continuation—a regulatory obsession some have termed a dubious, perhaps pseudo-, "super due process."[33] The law today in the United States, in the thirty-two jurisdictions in which the death penalty continues to be imposed (thirty-one states plus the federal government), severely limits the numbers of crimes for which death may be prescribed and requires that the decision for death be made by a jury, not by a judge;[34] the decision of the jury, discretionary and largely nonreviewable, must be founded in an individualized moral judgment about the defendant without legally mandated penalties or any generalizing guidelines beyond the need for consideration of aggravating and mitigating circumstances. Every effort is made to ensure that each "death-qualified" juror assumes the entire responsibility for her decision as to whether the particular "death-eligible" individual defendant should live or die. "[I]n the final analysis, capital punishment rests not on a legal but on an ethical judgment—an assessment of . . . the 'moral guilt' of the defendant,"[35] a standard of terrifying vagueness. What has emerged in the post-*Furman* period is a penalty less and less frequently imposed and less and less frequently carried out (fewer than 1 percent of murder convictions result in the death penalty) but one that many believe continues to do a great deal of vital political work.[36] As David Garland argues in *The Peculiar Institution*, "Capital punishment in America today operates primarily on the plane of the imaginary, and the great majority of its deaths are imagined ones. But the political and economic effects of these grim fantasies are no less real for being imagined."[37]

Garland argues that the factors explaining the persistence of the death penalty in the United States are rooted in the distinctiveness of American political and social institutions. The European story has often been told. Following the emergence of spectacular forms of executions that featured in the rise of the early modern state in Europe, such displays soon declined as modern states sought to resist popular appropriation of the meaning of public executions, as ideas about rational governance and the sanctity of life preoccupied would-be enlightened monarchs, and as states developed other forms of social control.[38] Prerevolutionary America, in contrast, as Garland details, was not characterized by strong state formation but by individualism and a preference for local control. It was also a place of a distinctively high level of interpersonal violence. Those inclinations were accommodated by the Constitution. Regional differences continued to be significant even after periodic expansions of federal power, with the racial logic of slavery leading after emancipation into the brutality of Jim Crow and lynching. At least three thousand black people were lynched between 1880 and 1930. Furthermore, unlike many other modern states, the United States was and continues to be resistant to international norms.[39] While the United States has not always been an outlier in the history of abolition—the state of Wisconsin in 1845 was the first government in the world to abolish the death penalty—since the 1960s the United States has diverged, entrenching its commitment even while the actual numbers of executions decrease. Importantly, even with the decline of its imposition and with numerous judicial efforts to control for racial discrimination and disparity in sentencing, a disproportionate number of those sentenced to death are black and the presence of a white victim continues to be the best predictor of a death sentence.[40]

As comparative legal scholar Elisabetta Grande explains in her review of his work, Garland sees the current iteration of the death penalty in the United States as distinctively modern and American—that is, it is humane, rational, and democratic; it is not a throwback to the use of violence as a display of centralized top-down control by the state as in early modern Europe. Grande emphasizes that "only the jury, as the authentic voice of the community and safeguard against the governmental power represented by the judge, can impose any sentence of death."[41] Extending Garland's argument, Grande argues that the death penalty in its American guise serves not the state, as in early modern Europe, but the dispersed interests of various local actors, including victims' families, prison officials, prosecutors, defense attorneys and judges. Moreover, she says,

> In a world in which mortality, and the limits of human control associated with it, is a cause of deep discomfort, the death penalty ironically provides a kind of collective reassurance: for society to be able to control the passing away of a sentenced person actually reinforces a sense of collective empowerment. At the same time, as Garland points out, the fact that it is the death of someone else sends the public a subliminal message of its own immortality.[42]

It is the jury that is asked to perform the task of selection on behalf of the people.

Grande, like Garland, does not think that American exceptionalism in this area, contrasted, as it often is, with Europe, is baked in or inevitable. Both note that US distinction in this area is recent and contingent in ways that could change.[43] And while neither names religion as central to the current exceptionalism of US death penalty policy, each points to distinctive aspects of the American project that I will argue once again reveal the ways in which the formation of a federal government of limited powers and the disestablishment of religion created new religious possibilities.

CHURCH AND STATE IN THE UNITED STATES

Because both the continued presence of the death penalty and the anomalous religiosity of Americans are often remarked upon as evidence of US exceptionalism, the assumption is sometimes made that there must be a connection. Former US Supreme Court Justice Antonin Scalia, for example, boldly stated that it is because Americans are still churchgoing Christians that they favor the death penalty, bolstering the notion that religiously conservative people are natural believers in capital punishment: "It seems to me that the more Christian a country is the *less* likely it is to regard the death penalty as immoral. Abolition has taken its firmest hold in post-Christian Europe, and has least support in the church-going United States."[44] He went on to pronounce that "the Christian attitude is reflected in the words Robert Bolt's play has Thomas More saying to the headsman: 'Friend, be not afraid of your office. You send me to God.'"[45] Christians are not afraid to die, Scalia says, because of their belief in an afterlife.[46] "The current predominance of opposition to the death penalty is," he said, "the legacy of Napoleon, Hegel, and Freud rather than St. Paul and St. Augustine."[47]

Scalia further attributed any waning of support for the death penalty in the United States to the fact that Americans sadly no longer understand their leaders to rule by divine right. Quoting Paul's epistle to the Romans, "Let every soul be subject unto the higher powers. For there is no power but of God: the powers that be are ordained of God . . . if thou do that which is evil, be afraid; for he beareth not the sword in vain: for he is the minister of God, a revenger to execute wrath upon him that doeth evil" (Romans 13:1–5), Scalia explained that Christians believe government to be exercising divine power: "The *core* of [Paul's] message is that government—however you want to limit that concept—derives its moral authority from God. It is the 'minister of God' with powers to 'revenge,' to 'execute wrath,' including even wrath by the sword (which is unmistakably a reference to the death penalty)."[48] Scalia went on to explain that another reason why the death penalty is so popular in the United States, again in contrast to the countries of Europe, is because Americans believe in free will and sin: "The Christian is also *more* likely to regard punishment in general as deserved."[49] The implication would seem to be that any errors in the imposition of the death penalty, even racially disparate arbitrariness in its administration, are really, in the end, not of much importance in the larger scheme of things.[50]

Scalia speaks here and elsewhere of Christians—of *the* Christian—without any qualification, arrogating to himself authority to speak normatively for a singular orthodox Christian position. The verses from Romans quoted by Scalia are also favored by some prosecutors; they are sometimes quoted in closing arguments, apparently with the intention of suggesting biblical support for the authority of the state. Both Scalia and these prosecutors offer a reading of scripture as a place of moral certainty, faith in authority, and commitment to retribution, a moral certainty, respect for authority, and retribution that Scalia at least believes distinguishes the United States as a Christian nation and that he believes continues to underwrite popular support for the death penalty.[51]

There is something superficially attractive about Scalia's assertion that there is a tight link between American religiosity and enthusiasm for the death penalty. It fits with a broader narrative linking US religiosity to conservative political positions on other issues such as reproductive rights. But it is not at all clear that Scalia speaks for most Americans, or even most American Christians, when he speaks of the death penalty. Indeed, sociological evidence suggests otherwise. Support for the death penalty is not tightly linked to and explained simply by the fact of personal religious commitment.[52]

Scalia's invocation of Thomas More and his misreading of *A Man for All Seasons* provide a clue to the rigidity of his natural law position and helps to loosen up the compressed political-theological narrative that arguably links Paul and More to "Evangelicals & Catholics Together,"[53] the 1994 manifesto of a self-appointed group of evangelicals and Catholics seeking to promote conservative Christian intellectualism and their version of normative Christianity. The words given Thomas More by Robert Bolt and quoted by Scalia, "Friend, be not afraid of your office. You send me to God," might more properly be understood in the context of the play to be the ironic reflection of a very particular modern political theology and understanding of natural law, not necessarily that of the historical Thomas More.

Indeed, Patrick Whiteley, writing about Bolt's play, sees it as portraying not a More of moral certainty, but a More deeply conflicted: "More, reshaped in Bolt's drama, is a reluctant martyr who realizes a modern heroic ideal: making the ultimate sacrifice for ultimately uncertain reasons."[54] Whiteley sees Bolt's play, and in particular the struggle among Henry, More, and Roper, as enacting a far more sophisticated understanding of the epistemological challenges of natural law theory than is reflected in Scalia's article. Understanding this legacy in the contemporary United States also arguably requires attention to the nuances of Bolt's More rather than the certainties of Scalia's. It requires attention to the startlingly diverse biblical interpretative strategies and theological resources available in the United States to think the relationship of natural and positive law.[55] Scalia's use of the quote might also be understood to reflect what might be called a very particular modern understanding of the self and a theology of law that specifically incorporates the role of the civil magistrate into its understanding of God's plan and which understands God's role in juridical terms,[56] one that, again, does not speak for all Americans—or for all Christians.

Do Americans continue to favor death because they are Christians? How would we know? Such generalizations are notoriously unreliable, even unknowable, dependent on a definition of who is a Christian, about which there is little agreement and which, in the United States, law cannot constitutionally address. Recent scholarly accounts of the reasons for the persistence of the death penalty in the United States have offered a varied set of explanations, mostly located in the nature of an American politics characterized by localism, federalism, and law-and-order populism. These accounts also point to a frontier culture of individualism and violence.[57] Scalia sees democracy and the inevitable secularism that it brings as fatal to support for the death penalty. Social scientists would say that the particularities of US democracy account for the death penalty's persistence, not for its decline.

Like Scalia, legal historian James Whitman argues that the role of religion is quite different in the United States from that in Europe (although, unlike Scalia, he is quite critical of the American version). Whitman too believes that a difference in the church/state model makes all the difference in the way justice is administered in the United States:

> There are two different western models of the separation of church and state. The American model . . . demands that the state take a studiously hands-off approach to churches, while at the same time permitting nearly unlimited expression of religious views in all contexts, including the courtroom. . . . The continental European model, by contrast, aims at a separation of religion from politics. . . . At the same time, the continental model countenances what seem to Americans gross government interferences in the institutions of daily religious life and in freedom of religious expression.[58]

As Whitman further explains, "Northern continental countries . . . all show variants on the same long-term tendency of the state to constitute itself as a kind of updated, secularized church."[59] Correspondingly, "A church that has surrendered most of its mission to the state is a church that retains little independent political influence. To put it a little differently, when church functions become government functions, they become denatured."[60] Whitman regards the increasing bureaucratization of the churches in northern Europe as happily having robbed them of their charismatic power, freeing them to serve as neutered partners to a secular paternalistic state. One might say that it is also a state which, in turn, is enabled to imagine itself and its politics as secular, even while, in a Schmittian and Girardian sense, it benefits from the violence of its sacred founding and its continued claim to a monopoly of violence.

Meanwhile, in the United States, because of what Whitman calls institutional separation, religion has not lost its charisma and still retains its visible power to matter in politics—in presidential speeches, in the legislature, and in the courtroom. Particularly in the courtroom. Whitman deplores especially the use of scripture in closing arguments in death penalty cases, by prosecuting and defense attorneys alike, as constituting problematic appeals to nonrational understandings of human motivation and of law's purposes. For Whitman a Bible in a courtroom is symptomatic of the American failure to domesticate religion. It is matter out of place.[61] Whitman agrees with Scalia that the religiosity of Americans contributes to their continued support of the death penalty but finds that fact to be the problematic result of the particular church-state formation in the United States and its failure to denature its religion, not in the content of religious beliefs. They both see American religion as dogmatic and atavistic.

What if the religiousness of the death penalty in the United States is not to be explained by the lingering persistence of charismatic punitive religion, as Scalia and Whitman suggest, or by the nature of US democracy, as Garland suggests, but in the particular nature of churchstateness in the United States— that is, in the peculiar ways in which "the people" as bearers of sovereignty, as receivers of the remains of the king's two bodies in Santner's sense, are constituted after disestablishment? What if its religiousness reveals not God's wrath but the particular pathos and poignancy that is the lot of free religious people?

The role that religion in this broader sense does in fact play in the criminal justice process in the United States is hugely under-studied and mostly not discussed by death penalty scholars. Contra Scalia, Christian commitment does not correlate with a penchant for supporting the continued existence of the death penalty but contra Whitman, as we will see, it is not the presence or not of Bibles that signals the presence of religion.

The particular and varied religiosity of the administration of the death penalty in the United States can be seen, rather, on the one hand, in a more attenuated and complex cultural Protestantism, one characterized by a religious anthropology and vocabulary of free will and determinism that structures the jury's decision making, as well as in the never-ending political theological project of constituting the people as ekklesia. For some jurors, religious formation may lead to a belief in the possibility of redemption and therefore a tendency to argue against death rather than for it.[62] Indeed, it may be faith in the possibilities of this world that underwrites the place of religion in the death penalty jury room, not faith in the next. But the capital jury room as it exists today in the United States is a place singularly ill-suited to the resolution of these genuinely thorny ethical quandaries.

THE BIBLE AND THE DEATH PENALTY

In a capital case, two hearings are conducted, followed by two separate jury deliberations, with new evidence being offered and new arguments being put before the jury in the second penalty phase. It is in the penalty hearing, after guilt has been proven beyond a reasonable doubt and the exacerbating factors of the offense necessary to make the defendant eligible for the death penalty established, that, usually for the first time, the jury is allowed to hear about any other convictions the defendant might have as well as to hear from witnesses to his character. The tight evidentiary focus on the particular events of the guilt phase is released. Guilt has been established. The death-qualified juror is now asked to make a judgment as to whether the death-eligible defendant will live or die.[63] Now the defense attorney asks the jury to sentence the defendant to life in prison, while the prosecutor argues that the defendant should be executed.

What role does scripture play at this stage? Let us return

to the Bible-spouting lawyers so worrying to Whitman. In the *Bradford* case,[64] cited by Whitman as exemplifying the irrational presence of religion in American law, the defense attorney, in his closing argument, asked the jury to sentence Bradford to life in prison, sparing Bradford's life as God had spared Cain's:

> Mr. Bradford will die in prison. That is no longer an issue. . . . The only remaining question is who will decide when he dies, you or the Almighty. . . . When I contemplated the awesome responsibility that you will soon face, I thought about the punishment that God gave to Cain for the murder of his brother Abel. In chapter 4 of Genesis, the Lord said to Cain, "[Y]our brother's blood cries out to me. You shall be banished from the land on which you spilled your brother's blood. You shall become a restless wanderer in the wilderness." . . . Today there is hardly a place we call a wilderness. Instead we have to build our wildernesses. We call them maximum security prisons. The mark we put on people who have committed such crimes is a sentence of life in prison without the possibility of parole. Our banishment.[65]

In other words, the jury was invited by the defense to imagine a sentence to a maximum security prison as analogous to the mark of Cain and life in prison as akin to biblical exile. We know that jurors often worry that if they decide for life, defendants might eventually be paroled and kill again, so defense attorneys are anxious to assure jurors that defendants who receive a life sentence will in fact be in prison for the rest of their natural lives. The defense attorney in *Bradford* apparently wanted life in a maximum security prison to look like a permanent and divinely sanctioned punishment, not a capitulation; he wanted the jury to let go of the specter of a possible release and reoffense.[66]

The prosecutor in the *Bradford* case responded with her own vernacular biblical riff. Beginning with the notion that some jurors might have religious qualms about voting for death, she said, "I am not a biblical scholar. I want you to know that. But I did make a few notes on some things I read just in case any of you feel you're going against any religious tenets."[67] She had read about what she referred to as how "the Bible feels about the death penalty." She focused on what she understood to be a mistranslation of the Hebrew word "kill" as in "Thou shalt not kill," rather than "murder" as in "Thou shalt not murder":

> It seems that through the ages and the 10 Commandments when they talked about thou shalt not kill that is a misnomer and not true. It's the King James mistranslation of what should have been thou shalt not do murder.... Killing is one thing, and when I talked to you with the jury instructions and told you what murder was, it's the unlawful killing with malice. That's murder. To go on a little bit further. The original Hebrew word defined the word murder as well, not kill.[68]

She then went on to muse on the many crimes for which death was apparently prescribed in what she called "biblical times":

> Then in the book of Deuteronomy, chapter 22, it teaches that the death penalty was required for rape and adultery back in those biblical times. In chapter 21 of Deuteronomy as well, hanging was the method for carrying out that sentence. So they had the death penalty way back then. Also the death penalty isn't just an Old Testament or a New Testament. Both the Old Testament and New Testament are not against the death penalty. They do support it. In Acts chapter 5, it talks about [Ananias] and his wife [Sapphira] were punished with death for lying. In Exodus chapter 21, when a man kills another after maliciously seeming to do so, you must take him even from my own alt[a]r and put him to death. So I don't want this appeal to religion to dissuade any of you, because the Bible does not say thou shalt not kill. It says thou shalt not murder. And you have already decided we have had a murder here.[69]

Worried that the Bible might be seen to recommend mercy after the defense attorney's exegesis of the Cain and Abel story, the prosecutor, in her turn, wanted any hesitant jurors, particularly those who might have been persuaded by the defense attorney's possible appeal to divine mercy, to give themselves permission to condemn the defendant to death. She did this by asking them to consider how the Bible "feels" about the death penalty and what really went on in what she called "those biblical times."

In addition to introducing the jurors to issues in biblical translation the prosecutor had also responded to the defense attorney by inviting the jury to transfer responsibility for their decision to the defendant himself:

> [T]he defense attorney . . . said something to the effect that you should decide if you're going to kill Mark Bradford or if God is going to kill Mark Bradford in his time. I want to tell you that's kind of a psychological ploy, a psychological defense sometimes defense attorneys use in trying to make you feel or give you the impression that you are killing the defendant if you vote for the death penalty. But you're not killing him. He killed himself on April the 18th of 1988 when he chose to rape and sodomize and slit Lynea Kokes['s] throat and stab her and everything else that he did to her. He killed himself. You are not killing him if you come back with a penalty of death. You are following the law. Because the law is the thing that lets you decide whether life or death is appropriate so do not fall for that psychological ploy that you're killing him, because you are not.[70]

The prosecutor is skating close to the line here in offering the jury an escape from its obligation under law. Both prosecuting and defending attorneys are limited in closing argument as to what they can say beyond reminding the jurors of what they have heard from witnesses. Always a tension in these cases is created by the difficulty of ensuring that the jury is not abdicating responsibility for making an individuated decision by coming to believe that an agency other than themselves is actually making the decision. Scholars of the jury report on the strong psychological pull jurors have toward any theory that might make the decision for them.[71] There is a surreal effort then, in the jury instructions and in the closing arguments, to walk the imagined line between offering law as the authorizing agent of a rational law-governed moral decision and offering law as a mandate. In *Bradford* the prosecutor seems to want the jurors to let themselves off the hook either by attributing responsibility to the defendant himself or by seeing the law as pointing definitively toward death.

Both courts and writers of law review articles understand biblical citations to threaten invasion by an alien authority into the jury room. The US Supreme Court has insisted that the decision for death be entirely the decision of each juror independently. Eschewing any version of communal wisdom and responsibility, it is the individuation of the decision that makes it constitutional.[72] Justice Stewart, writing for the majority in a Supreme Court opinion finding on the then North Carolina statute mandating death for certain crimes, said:

> we believe that in capital cases the fundamental respect for humanity underlying the Eighth Amendment, requires consideration of the character and record of the individual offender and the circumstances of the particular offense as a constitutionally indispensable part of the process of inflicting the penalty of death.

This conclusion rests squarely on the predicate that the penalty of death is qualitatively different from a sentence of imprisonment, however long. Death, in its finality, differs more from life imprisonment than a 100-year prison term differs from one of only a year or two. Because of that qualitative difference, there is a corresponding difference in the need for reliability in the determination that death is the appropriate punishment in a specific case.[73]

Cruelly almost, the law pulls the juror back toward the lonely empty place that is her lot, the empty space of David's Marat painting.

Bradford was condemned to death. On appeal, the court, refusing to overturn the decision on the ground of extraneous material having invaded the jury room, found that the prosecutor had done nothing improper in referring to the Bible; she was, they said, just reminding the jurors that they were required to follow the law.[74]

The biblical back and forth between prosecutor and defense attorney in the *Bradford* case features a grab bag of biblical references by both lawyers. There is strikingly little that is dogmatic or certain about these appeals to scriptural authority. The defense attorney speaks in the first person. He does not invoke divine authority—for justice or for mercy. The prosecutor just wants to give the jurors "some other ideas." There is no thundering appeal to the law's divinely authorized power to wield the sword. The appeal in each case is to the individual juror, to the private citizen tasked with an awesome power. Each lawyer is clumsily offering a lifeline—something to think about, as they say. We don't know what the jury in this case did with the biblical musings by the two lawyers, although the defense did argue on appeal that, among a raft of other claims of errors by the trial judge, the prosecutor's invocation of Deuteronomy was necessarily prejudicial, as a matter of law.

A raft of law review articles have been written agreeing with Whitman that the Bible should be excluded from the courtroom and the jury room.[75] Pennsylvania and Tennessee have judicially ruled in favor of complete exclusion. Other jurisdictions judge these appeals on a case-by-case basis, deciding whether there was likely an improper influence on the jury. Law professors and judges seem to imagine such references to the Bible as having an uncanny capacity to distract the jurors from their purpose. What is the precise force that opponents imagine these passages to have? And how exactly is it supposed to operate? Do they imagine religious material, perhaps especially the Bible, as effecting a kind of possession? Is it that "the church" is exerting a form of premodern authority? Or God himself?

Interestingly, those opposed to the invocation of scripture seem to be undecided as to whether the constitutional problem is that reference to these passages constitute unconstitutional appeals to foreign law or the problem is that they are an establishment of religion and therefore prohibited by the First Amendment. Religion as law or law as religion. Some say that the biblical quotes make the juror's job harder. Some say that they make it easier—all too easy. But the worry that the problem with biblical references is that they are too much like law dominates the critiques. The fear seems to be that jurors will be applying biblical law rather than American law.[76] Yet, as we've seen, the transcripts suggest the risk is actually quite low. In Whitman's exemplary case, for example, each side had a shot at the story of Cain and Abel. The lawyers were suggestive, not dogmatic, guessing at ways to insert themselves into the jurors decision-making process. In the end, the jury was presented with a Bible with an ambiguous—perhaps opaque—view of judicial killing. And the expectation of each lawyer seems to have been that each juror would be familiar with the story and was merely being invited to arrive at his own interpretation as well as any implication such an interpretation might have for the fate of Mr. Bradford.

The ambiguity and ambivalence of the *Bradford* example resonates strongly with the history of the American Bible, as discussed in the next section. Scholars of the Bible in American history emphasize the radical indeterminism of scripture in American cultural contexts. Biblical authority was famously appealed to by both sides in the fight over slavery, as Abraham Lincoln noted in his second inaugural address: "Both read the same Bible and pray to the same God, and each invokes His aid against the other." Likewise on other matters of public import, including marriage, abortion, economics, war and peace.

Pennsylvania is the only state that categorically bans all references to the Bible by the prosecutor.[77] In the leading Pennsylvania case, *Commonwealth v. Chambers*,[78] the prosecutor had said in his closing argument, "As the Bible says, 'and the murderer shall be put to death.'" On appeal to the Supreme Court of Pennsylvania, the court after considering the matter concluded about the jury's vote for death that "we are not convinced that the penalty was not the product of passion, prejudice or an arbitrary factor":

> More than allegorical reference, this argument by the prosecutor advocates to the jury that an independent source of law exists for the conclusion that the death penalty is the appropriate punishment for Appellant. By arguing that the Bible dogmatically commands that "the murderer shall be put to death," the prosecutor interjected religious law as an additional factor for the jury's consideration which neither flows from the evidence or any legitimate inference to be drawn therefrom. We believe that such an argument is a deliberate attempt to destroy the objectivity and impartiality of the jury which cannot be cured and which we will not countenance. Our courts are not ecclesiastical courts and, therefore, there is no reason to refer to religious rules or commandments to support the imposition of a death penalty.[79]

Affirming its decision in a later opinion, the Pennsylvania Supreme Court put it more forcefully: "any reference to the Bible during the penalty phase is improper and requires reversal."[80]

Juror reference to the Bible has also been condemned whether or not prompted by the lawyers. In *Oliver v. Quarterman*,[81] a Texas case, the Court of Appeals for the Fifth Circuit found no error in the district court's denial of a writ of habeas corpus on the ground that the jury's consultation of the Bible had been improper. At a state court evidentiary hearing on his motion for a new trial, Oliver called four jurors to testify. Juror Kenneth McHaney spoke of four Bibles in the jury room:

> McHaney stated that during the jury's deliberations, one juror, Kenneth Grace, read the Bible aloud to a small group of jurors in the corner of the jury room. McHaney also testified that fellow juror Donna Matheny mentioned to him that the Bible contained a passage discussing who is a murderer and who should be put to death, and that he asked Matheny if he could read her Bible, which Matheny had highlighted. McHaney recalled reading verses pertaining to the importance of obeying the law of the land, the commandment that "thou shalt not kill," and the passage Matheny pointed out that discussed who is a murderer and who deserves a death sentence. In particular, he recalled reading a passage that says that if a man strikes someone with an iron object so that he dies, then he is a murderer and should be put to death. McHaney also witnessed juror Rhonda Robinson reading the same passage from the Bible. McHaney believed that there were approximately four Bibles in the jury room, but he could not recall the exact number. He said that many jurors had Bibles with them because they went to church or Bible study at night.

Another juror, Maxine Symmank recalled reading the Bible to herself:

> Juror Maxine Symmank stated that she read the Bible to herself while in the jury room and that there was another male juror who read the Bible aloud to a small group of jurors at one end of the table. Symmank could not recall exactly when she read the Bible, although she believed it was after the jury made its punishment determination while the jurors waited for the court to reconvene. She admitted, however, that it is possible that she also read the Bible during earlier parts of the proceedings. Symmank recalled reading the same passage that McHaney had consulted from the Book of Numbers: "And if he smite him with an instrument of

iron, so that he die, he is a murderer: the murderer shall surely be put to death." Symmank had decided to read this passage after a fellow juror opened the Bible to that page. Symmank confirmed, however, that no juror explicitly stated that the jury should use the Bible as evidence in its deliberations.

The aimless quality of this testimony continued:

Rodney Rodrigues corroborated the testimony of the previous two jurors that at least one juror read Biblical passages aloud to a small group of jurors at some point during the deliberations. He testified that he did not read the Bible, but that some of his fellow jurors did. He did not know which passages the other jurors read. Finally, Glenda Webb recalled seeing more than one Bible in the jury room, but she stated that the Bible was not a focus of the jury's discussions. She recalled that some jurors consulted the Bible after they had made their decision on the appropriate punishment.[82]

What to make of this? In the end the Fifth Circuit Court found no reason to overturn the trial court's conclusion that there was no improper "external influence" on the jury, the relevant federal standard.[83]

Why are Bibles and biblical citation in the courtroom so scary? What are they imagined to do? There is little evidence that the words have the coercive power imagined by appellate courts and law professors. Transcripts of courtroom arguments reveal lawyers on both sides quoting and misquoting scripture to a not always obvious purpose. The way Bibles are used in US courtrooms might better be understood not as resulting from a failure of separation but as a symptom of disestablishment, of deep skepticism about the authority of both church and state—as well as that of political, legal, and ecclesiastical professionals. Bible talk is not, I would suggest, a symbol of continuing church authority, as Scalia would have it, but a site of vernacular philosophizing and the endless creation of new ekklesia, church-statenesses specifically enabled by US law in the context of the American jury trial.

BIBLES IN THE UNITED STATES

The Bible, some would say biblicism or even bibliolatry, has a distinctive cultural place in the United States.[84] As American religious historian Mark Noll says in the introduction to the first of his projected two-volume history of the Bible in American public life, "It is no exaggeration to claim that the Bible has been—and by far—the single most widely read text, distributed object, and referenced book in all of American history."[85] While historians see some decline in the extent of the Bible's dominance in published sources in American public life over the course of the nineteenth century, an estimated twenty-five million Bibles are still produced in the United States each year.[86]

American biblicism was produced by a particular confluence of religious and political factors: the dominance of various forms of low-church Protestantism from colonial times, the effects of disestablishment on church formation, competition among Protestant denominations, suspicion of secular literature, and anti-Catholicism. Beginning with Martin Luther, Protestants were taught that Christians did not need clerical intermediaries to interpret biblical text. As vernacular translations became available, Protestant Christians were urged to read and interpret the text for themselves—and to rely on the Bible as their sole guide to Christian living—*sola scriptura*. As historian Jonathan Sheehan describes it, "Translating afresh would release the Bible from the grip of the Catholic Church and, at the same time, allow reformers and their 'universal priesthood of all believers' to take possession of the Bible and make it once more the divine foundation of their own religious institutions."[87] Rejection of established church authority was accompanied by a heightened reliance on the text in all aspects of life, resulting in the United

States in what Noll calls an "informal Christendom"—what others have called de facto establishment.[88] Noll further comments that "Europeans have never fathomed this distinction between institutional and informal Christendom."[89]

As Noll and other historians have insisted, pervasive biblicism by no means implies that Americans have agreed on what the biblical text means—or even what the text is. Protestants have largely agreed that Catholics corrupted true Christianity and have seen fidelity to the biblical text as a way to return to a pure primitive Christian way of life. But the actual practices of biblicism—notwithstanding the ubiquity of references to "the" Bible as a unified object—tends to reflect the complexity of the text, a diffuse interpretive authority, and the proliferation of translations and versions and popularizations.[90] As Noll emphasizes, "By 1880, nearly two thousand different editions of the Bible were available to Americans."[91] Paul Gutjahr, another historian of the American Bible, argues that the movement away from the center of American consciousness of a singular Bible was the result, in part, of the enormously competitive Bible publishing industry: "In attempting to woo buyers and readers to their bible editions, American publishers helped erode the timeless, changeless aura surrounding 'the Book' by making it 'the books' . . . [I]n mass-producing the Bible and producing it in so many different formats and translations, its producers often made the Scriptures seem more ordinary than extraordinary."[92]

Other historians of American religion point to the effect of higher criticism, of scientism, and of the growing importance of religious experience to American Protestantism in the decentering of a singular biblical text.[93] Historian Peter Thuesen has shown how translation battles between liberals and conservatives over the New Revised Version ironically brought them together in a literalist dismissal of other ways of reading the text bolstered by appeals to institutionalized authorities.[94] Together, then, there is a real sense that, given this history, banning Bibles in the United States should be perceived as a quixotic effort in the biblically promiscuous yet still Bible-saturated United States described by historians. Many Americans read Bibles without belonging to a religious community of any kind or ever attending worship services, arrogating to themselves the role of interpreter of a text understood in some ways to be self-interpreting.

In this context, then, what is it exactly that Bibles and biblical quotations are imagined to do in the courtroom and how is that effected? One might argue that the principal reason for the continued presence of the Bible in US courtrooms and jury rooms is not the dogmatic threat of religious authority but the very dispersal into the culture that this history reflects. The Bible in America is perhaps less significant for its singular authority than for its historic function as a site for serious play, for what Cooper Harriss calls the eirobiblical.[95] Harriss "explores how the enslaved wielded the inherent imprecision of their biblical language to articulate coherent, if ironic, biblical worldviews."[96] He suggests that oral biblical citation is a specific cultural form, one particularly refined in the African American oral tradition— one that "served as an ironic weapon wielded against the overwrought determinism of a paternalistic social order."[97] Oral citation, on Harriss's reading, was used to fight against those who defended slavery on biblical grounds.

Harriss shows how the very instability of oral form underlines the radical openness of the text itself:

> Eirobiblical rhetoric in this way may be understood to speak God's own correction, to offer a divine judgment against the presumptive fixity of the theological conceptions; the canons of thought, belief, and society that attend and extend from them; and the human language that expresses them. In this way it rewrites the Bible according to an oral tradition that interrogates the notion of canon and its institutions.[98]

Harriss uses the word to describe the particular way that African American oral citation took ownership of the text—but it might be extended to the criminal justice context. In their clumsy ways, the lawyers too participate in the eirobiblical.

Bible talk is ubiquitous in the United States. Often invoked on social issues, it is the text of abolitionists and civil rights activists. But it has also been the text of slaveholders and would-be controllers of women; it is the text of warmongers and peacemakers. One can see this instability of reference in the reported cases challenging the presence of Bibles in the death penalty courtroom. Scripture is invoked by all sides in a deeply unstable semantic field.

THE JURY AS EKKLESIA

What does a jury's deliberation look like apart from Bible talk? Does banning the Bible make its work secular? The hearing in the penalty phase of a capital case, during which aggravating and mitigating evidence not admissible in the guilt phase is presented to the jury, opens a radically new moment in the trial. For the first time, the jury hears about the defendant's whole life and is invited, in effect, to judge that life, as *Woodson* anticipated.[99] As Sundby describes it, "Not wholly unlike the popular image of the Pearly Gates where St. Peter reviews one's life from birth to death, weighing good deeds against malevolent acts, the capital jury is likely to hear about the defendant's life from infancy (or even prenatally if a condition such as fetal alcohol syndrome is involved) on through the defendant's incarceration awaiting trial."[100] This second hearing has distinctive evidentiary rules, among them a particular policing of the words that can be used by the prosecutor and the defense attorney. In recent years, the permissibility of the use of biblical narratives and allusions by those lawyers in death penalty cases, once fairly common among American trial lawyers in general, has become a matter of debate among courts.[101] There is also debate about whether jurors themselves can introduce Bibles and biblical material into their deliberations. As Sundby insists, "The rules cannot change, however, the fundamental fact that, in the end, we ask jurors in death penalty cases to draw on their own senses of morality, outrage, and mercy in deciding whether the defendant deserves to live or die."[102]

If we set the presence of the Bible aside then, is there anything religious about the work done by the capital jury in the penalty phase? In other words, does banning Bibles effectively secularize the jury's work?[103] Let us consider the work of one jury that has been described by Sundby in his book *A Life and Death Decision*. Sundby details anonymously the jury's process in one death penalty case, one he names *People v. Lane*, one in which jurors were extensively interviewed about the experience.[104] No biblical language was used by the lawyers or the jurors in the *Lane* case. All of the jurors took their work seriously. No one thought it was easy.

In the guilt phase of the trial, the defendant, Steven Lane, had been convicted of shooting and killing a convenience store clerk during a robbery; the principle piece of evidence was an in-store video that recorded the event, although there was also testimony from witnesses present in the store at the time. The jury heard in the penalty phase previously excluded evidence that showed that Lane had numerous previous convictions and had been in and out of jail. They also learned of his neglectful childhood and his younger brother's death in junior high school from alcohol poisoning after a night of drinking by the two brothers. A psychiatrist testified about the trauma experienced by the defendant as a result of his brother's death. The jury also learned of his good behavior in prison.

The first time the *Lane* jury took a vote, nine voted for death and three for life. The second day it was down to two for life and on the third down to one. The eleven now focused on convincing the holdout, Peggy, the one Sundby terms "the hope juror." In describing the personalities of the members of the jury, Sundby divides the jury into types: the idealist, the chorus, the hope juror, and the fundamentalist. The foreman of the *Lane* jury, "the idealist," had begun their deliberations in the guilt phase by suggesting that they develop a list of written "norms" to guide their decision making—norms such as equality among jurors, respectful listening to one another, and an agreement to take a five-minute break if things got too emotional. The norms were posted on the wall of the jury room and remained there for the duration of their deliberations in both phases. Deprived of rules governing their decision making, they invented their own.

Ken, the idealist and foreman, told interviewers that he believed that the defendant "knows right from wrong, his life was a life of poor choices." He rejected the psychiatrist's argument that Lane had been traumatized by his childhood experiences and deprivations. The group Sundby calls "the chorus" was a group of five middle-class women. They were struck by their observation that Lane had shown no remorse, but they were also convinced that if given life he might get parole someday. They found him frightening and dreaded having the responsibility of another crime should he be released. The chorus was particularly moved by testimony from his previous robbery victims. They saw the death penalty as a way to prevent him from ever killing again. The twelfth juror, referred to by the others as a "Harley-Davidson" type of guy, Sundby termed a "fundamentalist," not in the religious sense but in the sense that this type of juror simply thinks that some kinds of killing require death.[105] It isn't a case of retribution but of moral balance.

Although she was eventually convinced to vote with the others after a campaign of subtle and not-so-subtle coercion that Sundby details with skill, Peggy, the hope juror, saw and heard the same testimony as the others but each piece of evidence she saw from a somewhat different angle. A careful and thoughtful observer, she concluded that the video showed a man in the grip of an unexplained passion rather than a man simply executing a cold-blooded murder. She remained puzzled throughout the trial by the fact that he shot the clerk before he had opened the cash drawer, making the robbery impossible. While the others saw a remorseless murderer, Peggy was not sure he had the requisite intent.

Mostly, though, Peggy was deeply empathetic. She observed the defendant carefully each day. As Sundby tells it:

> Peggy held on to the hope of redemption for Steven. Peggy had strong religious convictions that included the idea that any individual can redeem himself and become a better person. One of her first comments was "I believe change in a person is possible," and the attitude constantly surfaced when she discussed the evidence. . . . [W]hen Peggy heard the defendant's mother and sister testify about the loss of his brother and how he felt responsible for his brother's death, Peggy was deeply moved. . . . [I]n that traumatized thirteen-year-old kid, Peggy saw the embers of a person still worth saving.[106]

For Sundby, what he calls her "deep religiosity" correlates with life, not death. Peggy spoke of praying, but it was her hope for redemption that most characterized her attitude. Sundby contrasts Peggy's changed vote as the result of the intolerable pressure put on her with another case in another jurisdiction, a much more brutal murder/rape by a defendant with a severely abusive father; in this other case, the presence of two hope jurors able to support one another was enough apparently to change the dynamics of the jury deliberations and lead to a sentence of life in prison.[107]

Sundby is particularly effective at describing the way the death penalty jury becomes isolated during the trial. Prohibited from discussing the trial with anyone else, the twelve become a little society—an ekklesia, if you will—a highly complex little society, a miniature temporary church/state tasked with representing the people, finding truth, exercising judgment, voting, and dispensing grace, doing the work of religio-legal creation described by Robert Cover in his "Nomos and Narrative" in a highly compressed time frame. As in David and Jaruwan Engel's modern classic about contemporary legal consciousness, *Tort, Custom and Karma*, discussing the decline in the use of law by Thai accident victims, each person chooses among a set of received frames for understanding fault and recompense in a world in which they are largely removed from traditional communal cultural norms and procedures.[108] *A Life and Death Decision* is chilling reading. The sense of abandonment of the jury—and of the defendant—at this point in the trial, is palpable. The excessive pseudo process that has developed to preserve the constitutionality of the death penalty builds up to this? In spite of the post-*Furman* effort to cure the arbitrariness and overt racism of prior death penalty regimes, the decision, however seriously undertaken, still ends up being a deeply accidental one. As Sundby says, "Although a jury of twelve individuals is more likely than a single judge to express the community's conscience, it remains a relatively small deliberative body that can change 'personality' with even a minor variation in the mix of individual members."[109] They encapsulate the whole history of criminal justice, searching the defendant's words and actions for the avowal Foucault finds to be at the heart of the criminal process, while also embodying a modernist form of biopolitics.[110]

Putting Garland's and Sundby's accounts together, one sees the anomaly that is the American death penalty. Garland sees its persistence in the energy provided by law-and-order populism, the culture wars, states' rights politics, the legacy of slavery, and a desire for retribution. This energy has become, at this point, on Garland's reading, a perpetual motion machine, continuing to do political work even while the actual numbers of executions decline. The narrative of the heinous murder is normalized through patterned news accounts. As Garland observes, "Death is what exerts the gravitational pull, the cultural and psychic force that sparks anxiety and energizes action."[111] Sundby's account allows us to individuate Garland's story, focusing intensely on the way in which the small group that is the jury, bereft of other measures, scrutinizes the defendant for any sign of remorse, judging him by personal mannerisms, facial expressions, clothing choices, perceived attitudes toward testimony during trial, etc., all observations deeply compromised by social scientific studies of low reliability. Bringing together veridiction and jurisdiction—it is that fusion of individual intent and the law that is sought—the truth of the person but without a shared narrative to ground it.[112] The death penalty jury, representing the people, is asked to decide whether the defendant is of the people with all twenty-four of its hands tied behind their collective backs.[113]

CONSTITUTING THE PEOPLE

Religion in the United States is legally managed through a reading of the First Amendment religion clause that is commonly understood to mandate "a wall of separation between church and state," suppressing bad religion, that is, established religion, while freeing good religion, disestablished religion, to create a moral citizenry. And yet disestablishment also prohibits legal recognition of religion, so separation and freedom are ever-receding goals. Attending to the wall is never ending. The work of purification is never complete.[114] In lieu, perhaps, of enough other material manifestations of bad religion because of the iconoclasm of American Protestantism, one place this legal work is and has been accomplished over the last 150 years or so is in the control of Bibles and biblical material.[115] In schools, the Bible may be read as literature, but it cannot be used in what the court terms a "sectarian" manner. In classrooms Bibles can by law be either religious or secular depending on who is reading them and when and how.[116] In the courtroom, Bibles can be used for oath taking, and occasional biblical references may be made by defense attorneys, but the Bible should not be quoted by prosecutors or judges (even though such references that are made, like many dubiously legal references made by prosecutors in closing arguments, are rarely found to be ground for reversible error). In the jury room, Bibles can be present as interior mental furniture but not in the flesh; they can—perhaps should—inform decision making but they may not be discussed. In prisons, Bibles are good for ensuring good behavior and reducing recidivism as long as they are voluntarily accessed; other religious materials are more tightly controlled. As Nicholas Howe concludes in his *Landscapes of the Secular*,

> In America, therefore, one might say that what lawyers call "First Amendment rights" are a promiscuously blended set of cultural scripts that orient Americans toward a certain view of religious speech, one that stringently—one might say "obsessively"—homologizes the nation and "the public square." In other words, they are as much about making and maintaining particular kinds of places as protecting particular kinds of rights.[117]

Fixing on the Bible seems to promise that the law has hold of a really religious object. Its proper placement seems to promise justice founded in secular reason. In constituting the people of the Constitution, the need to ban Bibles from the capital trial seems obvious to many in the legal community and beyond. Banning Bibles in the courtroom and jury room, as in the classroom, serves to bolster the illusion that the post-*Furman* death penalty process is rational, but it also further exposes the futile effort that is disestablishment, leaving Americans with few acknowledged shared resources to think life and death together. We see instead more clearly perhaps the inchoate American religious world that Noll calls informal Christendom.

Scholars of the death-qualified jury see jurors as taking on an impossible task—on behalf of the nation—with few resources. Taking away their Bibles has epistemological and political motivations, but it also misses the point. The jury is asked to make a "reasoned moral decision" whether to impose the death penalty. They are told that they "must not be swayed by mere sentiment, conjecture, sympathy, passion, prejudice, public opinion or public feeling."[118] They may not consult extraneous sources or be externally influenced. That is, in theory, they may not bring anything into the jury room other than the evidence they have heard in the trial, the instructions from the judge, and their own moral compasses. A wide range of practices are reported, from group prayer or private consultation to the citation of particular verses advocating either mercy or condemnation, even those from the book of Numbers discussing particular penalties for particular acts. One of the challenges of these cases on appeal is the difficulty of finding out what exactly happened, as jurors cannot normally be compelled to testify about their deliberations because of the high value placed on the secrecy of the jury room.

There have been many attempts to describe what is distinctive about religion in the United States. Many of these efforts ground the difference in the constitutional arrangements created with the adoption of the federal Constitution, suggesting that religion in the United States is distinctively free—free by law. This essay assumes, as I have argued elsewhere, that the mutual articulation of law and religion in the formation of US ekklesia, not unlike the cases of Canada and Brazil discussed by Klassen and Johnson in this volume, results not in freedom or separation, but in a distinctively unstable and adaptable field of agonistic contest, one that operates very close to the ground. It is also fissiparous, resulting in a continuous creative spawning of new communities, formed by those trusting local more than distant authority.

It is not simply the continued use of the death penalty in the United States that makes it exceptional. It is the role of the jury in the administration of the death penalty. The jury's role in the penalty phase of US capital trials is distinctive in the world. Nowhere else do untrained laypersons make such a decision with virtually no guidance. US jurors are instructed to do so entirely on an individualized basis, employing what is termed moral and reasoned consideration, without external influences, weighing aggravating and mitigating factors. The jury room in these cases operates as a kind of black box, difficult to penetrate, what happens within deliberately obfuscated. The jury room in the penalty phase is akin to the holy of holies, a place with no law.[119] A place of exception, perhaps by design, the violence invented anew each time.

David Garland's book on the reasons for the persistence of the death penalty in the United States asks what social and cultural work the death penalty does. As one of Garland's reviewers says,

> Garland . . . argues—convincingly—that American capital punishment is "productive, performative, and generative—that it *makes things happen*—even if much of what happens is in the cultural realm of death penalty discourse rather than in the biological realm of life and death" (286). The core of America's cultural engagement with capital punishment is "the idea of death" (301). Death releases a power—"a sacred, irresistible energy"—that the institution of capital punishment exploits in many ways (302). Above all, capital punishment matters in America because "it talks of killing and makes that talk pleasurable and empowering" (304). Americans have substituted rituals of capital punishment debate for the lost rituals of public execution, and voters and viewers have usurped God's role by acquiring the capacity to put death to use against their enemies. In this way, "playing God" constitutes an important part of the death penalty's appeal (305).[120]

Liberal observers of American politics often bemoan the undue influence of religion in American life—threatening imminent theocratic rule. Getting this correct seems to promise so much. This ongoing debate is part of what the United States is. It won't get resolved. It can't get resolved, fueled as it is by the instability of the federal constitutional structure, the indeterminacy of religious formations, and the failure to create a welfare state, as well as the many ways in which US law enables religion, formally and informally, not as an arm of and contained by the state, as in Europe—but as creative coproducers of the sacred.

Historians and social scientists have increasingly described the secular polity as one profoundly engaged in the business of setting the boundaries of and regulating religion. This complicated effort at slicing and dicing is evident in American law. There is often, however, a misunderstanding of law's role. Law does not settle things. The peculiarly low ecclesiology of American religion and an anti-intellectual bent fosters continuous transformation and reinvention. Bibles in the courtroom should not be understood as a failure of separation. They should be understood as intrinsic to American churchstateness—to the do-it-yourself quality of American ekklesia. The American jury trial, better understood, as Robert Burns argues, as a collaborative ritual performance, rather than as a search for truth, is a distinctive phenomenon, and acceptance of the possibility of jury nullification arguably quintessentially embodies American ambivalence about government.[121] The persistence of nonexpert fact finding distinguishes the US trial from its continental counterparts.

Whitman's picture of religion in the United States as something uncontrolled, atavistic, and opportunistic is typical of the view of American religion of many secularists. Religion in the United States is viewed as insufficiently domesticated—a wilder form of religion, one quick to slip into spaces between and quick to take advantage of the myriad legal advantages for individuals and groups styling themselves as religious. But, as Garland emphasized, it is not just religion that has failed to be domesticated in the United States. Politics is also wilder. The United States as a state has always been one of mixed government because of federalism and because of deep popular skepticism about both centralized state power and the private government of big business. The US federal government did not (and was not even imagined to) directly succeed to and assume the powers of the absolute monarchs and churches as the countries of northern Europe did. There was and is no state in that European sense. The Constitution created a secular federated government of limited powers. State conventions did the same. The ongoing appropriation of Indian country and the presence of slavery created a deep undertow of illegitimacy and inauthenticity. All of these experiments in governance supported a constant flow of rival sovereignties, as did the invention of the business corporation.[122] New ekklesia were and continue to be formed, both religious and secular.

Migration away from the geographically based religious forms of the Old World, followed by legal disestablishment in the New, created an immediate need for a fundamental reconceptualization of the legal terms under which religion would do business. In many ways, the result was not in fact institutional separation, as Whitman suggests, but a deep entanglement of the twin affair of reinventing government and reinventing religion. While the revolutionary moment is usually understood to have been the time at which there was the lowest number of "churched" Americans, it was not long before evangelical Christians and others came together across church denominations to work for the creation of a moral society. Importantly, they did this not through the institutional church but through voluntary societies, parachurch organizations—including the American Bible Society. In other words, there is a partnership of sorts between religion and government in the United States as there is in Europe. But it works because they conspire together to deny the existence of a church or a state—in the name of freedom. Teresa Bejan calls this "*established* disestablishmentarian congregationalism."[123] Christianity is not a religion on this understanding but a deeply pervasive metaphor for reality. And the government is not a state in the paternalistic sense but a deeply regrettable necessity.

What so disturbs Whitman and others, the use of biblical analogies in closing arguments in capital cases in the United States or the introduction of biblical language into the jury room, cannot be handled by a better separation of church and state in the United States. Religion seems to be misapprehended as something that could be disestablished if only the will were there. It is in fact much more intractable than that. There is no "there" there to be separated. There is rather a shadowy shape-shifting churchness taken from the flotsam and jetsam of religious life washed up on the US shore, ever adaptable to sustain national projects or to resist them. As Eric Santner says, the decapitation of the king resulted in the inability to secure the body of the people. It also resulted in an inability to secure the body of the church.[124]

The death penalty has had wide public support in the United States, across religious communities and outside them. Opposing the death penalty can be fatal to a political career. There is something particularly disturbing about efforts to secularize death penalty cases through the banning of the Bible. A kind of whitewashing. The presence of religion in law in the United States might rather be seen as diagnostic of the gaps in the would-be hyperrationalism of the modern state, not in Scalia's sense of affirming our greater faithfulness, but in affirming a tragic eirobiblical sensibility. The American jury in the penalty phase encapsulates US churchstateness in the way in which it shows the paradoxically empty and lawless place at the heart of popular sovereignty / free religion, a place of irreducible surplus and entanglement—and suffering. The jury room is a largely unregulated space in the sense that the capital jury is abandoned—left holding the bag—asked to decide on the value of a single individual life. Banning Bibles distracts from the actual law/religion of death. This is profoundly theopolitical work. The decentralization of politics works in, among other things, the failure to resolve racial divisions among people and the way in which an ideology of individualism is betrayed by the state.[125] The death penalty and massive incarceration in the US ensure the continuation of the state through a blood sacrifice on the scale of the Aztecs.[126] There are two metonymies for working out who "we the people" are, the jury and the condemned.

In *The Weight of All Flesh*, Santner describes the loss of the "little piece of the real," in Slavoj Žižek's words, that underwrote the king's virtual body:

> To put it in terms I have used in earlier work, what I am calling the "flesh"—the stuff out of which the sovereign's sublime body is composed—emerges out of the entanglement of the somatic and normative pressures that constitute creaturely life. . . . It signifies a mode of *exposure* that distinguishes human beings from other kinds of life: not simply to the elements or to the fragility, vulnerability, and precariousness of our mortal, finite lives, but also to an ultimate *lack of foundation* for the historical forms of life in which human life unfolds. This is what Žižek means when he speaks of the law's rotation in a vicious circle; it is a rotation around a gap that opens at the jointure of the somatic and the normative, life and forms of life.[127]

Returning to Justice Scalia on Thomas More, is the persistence of the death penalty in the United States best understood as exemplifying a US law still saturated with biblical morality, a law that has failed properly to secularize by enshrining positive law and banning natural law? Or might we better understand the persistence of the death penalty as revealing a deep uncertainty about sovereignty at the heart of the American project—maybe of the secular project more broadly, one not unlike the uncertainty that haunts Henry in *A Man for All Seasons*? There is something at once modern and barbaric about the effort to insist on individuation of the death penalty by an ekklesia especially constituted for the purpose—the people both made and unmade.

NOTES

1. Kantorowicz, *The King's Two Bodies*; Santner, *The Royal Remains*; Santner, *The Weight of All Flesh*.

2. Santner, *The Weight of All Flesh*, 25.

3. *The Death of Marat*, Wikipedia, accessed February 21, 2017, https://en.wikipedia.org/wiki/The_Death_of_Marat#/media /File:Jacques-Louis_David_-_Marat_assassinated_-_Google_Art _Project_2.jpg.

4. Santner, *The Weight of All Flesh*, 117.

5. While beyond the scope of this volume, comparison could and should be extended beyond Europe. See p. 24, n. 2.

6. See, e.g., Edmund Morgan, *Inventing the People: The Rise of Popular Sovereignty in England and America* (New York: Norton, 1988); Larry Kramer, *The People Themselves: Popular Constitutionalism and Judicial Review* (Oxford: Oxford University Press, 2005); and Thomas Green, *Verdict According to Conscience: Perspectives on the English Criminal Trial Jury, 1200–1800* (Chicago: University of Chicago Press, 1988).

7. David Garland, *The Peculiar Institution: America's Death Penalty in an Age of Abolition* (Harvard: Harvard University Press, 2010); Kenneth Stampp, *The Peculiar Institution: Slavery in the Ante-Bellum South* (New York: Vintage Books, 1956).

8. See, e.g., James Q. Whitman, *Harsh Justice: Criminal Punishment and the Widening Divide between America and Europe* (Oxford: Oxford University Press, 2005), comparing the United States to Germany and France.

9. See, e.g., Charles J. Ogletree Jr. and Austin Sarat, eds., *From Lynch Mobs to the Killing State: Race and the Death Penalty in America* (New York: NYU Press, 2006); and Michelle Alexander, *The New Jim Crow: Mass Incarceration in the Age of Colorblindness* (New York: New Press, 2012).

10. Section 2 of Article 3 provides, "The Trial of all Crimes, except in Cases of Impeachment, shall be by Jury." The Sixth Amendment provides, "In all criminal prosecutions, the accused shall enjoy the right to a speedy and public trial, by an impartial jury of the state and district wherein the crime shall have been committed, which district shall have been previously ascertained by law, and to be informed of the nature and cause of the accusation; to be confronted with the witnesses against him; to have compulsory process

for obtaining witnesses in his favor, and to have the assistance of counsel for his defense."

11. In the most recent Supreme Court decision to regulate the circumstances under which the decision of a criminal jury may be impeached by testimony about what occurred in the jury room, *Peña-Rodriguez v. Colorado*, 580 US __ (2017), Justice Kennedy, writing for the majority, found, "For the reasons explained above, the Court now holds that where a juror makes a clear statement that indicates he or she relied on racial stereotypes or animus to convict a criminal defendant, the Sixth Amendment requires that the no-impeachment rule give way in order to permit the trial court to consider the evidence of the juror's statement and any resulting denial of the jury trial guarantee."

12. Diane E. Courselle, "Struggling with Deliberative Secrecy, Jury Independence, and Jury Reform," *South Carolina Law Review* 57 (2005): 203–53.

13. The term "death-qualified juror" refers to the standard that permits prosecutors to exclude only those potential jurors who have an absolute ideological bias against the death penalty, following the Court's decision in *Witherspoon v. Illinois*, 391 US 510 (1968). A defendant is death-eligible once the jury has concluded that he is a member of that narrow class of criminal defendants who have committed specific crimes as defined by the relevant jurisdiction. *Gregg v. Georgia, Proffitt v. Florida, Jurek v. Texas, Woodson v. North Carolina*, and *Roberts v. Louisiana*, 428 US 153 (1976).

14. *People v. Harlan*, 109 P.3d at 616 (2005).

15. 18-1.3-1201, CRS (2004).

16. The Colorado rules of evidence specify the conditions under which a court can inquire into the validity of a jury verdict: "(b) Inquiry into validity of verdict or indictment. Upon an inquiry into the validity of a verdict or indictment, a juror may not testify as to any matter or statement occurring during the course of the jury's deliberations or to the effect of anything upon his or any other juror's mind or emotions as influencing him to assent to or dissent from the verdict or indictment or concerning his mental processes

in connection therewith. But a juror may testify about (1) whether extraneous prejudicial information was improperly brought to the jurors' attention, (2) whether any outside influence was improperly brought to bear upon any juror, or (3) whether there was a mistake in entering the verdict onto the verdict form. A juror's affidavit or evidence of any statement by the juror may not be received on a matter about which the juror would be precluded from testifying." CRE 606(b).

17. This curious reference might reflect the ways in which the pope is becoming a religious leader for Protestants as well as Catholics, an instance of celebrity culture transcending the old Reformation divisions, perhaps.

18. 109 P.3d at 630.

19. Ibid.

20. Ibid. at 630–31.

21. The significant question as to how courts make decisions about human decision making and emotion is a matter of serious concern to court watchers. See, for example, Adam Liptak, "Did the Supreme Court Base a Ruling on a Myth?," *New York Times*, March 6, 2017, accessed March 12, 2017, https://www.nytimes.com /2017/03/06/us/politics/supreme-court-repeat-sex-offenders .html.

22. 109 P.3d at 632.

23. See Susan Bandes, "Repellent Crimes and Rational Deliberation: Emotion and the Death Penalty," *Vermont Law Review* 33 (2009): 489–518, for a discussion of the ways in which courts deliberately exclude emotion from their deliberations.

24. 109 P.3d at 632.

25. Ibid. at 638.

26. Law review articles surveying the cases include John H. Blume and Sheri Lynn Johnson, "Don't Take His Eye, Don't Take His Tooth, and Don't Cast the First Stone: Limiting Religious Arguments in Capital Cases," *William & Mary Bill of Rights Journal* 9 (2000): 61; Elizabeth A. Brooks, "Thou Shalt Not Quote the Bible: Determining the Propriety of Attorney Use of Religious Philosophy

and Themes in Oral Arguments," *Georgia Law Review* 33 (1999): 1113;
Terrence T. Egland, "Prejudiced by the Presence of God: Keeping
Religious Material Out of Death Penalty Deliberations," *Capital
Defense Journal* 16 (2004): 337; and Monica K. Miller et al., "Bibles in
the Jury Room: Psychological Theories Question Judicial Assump-
tions," *Ohio Northern University Law Review* 39 (2013): 579.

27. Guidelines as to when death is appropriate have been found
to be unconstitutionally arbitrary. *Woodson v. North Carolina*, 428
US 280 (1976).

28. See below pp. 184–85.

29. Peña-Rodriguez v. Colorado.

30. On free will and determinism in contemporary life: Constance Furey, "Calvin's Questions: A Response to Jonathan Sheehan," SSRC, http://blogs.ssrc.org/tif/2016/09/21/calvins-questions/.
See also Webb Keane, *Christian Moderns: Freedom and Fetish in the
Mission Encounter* (Berkeley: University of California Press, 2007).

31. Scott E. Sundby, *A Life and Death Decision: A Jury Weighs the
Death Penalty* (New York: St. Martin's, 2005), 15.

32. Several of my readers have asked whether I advocate permit-
ting references to the Bible by judges and lawyers and jurors in the
United States today. I have no opinion on that subject. Like David
Garland, who discusses the problem of a too short recourse to normative positions in this arena in his book, I hope here to contribute
to a conversation aiming to understand the phenomenon. Advo-
cacy has its place in other conversations.

33. *Furman v. Georgia*, 408 US 238 (1972). From the Death Penalty
Information Center website:

In *Furman*, the Court effectively voided every state's death penalty
law, commuted the sentences of all death row inmates around the
country, and suspended the future use of the death penalty. Following *Furman*, many states enacted new statutes that they believed
would decrease arbitrariness in capital sentencing. To address
the unconstitutionality of unguided jury discretion, some states
removed all of that discretion by mandating capital punishment for

those convicted of capital crimes. However, this practice was held unconstitutional by the Supreme Court in *Woodson v. North Carolina*, 428 U.S. 280 (1976) because it did not allow for consideration of individual differences among defendants. Other states sought to focus the jury's discretion by providing sentencing guidelines to direct the jury when deciding whether to impose death. Georgia provided bifurcated proceedings, in which guilt and sentence are determined in separate trials. In the penalty phase, the jury must find at least one aggravating circumstance (characteristics that make certain murders worse than others) beyond a reasonable doubt before considering other evidence and making a decision between life or death. In an effort to safeguard against arbitrary sentencing, Georgia also created specialized appellate review. In 1976, Georgia's guided discretion statute, as well as statutes in Florida and Texas, were approved when the Supreme Court decided *Gregg v. Georgia*, 428 US 153. This landmark decision held that the new death penalty statutes were constitutional, thus reinstating the death penalty in those states. The Court also held that the death penalty itself was constitutional under the Eighth Amendment.

Accessed February 21, 2017, http://www.deathpenaltyinfo.org /arbitrariness#Legal.

34. Alabama is the only state left in which a judge may overrule a jury's decision for life. On January 12, 2016, in *Hurst v. Florida*, 577 U.S. ___ (2016), the US Supreme Court held that the Florida judicial override statute was unconstitutional. A bill cleared the Alabama House in March 2017 that would end the practice in Alabama.

35. *Spaziano v. Florida* 468 US 447, 487 (1984), J. Stevens, dissenting. Scott Sundby emphasizes the difficulty of the post-*Furman* task:

The Court's struggles in the ensuing decades to design and maintain a constitutional system of capital punishment has consumed more of the Court's docket and energy than perhaps any other constitutional controversy. Out of fairness to the Court, it is hard to imagine a task of greater difficulty and immensity—how does one bring rationality, reliability, and consistency to the moral and highly emotional judgment by one human being over another as to whether that person should live or die? The challenge would be difficult enough for a philosopher or a theologian, but it is especially daunting for a Court tasked with bringing the decision within the bounds of the rule of law. In fact, but a year before *Furman*, Justice Harlan had suggested that the task was impossible: 'To identify before the fact those characteristics of criminal homicides and their perpetrators which call for the death penalty, and to express these characteristics in language which can be fairly understood and applied by the sentencing authority, appear to be tasks which are beyond present human ability.' Yet, despite Justice Harlan's warning, five years later the Court found itself trying to do exactly what Harlan had declared as 'beyond present human ability,' and, as a result, the Court has found itself engaged in an unparalleled level of constitutional micromanagement.

Scott Sundby, "The True Legacy of *Atkins* and *Roper*: The Unreliability Principle, Mentally Ill Defendants, and the Death Penalty's Unraveling," *William & Mary Bill of Rights Journal* 23 (2014): 489.

36. In 1999, ninety-eight prisoners were executed. In 2015, twenty-eight prisoners were executed. Between 1977 and 2014 there were 1,394 death sentences in all jurisdictions (35 percent black defendants; 79 percent white victims). There are approximately three thousand prisoners on death row. Extensive documentation of the death penalty can be found at Death Penalty Information Center, accessed February 21, 2017, http://www.deathpenaltyinfo.org/, and US Department of Justice, "Capital Punishment, 2013– Statistics Tables," December 19, 2014, http://www.bjs.gov/content/pub/pdf /cp13st.pdf. Furthermore, more than 90 percent of indictments result from a plea, not a trial.

37. Garland, *The Peculiar Institution*, 312.

38. Described and analyzed in many works, including Foucault,

Discipline and Punish; Michael Ignatieff, *A Just Measure of Pain: The Penitentiary in the Industrial Revolution* (New York: Peregrine, 1989); Michael Merback, *The Thief, the Cross and the Wheel: Pain and the Spectacle of Punishment in Medieval Europe* (Chicago: University of Chicago Press, 1999); and Norval Morris and David Rothman, eds., *The Oxford History of the Prison: The Practice of Punishment in Western Society* (New York: Oxford University Press, 1997). For an account of the invention of the electric chair, see Jürgen Martschukat, "'The Art of Killing by Electricity': The Sublime and the Electric Chair," *Journal of American History* 89 (2002): 900–921.

39. See Moshe Temkin, "The Great Divergence: The Death Penalty in the United States and the Failure of Abolition in Transatlantic Perspective" (Faculty Research Working Paper Series, Harvard Kennedy School, July 2015).

40. Garland, *The Peculiar Institution*.

41. Elisabetta Grande, review of *The Peculiar Institution* by David Garland, *American Journal of Comparative Law* 60 (2012): 1113.

42. Ibid., 1118.

43. Ibid. Importantly, abolition in France, for example, was an elite project, essentially that of a single man, Robert Badinter, and it happened fairly recently, in 1981. See Robert Badinter, *L'Abolition* (Paris: Fayard, 2000).

44. Antonin Scalia, "God's Justice and Ours," *First Things*, May 2002, accessed March 13, 2017, http://www.firstthings.com/article /2002/05/gods-justice-and-ours, 6.

45. Ibid. 6.

46. Ibid., 9. On the Catholic way of death, cf. Robert A. Orsi, *History and Presence* (Cambridge, MA: Harvard University Press, 2016).

47. Ibid., 9.

48. Ibid., 5.

49. Ibid., 6.

50. Scalia was frequently quoted as saying that he believed errors were very rarely made in the imposition of the death penalty.

For a refutation of his position, see Samuel R. Gross et al., "Rate of False Conviction of Criminal Defendants Who Are Sentenced to Death," *PNAS* 111 (2014): 7230–35.

51. Scalia also argued on occasion, employing his well-known originalist approach to interpretation of the US Constitution, that as a judge it was his obligation to apply the Constitution as it was understood at the time of the American founding, a time when, he said (incorrectly—see Garland, *The Peculiar Institution*, 101–26) no one questioned the morality of the death penalty. Scalia also announced in the *First Things* article that he did not understand the use of the death penalty by the state to be immoral under Catholic teaching, notwithstanding a recent papal encyclical taking such a position. See "The Church's Anti-Death Penalty Position," United States Conference of Catholic Bishops, accessed May 9, 2017, http://www.usccb.org/issues-and-action/human-life-and-dignity/death-penalty-capital-punishment/catholic-campaign-to-end-the-use-of-the-death-penalty.cfm. There are parallels between Scalia's theology and his originalism, as Anthony Crapanzano has argued. Anthony Crapanzano, *Serving the Word: Literalism in America from the Pulpit to the Bench* (New York: New Press, 2000).

52. Michael Lipka, "Some Major U.S. Religious Groups Differ from Their Members on the Death Penalty," Pew Research Center, July 13, 2015, accessed March 13, 2017, http://www.pewresearch.org/fact-tank/2015/07/13/some-major-u-s-religious-groups-differ-from-their-members-on-the-death-penalty/. See also a survey of attitudes in Indiana: Marla Sandys and Edmund F. McGarrell, "Beyond the Bible Belt: The Influence (or Lack Thereof) of Religion on Attitudes toward the Death Penalty," *Journal of Crime and Justice* 20 (1997): 179–90. This article reproduces in Indiana a study done in Oklahoma. The authors say they left out one of the Oklahoma survey questions, explaining that "their item concerning the existence of the Devil was excluded because, according to the Director of the POL that conducted the interviews, several respondents laughed during the pretest when asked this item." Ibid., 182.

53. "Evangelicals & Catholics Together: The Christian Mis-

sion in the Third Millennium," *First Things*, May 1994, accessed March 10, 2017, https://www.firstthings.com/article/1994/05/evangelicals-catholics-together-the-christian-mission-in-the-third-millennium.

54. Patrick J. Whiteley, "Natural Law and the Problem of Certainty: Robert Bolt's *A Man for All Seasons*," *Contemporary Literature* 43 (2002): 760–83. Whiteley contrasts the moral complexity of *A Man for All Seasons* with what is usually taken to be the moral absolutism of *Antigone*.

55. See, for example, Vincent Lloyd, *Black Natural Law* (Oxford: Oxford University Press, 2016).

56. See John Witte Jr. and Frank S. Alexander, eds., *The Teachings of Modern Protestantism on Law, Politics & Human Nature* (New York: Columbia University Press, 2007).

57. For another perspective on the reasons for US support for the death penalty, see Bandes, "Repellent Crimes and Rational Deliberation.". Susan Bandes, a leading scholar of law and emotion, sees the persistence of support for the death penalty in a pervasive refusal in American law to deal with emotions. Bandes sees the American insistence that the death penalty, as an abstract matter, can be rationally defended and administered as an instance of this emotional refusal. Arguing for abolition, she says,

> The death penalty thrives under a set of rules, explicit and implicit, about what sorts of emotions can be displayed and even experienced in the legal arena. These rules encourage moral disengagement and discourage empathy. They keep the concrete reality of the death penalty at a safe remove. Most of those who support the death penalty do so in the abstract. Their support often wanes when they become viscerally aware of the fact that capital punishment involves the killing of human beings. Certain realities need to be made salient: the humanity and individuality of each capital defendant, the horror of the execution itself, and the fact that each of us is implicated in and responsible for each execution and for the system that facilitates state-sponsored killing. These realities are at

the moral and emotional center of the American system of capital punishment, and they should be at the center of the debate about its fate. They should incite passion and commitment. When that happens on a broad scale, the death penalty will die its well-deserved death.

Susan Bandes, "The Heart Has Its Reasons: Examining the Strange Persistence of the American Death Penalty," in "Is the Death Penalty Dying?," ed. Austin Sarat, special issue, *Studies in Law, Politics and Society* 42 (2008): 52.

58. Whitman, "Separating Church and State," 89–90.

59. Ibid., 95. It is important to note that when Whitman talks about Europe he means northern Europe. When he talks about church and state he means the state churches of northern Europe. On the different patterns of southern Europe, cf. Alessandro Ferrari, "Dove va la libertà religiosa: Corsi e ricorsi tra le due sponde del Mediterraneo," *Stato, Chiese e pluralismo confessionale* 5 (2014): 1–41.

60. Whitman, "Separating Church and State," 96.

61. Whitman has argued that the harshness of the US criminal justice system can be explained, in part, by different popular attitudes toward the state and the political prisoner. In his comparative study of criminal justice in the United States, France, and Germany, Whitman shows how the two diverged in the early nineteenth century, the United States opting to generalize down, treating all defendants as common criminals, while Europeans generalized up, treating all defendants as potential political prisoners. He also shows how the difference plays out in the percentage of crimes in the United States that are categorized *malum in se* rather than *malum prohibitum*, in the severity of punishments, and in the treatment of prisoners. Whitman, *Harsh Justice*.

62. Sundby, *A Life and Death Decision*, 70.

63. See above, n. 14.

64. *People v. Bradford*, 14 Cal. 4th 1005 (1997).

65. Ibid., 1061–62.

66. Attention to the jury's fear of reoffense might be seen to be an index of a management rather than a moral view of criminal justice. The jury here is being invited to make a risk assessment rather than a judgment of degrees of depravity. Sentencing then becomes a question of security rather than of punishment. Cf. Foucault, *Wrong-Doing, Truth-Telling*, 223.

67. 14 Cal. 4th at 1062.

68. Ibid.

69. Ibid., 1062–63.

70. Ibid., 1062.

71. Joseph L. Hoffmann, "Where's the Buck? Juror Misperception of Sentencing Responsibility in Death Penalty Cases," *Indiana Law Journal* 70 (1995): 1137–60.

72. *Woodson v. North Carolina*, 428 US 280 (1976).

73. Ibid., 304–5.

74. Bradford had been convicted of the brutal rape and murder of a motel owner's wife. The associated conviction for robbery was overturned on appeal, but the murder and death penalty sentence were affirmed. 14 Cal. 4th at 1017.

75. See above at n. 27.

76. This argument is a corollary to the argument for religious accommodation and conscientious exemption. The religiously motivated person is imagined by law to be a person subject to a kind of irrational divine coercion that is impossible to resist. For a subtle comparison of religious conscience and disability, see Cathleen Kaveny, *Law's Virtues: Fostering Autonomy and Solidarity in American Society* (Washington, DC: Georgetown University Press, 2012).

77. Blume and Johnson, "Don't Take His Eye,"; Andrea D. Walker, "'The Murderer Shall Surely be Put to Death': The Impropriety of Biblical Arguments in the Penalty Phase of Capital Cases," *Washburn Law Journal*: 43 (2003): 197–223.

78. *Commonwealth v. Chambers*, 528 Pa. 558 (1991).

79. 528 Pa. at 643.

80. *Commonwealth v. Brown*, 551 Pa. 465, 494 (1998).

81. *Oliver v. Quarterman* 541 F. 3rd 329 (2008) (cert. denied).

82. 541 F. 3rd at 331–33.

83. For an argument that jurors have a constitutional right to consult the Bible, see Kathleen Rupp, "Capital Hypocrisy: Does Compelling Jurors to Impose the Death Penalty without Spiritual Guidance Violate Jurors' First Amendment Rights?," *American Criminal Law Review* 48 (2011): 217–40.

84. Martin Marty, *Religion and Republic: The American Circumstance* (Boston: Beacon, 1989).

85. Mark Noll, *In the Beginning Was the Word: The Bible in American Public Life, 1492–1783* (Oxford: Oxford University Press, 2016), 1. See also Lincoln Mullen, "*America's Public Bible: Biblical Quotations in U.S. Newspapers*," 2016, accessed March 14, 2017, http://americaspublicbible.org.

86. Daniel Radosh, "The Good Book Business: Why Publishers Love the Bible," *New Yorker*, December 18, 2006, 1. See also, on the distribution of Bibles, John Fea, *The Bible Cause: A History of the American Bible Society* (Oxford: Oxford University Press, 2016); and Matthew Engelke, *God's Agents: Biblical Publicity in Contemporary England* (Berkeley: University of California Press, 2013).

87. Jonathan Sheehan, *The Enlightenment Bible: Translation, Scholarship, Culture* (Princeton, NJ: Princeton University Press, 2005), 4.

88. Mark De Wolfe Howe, *The Garden and the Wilderness: Religion and Government in American Constitutional History* (Chicago: University of Chicago Press, 1965).

89. Ibid., 3.

90. And one cannot forget Jefferson's Bible, carefully redacted to remove all miracles!

91. Noll, *In the Beginning*, 3.

92. Paul Gutjahr, *An American Bible: A History of the Good Book in the United States, 1777–1880* (Stanford, CA: Stanford University Press, 1999), 3–4, 176; cf. John Modern, *Secularism in Antebellum America* (Chicago: University of Chicago Press, 2011). As if confirming all of this scholarship, a new "Lawyers' Bible" has been proposed. See J. Nelson Happy and Samuel Pyeatt Menefee, "Genesis!:

Scriptural Citation and the Lawyer's Bible Project," *Regent University Law Review* 9 (1997): 89–144.

93. See, e.g., Leigh Schmidt, review of *An American Bible*, by Paul Gutjahr, *Church History* 69 (2000): 445–46.

94. Peter Thuesen, *In Discordance with the Scriptures: American Protestant Battles over Translating the Bible* (New York: Oxford University Press, 1999).

95. Harriss, "On the Eirobiblical."

96. Ibid., 476.

97. Ibid., 474.

98. Ibid., 480.

99. Sundby, *A Life and Death Decision*, 15–16.

100. Ibid., 15.

101. Two leading death penalty researchers argue that prosecutors should never refer to religion because such references constitute an impermissible endorsement of religion in violation of the establishment clause, lower the responsibility of the jurors, violate individualized sentencing principles, and distract the jury from its job; it should be acceptable for defense counsel to make biblical references, however, because they are not state actors and because of the constitutional rights of defendant to a full defense. Blume and Johnson, "Don't Take His Eye."

102. Sundby, *A Life and Death Decision*, 16.

103. Accounts and theories of secularization abound. Legal thinkers pushing for the banning of Bibles seem to be relying on a vernacular version of the subtraction thesis, understanding secularization and a concomitant advance of reason since the Reformation as being characterized by the progressive evacuation of religious objects and institutions from public space. An iconic riposte to this thesis was, of course, Richard John Neuhaus, *The Naked Public Square: Religion and Democracy in America* (Grand Rapids, MI: Eerdmans, 1988). See also Mariana Valverde, "The Ethic of Diversity: Local Law and the Negotiation of Urban Norms," *Law & Social Inquiry* 33 (2008): 895–923, for a discussion of the ways in which a focus on content in law—here progressive regulation to

recognize diversity—can obscure the ways in which administration continues to be based in restrictive norms.

104. Sundby relies in telling his story on the extensive interviews conducted by the Capital Jury Project led by William Bowers. See William Bowers, "What Is the Capital Jury Project?," School of Criminal Justice, University at Albany, State University of New York. n.d., accessed May 9, 2017, http://www.albany.edu/scj/13189.php. The names of the participants in the case were changed by Sundby to conceal their identities. This is a deceptively simple little book, presented as the account of one trial, but Sundby, an expert on the death penalty jury, skillfully incorporates years of research into the many complexities and failures of the capital jury trial into the story. I won't try to represent them all here. I will use his account to set up the predicament of the capital jury in the penalty phase.

105. Marla Sandys and Adam Trahan call these jurors latent ADPs (automatic death penalty voters) because, although they can survive voir dire as jurors who are open to a lesser sentence; in fact for them guilt of a certain offense carries an automatic death penalty vote. Marla Sandys and Adam Trahan, "Life Qualification, Automatic Death Penalty Voter Status, and Juror Decision Making in Capital Cases," *Justice System Journal* 29 (2008): 385–95.

106. Sundby, *A Life and Death Decision*, 70–71.

107. Ibid., 138–59. Sundby says that his own opposition to the death penalty is partly motivated by the randomness of jury selection and the ways in which life depends on the happenstance of who is chosen, whether, in other words, the defendant is judged by a jury containing more than one hope juror.

108. David Engel and Jaruwan Engel, *Tort, Custom and Karma: Globalization and the Decline of Legal Consciousness in Thailand* (Palo Alto: Stanford University Press, 2010).

109. Sundby, *A Life and Death Decision*, 183.

110. Foucault, *Wrong-Doing, Truth Telling*.

111. Garland, *The Peculiar Institution*, 302.

112. Foucault, *Wrong-Doing, Truth-Telling*, 178, 207–8.

113. This essay focuses only on the penalty phase of the current death penalty jury. It is one piece of a long and complex story. See Albert Alschuler and Andrew G. Deiss, "A Brief History of the Criminal Jury in the United States," *University of Chicago Law Review* 61 (1994): 867–928. Its value is deeply contested. See Robert P. Burns, "The History and Theory of the American Jury," *California Law Review* 83, no. 6 (1995): 1477–94.

114. Cf. Bruno Latour, *We Have Never Been Modern*, trans. Catherine Porter (Cambridge, MA: Harvard University Press, 1991).

115. The American Civil Liberties Union, Americans United for the Separation of Church and State, and the Freedom from Religion Foundation, all dedicated to ridding the landscape of religion, also vigilantly monitor crosses and Ten Commandment monuments. See Nicolas Howe, *Landscapes of the Secular: Law, Religion and American Sacred Space* (Chicago: University of Chicago Press, 2016) for a perspicacious reading of the spatial secular and sacred in the United States.

116. *Abingdon v. Schempp*, 374 US 203 (1963). Litigation challenging statutes mandating the reading of the Bible in schools proliferated in the nineteenth century as Catholics, and Jews, challenged the Protestant monopoly over public education. Known as the Bible wars, they found an eloquent spokesperson in Judge Welch of the Ohio Supreme Court in *Board of Education v. Minor*, 23 Ohio St. 211 (1872). Whether and precisely in what way these efforts resulted in the secularization of US public education is debated.

117. Howe, *Landscapes of the Secular*, 77.

118. Bandes, "Repellent Crimes and Rational Deliberation."

119. See Faisal Devji, *The Terrorist in Search of Humanity: Militant Islam and Global Politics* (New York: Columbia University Press, 2009), 147, for a discussion of the effects in the "war on terror" of setting up situations in which morality governs unchecked by law.

120. David T. Johnson, "American Capital Punishment in Comparative Perspective," *Law & Social Inquiry* 36 (2011): 1033–61.

121. Robert Burns, *A Theory of the Trial* (Princeton, NJ: Princeton University Press, 2001).

122. Pauline Maier, "The Revolutionary Origins of the American Corporation," *William and Mary Quarterly*, 3rd series, 50, no. 1 (1993): 51–84.

123. Teresa M. Bejean, *Mere Civility: Disagreement and the Limits of Toleration* (Cambridge, MA: Harvard University Press, 2017), 172.

124. Santner, *Royal Remains*.

125. See Sally Engle *Merry, Getting Justice and Getting Even: Legal Consciousness among Working-Class Americans* (Chicago: University of Chicago Press, 1990).

126. For reflection on execution as sacrifice, see Merback, *The Thief, the Cross and the Wheel*; and Mark Lewis Taylor, *The Executed God: The Way of the Cross in Lockdown America* (Minneapolis: Fortress, 2001).

127. Santner, *Weight of All Flesh*, 84.

ACKNOWLEDGMENTS

This book has been a true work of collaboration that has benefitted from the help of many people and institutions. The idea was sparked at a panel at an American Academy of Religion Annual Meeting and grew into a work of joint authorship with the support and guidance of Alan Thomas at the University of Chicago Press. Collectively, we would like to thank the Jackman Humanities Institute at the University of Toronto for giving us a beautiful space to gather and talk through early versions of the book. We are also grateful to the two anonymous reviewers who provided critical feedback on how to make our collective and specific arguments much clearer. As we brought the final manuscript together, Gregory Fewster and Suzanne van Geuns, two doctoral students at the University of Toronto, worked with great care to ensure that we were consistent and clear in our style, prose, and arguments.

Paul Johnson thanks Matthew Hull, Richard Reinhardt, Winnifred Fallers Sullivan, Pamela E. Klassen, Geneviève Zubrzycki, and two anonymous reviewers for comments on earlier versions of his essay. Winnifred Fallers Sullivan is particularly grateful to Susan Bandes, Marla Sandys, and Scott Sundby for sharing their expertise on the death penalty and to Jeffrey Siker and Peter Thuesen for conversations about the American use of scripture. She is also grateful to the Law and Religion reading group at Indiana University, Bloomington, for reading and commenting on an early version of the essay. She also thanks Helge Arsheim, Benjamin Berger, Elizabeth Shakman Hurd, Barry Sullivan, and

Robert Yelle, each of whom kindly read and commented on the manuscript. She thanks Fred Konefsky, as always, for excellent counsel.

Pamela Klassen would like to thank her coauthors and several research assistants, including Magdalene Klassen, Suzanne van Geuns, and Gregory Fewster, all of whom read and commented on her essay. Artemisia Robins provided helpful research on the question of clergy reserves. Klassen also thanks several people who provided critical insights and directions for further inquiry, especially John Borrows of the University of Victoria, Delaine Friedrich of the British Columbia Assembly of First Nations, Benjamin Berger of Osgoode Hall Law School, Elizabeth Elbourne of McGill University, and her colleagues Kevin O'Neill, Jill Carter, Heidi Bohaker, and Cara Krmpotich at the University of Toronto. She presented an earlier version of her essay at the Department of Religious Studies at the University of Waterloo, as well as at the Sites of Memory workshop at the University of Toronto, and benefited from questions raised by the audience.

Anne-Marie Holland, associate librarian of Rare Books and Special Collections at the McGill University Library, generously provided access to the library's copy of the Royal Proclamation. Maureen Matthews, curator of ethnology at the Manitoba Museum, offered a tour of the museum's Indigenous collections and recounted the history and process of the Treaty People exhibit. Vicki Sharp kindly took photos of the Royal Proclamation on display at the Canadian Museum of Human Rights. The research for Klassen's chapter was generously supported by a Social Sciences and Humanities Research Council Insight Grant and the Anneliese Maier Research Award from the Alexander von Humboldt Foundation. Finally, Klassen thanks her colleague and husband John Marshall, not only for reading and commenting on the manuscript, but also for feeding all the coauthors during our summer meeting in Toronto.

BIBLIOGRAPHY

Abray, Lorna Jane. *The People's Reformation: Magistrates, Clergy, and Commons in Strasbourg, 1500–1598*. Ithaca, NY: Cornell University Press, 1985.

Agamben, Giorgio. *Homo Sacer: Sovereign Power and Bare Life*. Translated by Daniel Heller-Roazen. Stanford, CA: Stanford University Press, 1998.

———. *The Kingdom and the Glory: For a Theological Genealogy of Economy and Government*. Translated by Lorenzo Chiesa. Stanford, CA: Stanford University Press, 2011.

———. *The Open: Man and Animal*. Stanford, CA: Stanford University Press, 2004.

Agrama, Ali Hussein. *Questioning Secularism: Islam, Sovereignty, and the Rule of Law in Modern Egypt*. Chicago: University of Chicago Press, 2012.

Aguiar, Durval Vieira de. *Descrições práticas da provincia da Bahia*. Rio de Janeiro: Editora Cátedra, 1979.

Aldridge, Jim. *Keeping Promises: The Royal Proclamation of 1763, Aboriginal Rights, and Treaties in Canada*. Montreal: McGill-Queen's University Press, 2015.

Alexander, Michelle. *The New Jim Crow: Mass Incarceration in the Age of Colorblindness*. New York: New Press, 2012.

Almeida, Cícero Antônio F. de. *Canudos: Imagens da guerra*. Rio de Janeiro: Lacerda, 1997.

Alschuler, Albert, and Andrew Deiss. "A Brief History of the Criminal Jury in the United States." *University of Chicago Law Review* 61, no. 3 (1994): 867–928.

"Arbitrariness: Legal and Historical Background." Death Penalty Information Center, July 16, 2015. http://www.deathpenaltyinfo.org/arbitrariness#Legal.

Arendt, Hannah. *The Human Condition*. 2nd ed. Chicago: University of Chicago Press, 2011.

Arnot, David. "The Honour of the First Nations—The Honour of the Crown: The Unique Relationship of First Nations with the Crown." In *The Evolving Canadian Crown*, edited by Jennifer Smith and D. Michael Jackson, 155–76. Montreal: McGill-Queen's University Press, 2012.

Asad, Talal. *Genealogies of Religion: Discipline and Reasons of Power in Christianity and Islam*. Baltimore: Johns Hopkins University Press, 1993.

Ataide, Yara Dulce Bandeira de. "As origens do povo do Bom Jesus Conselheiro." *Revista USP* 20 (1994): 89–99.

Badinter, Robert. *L'Abolition*. Paris: Fayard, 2000.

Bandes, Susan. "The Heart Has Its Reasons: Examining the Strange Persistence of the American Death Penalty." In "Is the Death Penalty Dying?," edited by Austin Sarat, special issue, *Studies in Law, Politics and Society* 42 (2008): 21–52.

———. "Repellant Crimes and Rational Deliberation: Emotion and the Death Penalty." *Vermont Law Review* 33, no. 3 (2009): 489–518.

Barbosa, Rui. "Terminação da guerra de Canudos." In *Obras completas*, vol. 24. Rio de Janeiro: Ministério da Educação, 1897.

Bataille, Georges. *Guilty*. Translated by Bruce Boone. Venice, CA: Lapis, 1988.

Beal, Bob. "An Indian Chief, an English Tourist, A Doctor, A Reverend, and a Member of Parliament: The Journeys of Pasqua's Pictographs and the Meaning of Treaty Four." *Canadian Journal of Native Studies* 27, no. 1 (January 1, 2007): 109–88.

Bell, Lynne. "Buffalo Boy Testifies: Decolonising Visual Testimony in a Colonial-Settler Society." In *Decolonising Testimony: On the Possibilities and Limits of Witnessing*, edited by Rosanne Kennedy, Lynne Bell, and Julia Emberley, Humanities Research, vol. 15, no. 3, 81–96. Canberra: Australian National University Press, 2009.

Benicio, Manoel. *O rei dos jagunços: Chronica historica e de costumes sertanejos sobre os acontecimentos de Canudos*. Rio de Janeiro: Typographia do Jornal do Commercio, 1899.

Benjamin, Walter. "Critique of Violence." In *Reflections: Essays, Aphorisms, Autobiographical Writings*, translated by Edmund Jephcott, 277–300. New York: Schocken Books, 1986.

Benoit, Paul. "State Ceremonial: The Constitutional Monarch's Liturgical Authority." In *The Evolving Canadian Crown*, edited by Jennifer Smith and D. Michael Jackson, 119–38. Montreal: McGill-Queen's University Press, 2012.

Benton, Lauren. *Law and Colonial Cultures: Legal Regimes in World History, 1400–1900*. New York: Cambridge University Press, 2002.

Berger, Benjamin L. *Law's Religion: Religious Difference and the Claims of Constitutionalism*. Toronto: University of Toronto Press, 2015.

Blume, John, and Sheri Lynn Johnson. "Don't Take His Eye, Don't Take His Tooth, and Don't Cast the First Stone: Limiting Religious Arguments in Capital Cases." *William & Mary Bill of Rights Journal* 9, no. 1 (2000): 61–104.

Bohaker, Heidi. "Reading Anishinaabe Identities: Meaning and Metaphor in Nindoodem Pictographs." *Ethnohistory* 57, no. 1 (January 1, 2010): 11–33.

Bohaker, Heidi, Alan Ojiig Corbiere, and Ruth B. Phillips. "Wampum Unites Us: Digital Access, Interdisciplinarity and Indigenous Knowledge—Situating the GRASAC Knowledge Sharing Database." In *Museum as Process: Translating Local and Global Knowledges*, edited by Raymond Silverman, 45–66. New York: Routledge, 2015.

Borrows, John. *Canada's Indigenous Constitution*. Toronto: University of Toronto Press, 2010.

———. *Drawing Out Law: A Spirit's Guide*. Toronto: University of Toronto Press, 2010.

———. "Legislation and Indigenous Self-Determination in Canada and the United States." In *From Recognition to Reconciliation: Essays on the Constitutional Entrenchment of Aboriginal and Treaty Rights*, edited by Patrick Macklem and Douglas Sanderson, 474–505. Toronto: University of Toronto Press, 2016.

———. "Origin Stories & the Law: Treaty Metaphysics in Canada and New Zealand." n.d.

———. *Recovering Canada: The Resurgence of Indigenous Law*. Toronto: University of Toronto Press, 2002.

———. "Unextinguished: Rights and the Indian Act." *University of New Brunswick Law Journal* 67 (2016): 3–35.

———. "Wampum at Niagara: The Royal Proclamation, Canadian Legal History, and Self-Government." In *Aboriginal and Treaty Rights in Canada: Essays on Law, Equality, and Respect for Difference*, edited by Michael Asch, 155–72. Vancouver: University of British Columbia Press, 1997.

Bourdieu, Pierre. *Outline of a Theory of Practice*. Translated by Richard Nice. Cambridge: Cambridge University Press, 1977.

Bowers, William. "What Is the Capital Jury Project?" School of Criminal Justice, University at Albany, State University of New York. n.d. http://www.albany.edu/scj/13189.php.

Brake, Justin. "'We . . . Do Not Recognize Your Authority at Muskrat Falls': Land Protectors." *TheIndependent.ca*, October 7, 2016. http://theindependent.ca/2016/10/07/we-do-not-recognize-your-authority-at-muskrat-falls-land-protectors/.

Brandão, Marina. "No dia do santo casamenteiro, pedidos agora são por emprego." *O Globo*, June 14, 2016.

Brooks, Elizabeth. "Thou Shalt Not Quote the Bible: Determining the Propriety of Attorney Use of Religious Philosophy and Themes in Oral Arguments." *Georgia Law Review* 33, no. 4 (1998): 1113–80.

Brownstone, Arni. "Mysteries of the Sculptural Narrative Pipes from Manitoulin Island." *American Indian Art* 36, no. 3 (2011): 54–84.

Buck-Morss, Susan. "Hegel and Haiti." *Critical Inquiry* 26, no. 4 (2000): 821–65.

Burdick, John. *Blessed Anastácia: Women, Race, and Popular Christianity in Brazil*. New York: Routledge, 1998.

Burke, Edmund. *Reflections on the Revolution in France*. London: James Dodsley, 1790.

Burns, Robert P. "The History and Theory of the American Jury." *California Law Review* 83, no. 6 (1995): 1477–94.

———. *Kafka's Law: "The Trial" and American Criminal Justice*. Chicago: University of Chicago Press, 2014.

———. *A Theory of the Trial*. Princeton, NJ: Princeton University Press, 2001.

Butler, Judith. *Notes Toward a Performative Theory of Assembly*. Cambridge, MA: Harvard University Press, 2015.

Butler, Samuel. *Erewhon*. 1872; Mineola, NY: Dover, 2002.

Cable Public Affairs Channel. "CPAC Special: 2016 Royal Tour— B.C. Black Rod Ceremony." *CPAC*, 2016. Accessed November 1, 2016. http://www.cpac.ca/en/programs/cpac-special/episodes /49023425/.

Calasans, José. "Canudos não Euclidiano." In *Subsídios para a sua reavaliação histórica*. Rio de Janeiro: Fundação Casa de Rui Barbosa, 1986.

———. *Quase biografias de jagunços: O séquito de Antonio Conselheiro*. Salvador da Bahia: EDUFBA, 2013.

Calloway, Colin G. *The American Revolution in Indian Country: Crisis and Diversity in Native American Communities*. Cambridge University Press, 1995.

———. "The Proclamation of 1763: Indian Country Origins and American Impacts." In *Keeping Promises: The Royal Proclamation of 1763, Aboriginal Rights, and Treaties in Canada*, edited by Jim Aldridge and Terry Fenge, 33–48. Montreal: McGill-Queen's University Press, 2015.

———. *The Scratch of a Pen: 1763 and the Transformation of North America*. New York: Oxford University Press, 2006.

Camus, Albert. *The Stranger*. 1942; London: Vintage Books, 1988.

Canadian Museum of Human Rights. "Canada's Magna Carta: Meaning and Misconceptions." August 14, 2015. https:// humanrights.ca/newsbg-magnacarta-meaning-misconceptions.

Canovan, Margaret. "The People." In *The Oxford Handbook of Political Theory*, edited by John S. Dryzek, Bonnie Honig, and Anne Phillips, 349–62. New York: Oxford University Press, 2008.

Cardinal, Harold. *The Rebirth of Canada's Indians*. Edmonton: Hurtig, 1977.

Carter, Jill. "Discarding Sympathy, Disrupting Catharsis: The Mortification of Indigenous Flesh as Survivance-Intervention." *Theatre Journal* 67, no. 3 (October 29, 2015): 413–32.

Carvalho, Álvaro Dantas de, and Consuelo Novais Sampaio. "A posição do Barão de Jeremoabo." In *Canudos: Cartas para o barão*, 17–31. São Paulo: EdUSP, 1999.

Cavanaugh, William. *Torture and Eucharist: Theology, Politics, and the Body of Christ*. Oxford: Blackwell, 1998.

Chamberlin, J. Edward. *If This Is Your Land, Where Are Your Stories? Finding Common Ground*. New York: Random House, 2004.

Chatterjee, Nandini. *The Making of Indian Secularism: Empire, Law and Christianity, 1830–1960*. London: Palgrave Macmillan, 2011.

Chatterjee, Partha. *The Politics of the Governed*. New York: Columbia University Press, 2006.

Chiefs of Ontario. "250th Anniversary of the Treaty of Niagara." Chiefs of Ontario website. Accessed April 24, 2017. http://www.chiefs-of-ontario.org/node/920.

"The Church's Anti-Death Penalty Position." United States Conference of Catholic Bishops, n.d. http://www.usccb.org/issues-and-action/human-life-and-dignity/death-penalty-capital-punishment/catholic-campaign-to-end-the-use-of-the-death-penalty.cfm.

Cleary, Edward. "The Brazilian Catholic Church and Church-State Relations: Nation-Building." *Journal of Church and State* 39, no. 2 (1997): 253–72.

Coleman, Daniel. "Imposing subCitizenship: Canadian White Civility and the Two Row Wampum of the Six Nations." In *Narratives of Citizenship: Indigenous and Diasporic Peoples Unsettle the Nation-State*, edited by Aloys N. M. Fleischmann, Nancy Van Styvendale, and Cody McCarroll, 177–211. Edmonton: University of Alberta Press, 2011.

Collins, John F. *Revolt of the Saints: Memory and Redemption in the Twilight of Brazilian Racial Democracy*. Durham, NC: Duke University Press, 2015.

Corbiere, Alan Ojiig. "Treaty Medals." Paper presented at Metals and Memory: War, Metal, and Memory, Toronto, February 4, 2016.

Corbiere, Alan Ojiig, Mchigiing Njibaa, and Bne Doodeman. "Parchment, Wampum, Letters and Symbols: Expanding the Parameters of the Royal Proclamation Commemoration." *ActiveHistory.ca*, October 2, 2013. http://activehistory.ca/2013/10/parchment-wampum-letters-and-symbols-expanding-the-parameters-of-the-royal-proclamation-commemoration/.

Corntassel, Jeff, Chaw-win-is, and T'lakwadzi. "Indigenous Storytelling, Truth-Telling, and Community Approaches to Reconciliation." *English Studies in Canada* 35, no. 1 (2009): 137–59.

Coulthard, Glen Sean. *Red Skin, White Masks: Rejecting the Colonial Politics of Recognition*. Minneapolis: University of Minnesota Press, 2014.

Courselle, Diane E. "Struggling with Deliberative Secrecy, Jury Independence, and Jury Reform." *South Carolina Law Review* 57 (2005): 203–53.

Couto, Manoel José Gonçalves. *Missão abreviada*. Porto: Typographia de Sebastião José Pereira, 1859.

Crapanzano, Vincent. *Serving the Word: Literalism in America from the Pulpit to the Bench*. New York: New Press, 2000.

"The Crown." Government of Canada. Accessed May 22, 2017. http://canada.pch.gc.ca/eng/1444999462589/1444999462592.

Da Cunha, Euclides. *Caderneta de Campo*. Edited by Olimpio de Souza Andrade. Rio de Janeiro: Fundação Biblioteca Nacional, 2009.

———. *Diário de uma expedição*. Edited by Walnice Nogueira Galvão. São Paulo: Companhia das Letras, 2000.

———. *Rebellion in the Backlands*. Translated by Samuel Putnam. Chicago: University of Chicago Press, 1944.

Daly, Richard. *Our Box Was Full: An Ethnography for the Delgamuukw*

Plaintiffs. Vancouver: University of British Columbia Press, 2004.

Dantas, S. de Souza. *Aspectos e contrastes: Ligeiro estudo sobre o estadod da Bahia.* Rio de Janeiro: Revista dos Tribunaies, 1922.

"Declaration of Independence: A Transcription." *America's Founding Documents,* National Archives, Accessed November 1, 2016. https://www.archives.gov/founding-docs/declaration-transcript.

Deloria, Vine, Jr. *For This Land: Writings on Religion in America.* New York: Routledge, 1998.

Della Cava, Ralph. "Brazilian Messianism and National Institutions: A Reappraisal of Canudos and Joaseiro." *Hispanic American Historical Review* 48, no. 3 (1986): 402–20.

Derrida, Jacques. *Writing and Difference.* Translated by Alan Bass. Chicago: University of Chicago Press, 1978.

Desbiens, Caroline. *Power from the North: Territory, Identity, and the Culture of Hydroelectricity in Quebec.* Vancouver: University of British Columbia Press, 2013.

Devji, Faisal. *The Terrorist in Search of Humanity: Militant Islam and Global Politics.* New York: Columbia University Press, 2009.

De Vries, Hent. Introduction to *Political Theologies: Public Religions in a Post-Secular World,* edited by Hent de Vries and Lawrence Eugene Sullivan, 1–88. New York: Fordham University Press, 2006.

Diacon, Todd. *Millenarian Vision, Capitalist Reality: Brazil's Contestado Rebellion, 1912–1916.* Durham, NC: Duke University Press, 1991.

Die, Marguerite Van. "Religion and Law in British North America, 1800–1867." In *The Cambridge History of Religions in America,* edited by Stephen J. Stein, 2:717–45. Cambridge: Cambridge University Press, 2012.

"Editorial." *Journal of Church and State* 1, no. 1 (1959): 2–3.

Edmonds, Penelope. *Settler Colonialism and (Re)conciliation: Frontier Violence, Affective Performances, and Imaginative Refoundings.* Hampshire: Palgrave Macmillan, 2016.

Egland, Terrence. "Prejudiced by the Presence of God: Keeping Religious Material Out of Death Penalty Deliberations." *Capital Defense Journal* 16, no. 2 (2004): 337–66.

Eiss, Paul. *In the Name of El Pueblo: Place, Community, and the Politics of History in Yucatán*. Durham, NC: Duke University Press, 2010.

Elbourne, Elizabeth. "Managing Alliance, Negotiating Christianity: Haudenosaunee Uses of Anglicanism in Northeastern North America, 1760s–1830s." In *Mixed Blessings: Indigenous Encounters with Christianity in Canada*, edited by Tolly Bradford and Chelsea Horton, 38–60. Vancouver: University of British Columbia Press, 2016.

Engelke, Matthew. *God's Agents: Biblical Publicity in Contemporary England*. Berkeley: University of California Press, 2013.

———. "Material Religion." In *The Cambridge Companion to Religious Studies*, edited by Robert A. Orsi, 209–29. Cambridge: Cambridge University Press, 2012.

Erasmus, Georges. Introduction to *Drum Beat: Anger and Renewal in Indian Country*, edited by Boyce Richardson, 1–42. Toronto: Summerhill, 1989.

Essus, Ana Maria Mauad de Sousa Andrade. "O 'olho da história': Análise da imagem fotográfica na construção de uma memoria sobre o conflito de Canudos," *Acervo: Revista do Arquivo Nacional* 6, no. 1–2 (1993): 25–40.

"Evangelicals & Catholics Together: The Christian Mission in the Third Millennium." *First Things*, May 1994, accessed March 10, 2017. https://www.firstthings.com/article/1994/05/evangelicals -catholics-together-the-christian-mission-in-the-third -millennium.

Ewart, John Skirving. *The Kingdom of Canada: Imperial Federation, the Colonial Conferences, the Alaska Boundary and Other Essays*. Toronto: Morang, 1908.

Facó, Rui. *Cangaceiros e fanáticos: Gênese e lutas*. Rio de Janeiro: UFRJ, 2009.

Farr, James. "Locke, Natural Law, and New World Slavery." *Political Theory* 36, no. 4 (2008): 495–522.

Fea, John. *The Bible Cause: A History of the American Bible Society.* New York: Oxford University Press, 2016.

Ferrari, Alessandro. "Dove va la libertà religiosa: Corsi e ricorsi tra le due sponde del Mediterraneo." *Stato, Chiese e pluralismo confessionale* 5 (2014): 1–41.

"Fisheries and Justice Ministers Head to B.C. Diesel Spill Site to Talk to Heiltsuk First Nation." *CBC News.* Accessed November 1, 2016. http://www.cbc.ca/news/canada/british-columbia/bella-bella-diesel-oil-leaking-nathan-stewart-tugboat-accident-heiltsuk-1.3828347.

Flyaway, J. K., J. R. Badweather, S. A. Zeedawit, A. M. Nahneigh, J. Nakmauz, Amos G. Neesgwaksaw, Samuel Weeshakes, and Johnny O'Yea. "Indian Protest against White Settlers Coming in to the Aiyansh Valley, Naas River, British Columbia." May 17, 1910. Printed at Aiyansh. Image GR-0429, 2561/10, Royal British Columbia Museum and Archives.

Foster, Hamar, and Benjamin L. Berger. "From Humble Prayers to Legal Demands: The Cowichan Petition of 1909 and the British Columbia Indian Land Question." In *The Grand Experiment: Law and Legal Culture in British Settler Societies,* edited by A. R. Buck, Benjamin L. Berger, and Hamar Foster. 240–67. Vancouver: University of British Columbia Press, 2008.

Foucault, Michel. *Discipline and Punish: The Birth of the Prison.* Translated by Alan Sheridan. New York: Pantheon Books, 1977.

———. *History of Sexuality.* Vol. 1, *An Introduction.* Translated by Robert Hurley. New York: Vintage Books, 1990.

———. *Security, Territory, Population: Lectures at the College de France, 1977–78.* Edited by Arnold Davidson. Translated by Graham Burchell. London: Palgrave Macmillan, 2009.

———. *Wrong-Doing, Truth-Telling: The Function of Avowal in Justice.* Edited by Fabienne Brion and Bernard Harcourt. Translated by Stephen Sawyer. Chicago: University of Chicago Press, 2014.

Freeman, Victoria. "In Defence of Reconciliation Discourse and Negotiations across the Indigenous/Non-Indigenous Divide." *Canadian Journal of Law and Jurisprudence* 27 (2014): 213–24.

French, Jan. *Legalizing Identities: Becoming Black or Indian in Brazil's Northeast*. Chapel Hill: University of North Carolina Press, 2009.

Freyre, Gilberto. *The Masters and the Slaves*. Translated by Samuel Putnam. Berkeley: University of California Press, 1986.

Furey, Constance. "Calvin's Questions: A Response to Jonathan Sheehan." SSRC. *The Immanent Frame*, September 21, 2016. http://blogs.ssrc.org/tif/2016/09/21/calvins-questions/.

Garland, David. *The Peculiar Institution: America's Death Penalty in an Age of Abolition*. Cambridge, MA: Harvard University Press, 2010.

Gill, Anthony. *Rendering Unto Caesar: The Catholic Church and the State in Latin America*. Chicago: University of Chicago Press, 1998.

Gorski, Philip S. *The Disciplinary Revolution: Calvinism and the Rise of the State in Early Modern Europe*. Chicago: University of Chicago Press, 2003.

Graden, Dale Torsten. *From Slavery to Freedom in Brazil: Bahia, 1835–1900*. Albuquerque: University of New Mexico Press, 2006.

Grande, Elisabetta. Review of *The Peculiar Institution*, by David Garland. *American Journal of Comparative Law* 60 (2012): 1111–18.

Green, Thomas. *Verdict According to Conscience: Perspectives on the English Criminal Trial Jury, 1200–1800*. Chicago: University of Chicago Press, 1985.

Gross, Samuel R., et al. "Rate of False Conviction of Criminal Defendants Who Are Sentenced to Death." *PNAS* 111 (2014): 7230–35.

Gutjahr, Paul. *An American Bible: A History of the Good Book in the United States, 1777–1880*. Stanford, CA: Stanford University Press, 1999.

Hacking, Ian. *Historical Ontology*. Cambridge, MA: Harvard University Press, 2004.

"Haida Gwaii Reconciliation Act." British Columbia Laws, June 3, 2010. Accessed May 22, 2017. http://www.bclaws.ca/civix/document/id/complete/statreg/10017_01.

Hall, Anthony J. *Earth into Property: Colonization, Decolonization, and Capitalism*. Montreal: McGill-Queen's University Press, 2010.

Hamilton, Michelle A. *Collections and Objections: Aboriginal Material Culture in Southern Ontario, 1791–1914*. Montreal: McGill-Queens University Press, 2012.

Hansen, Thomas Blom, and Finn Stepputat. "Sovereignty Revisited." *Annual Review of Anthropology* 25 (2006): 289–315.

Happy, J. Nelson, and Samuel Pyeatt Menefee. "Genesis! Scriptural Citation and the Lawyer's Bible Project." *Regent University Law Review* 9 (1997): 89–144.

Harjo, Suzan Shown. *Nation to Nation: Treaties between the United States & American Indian Nations*. Washington, DC: Smithsonian Books, 2014.

Harring, Sidney L. *White Man's Law: Native People in Nineteenth-Century Canadian Jurisprudence*. Toronto: University of Toronto Press, 1998.

Harris, Cole. *Making Native Space: Colonialism, Resistance, and Reserves in British Columbia* Vancouver: University of British Columbia Press, 2002.

Harriss, M. Cooper. "On the Eirobiblical: Critical Mimesis and Ironic Resistance in 'The Confessions of Nat Turner.'" *Biblical Interpretation* 21, no. 4–5 (2013): 469–93.

Hegel, Georg Wilhelm Friedrich. *Grundlinien der Philosophie des Rechts*. Berlin: Nicolaischen Buchhandlung, 1821.

———. *The Philosophy of History*. Translated by John Sibree. London: Dover, 1956.

Henderson, James (Sákéj) Youngblood. "The Context of the State of Nature." In *Reclaiming Indigenous Voice and Vision*, edited by Marie Battiste, 11–38. Vancouver: University of British Columbia Press, 2000.

———. *Indigenous Diplomacy and the Rights of Peoples: Achieving UN Recognition*. Vancouver: University of British Columbia Press, 2008.

———. *The Mikmaw Concordat*. Halifax: Fernwood, 1997.

Herberg, Will. *Protestant, Catholic, Jew: An Essay in American Religious Sociology*. Chicago: University of Chicago Press, 1955.

Hildebrandt, Walter, Dorothy First Rider, and Sarah Carter. *The True Spirit and Original Intent of Treaty 7*. Montreal: McGill-Queen's University Press, 1996.

Hoffmann, Joseph L. "Where's the Buck? Juror Misperception of Sentencing Responsibility in Death Penalty Cases." *Indiana Law Journal* 70 (1995): 1137–60.

Hoornaert, Eduardo. *Os anjos de Canudos: Uma revisão histórica*. Petrópolis: Vozes, 1997.

Horcades, Alvim Martins. *Descrição de uma viagem a Canudos*. Bahia: Typographia Tourinho, 1899.

Howe, Mark De Wolfe. *The Garden and the Wilderness: Religion and Government in American Constitutional History*. Chicago: University of Chicago Press, 1965.

Howe, Nicolas. *Landscapes of the Secular: Law, Religion, and American Sacred Space*. Chicago: University of Chicago Press, 2016.

Ignatieff, Michael. *A Just Measure of Pain: The Penitentiary in the Industrial Revolution*. London: Puffin, 1989.

Indigenous Foundations, University of British Columbia. "Royal Proclamation, 1763." Indigenous Foundations UBC. Accessed October 18, 2016. http://indigenousfoundations.adm.arts.ubc.ca /royal_proclamation_1763/.

Jakobsen, Janet R., and Ann Pellegrini. *Secularisms*. Durham, NC: Duke University Press, 2008.

Jamieson, Keith. "The Haundenosaunee / Six Nations and the Royal Proclamation of 1763." *ActiveHistory.ca*, October 2, 2013. http:// activehistory.ca/2013/10/the-haundenosauneesix-nations-and -the-royal-proclamation-of-1763/.

Jasanoff, Maya. *Liberty's Exiles: American Loyalists in the Revolutionary World*. New York: Knopf Doubleday, 2012.

Johnson, Adriana Michéle Campos. *Sentencing Canudos: Subalternity in the Backlands of Brazil*. Pittsburgh: University of Pittsburgh Press, 2010.

Johnson, David T. "American Capital Punishment in Comparative Perspective." *Law & Social Inquiry* 36, no. 4 (2011): 1033–61.

Johnson, Harold. *Two Families: Treaties and Government*. Saskatoon: Purich, 2007.

Kahn, Jonathon S., and Vincent W. Lloyd, eds. *Race and Secularism in America*. New York: Columbia University Press, 2016.

Kahn, Paul. *Political Theology: Four New Chapters on the Concept of Sovereignty*. New York: Columbia University Press, 2012.

Kamloops This Week. "Chief Gottfriedson Witnesses Reconciliation Ceremony with Prince William." *Kamloops This Week*, September 27, 2016. http://www.kamloopsthisweek.com/chief-gottfriedson-witnesses-reconciliation-ceremony-with-prince-william/.

Kant, Immanuel. *Observations of the Feeling of the Sublime*. Translated by John T. Goldthwait. Berkeley: University of California Press, 1960.

Kantorowicz, Ernst. *The King's Two Bodies: A Study in Mediaeval Political Theology*. Princeton, NJ: Princeton University Press, 1957.

Kaveny, Cathleen. *Law's Virtues: Fostering Autonomy and Solidarity in American Society*. Washington, DC: Georgetown University Press, 2012.

Keane, Webb. *Christian Moderns: Freedom and Fetish in the Mission Encounter*. Berkeley: University of California Press, 2003.

Kennedy, W. P. M. *Documents of the Canadian Constitution, 1759–1915*. Toronto: Oxford University Press, 1963.

King, Thomas. *The Truth about Stories: A Native Narrative*. Toronto: House of Anansi, 2003.

Klassen, Pamela E. "Fantasies of Sovereignty: Civic Secularism in Canada." *Critical Research on Religion* 3, no. 1 (2015): 41–56.

———. "God Keep Our Land: The Legal Ritual of the McKenna-McBride Royal Commission, 1913–1916." In *Religion and the Exercise of Public Authority*, ed. Benjamin L. Berger and Richard Moon, 79–93. Oxford: Hart, 2016.

———. *The Story of Radio Mind: A Missionary's Journey on Indigenous Land*. Chicago: University of Chicago Press, forthcoming.

Kramer, Larry. *The People Themselves: Popular Constitutionalism and Judicial Review*. New York: Oxford University Press, 2005.

Laanela, Mike. "B.C.'s Grand Chief Stewart Phillip Won't Attend Royal Ceremony with Prince William." *CBC News*, September 26, 2016. Accessed November 1, 2016. http://www.cbc.ca /news/canada/british-columbia/royal-visit-black-rod-stewart -phillip-1.3778997.

———. "Black Rod Ceremony Comes with Lesson in Colonialism, Cultural Genocide for Prince William." *CBC News*, September 27, 2016. http://www.cbc.ca/news/canada/british-columbia /royal-visit-black-rod-prince-william-1.3780573.

Latour, Bruno. *Pandora's Hope: Essays on the Reality of Science Studies*. Cambridge, MA: Harvard University Press, 1999.

———. *We Have Never Been Modern*. Translated by Catherine Porter. Cambridge, MA: Harvard University Press, 1993.

Leakey, David. "Black Rod: Today's Role in Parliament—with a Glance Back to 1348." Lecture presented at the Open Lecture, UK Parliament, London, England, October 8, 2014. Accessed November 1, 2016. https://www.parliament.uk/get-involved /education-programmes/universities-programme/university -teaching-resources/black-rod-todays-role-in-parliament --with-a-glance-back-to-1348/.

Le Bon, Gustave. *Psychologie des foules*. Paris: Félix Alcan, 1895.

———. *The Psychology of Peoples*. New York: Macmillan, 1898.

Lefort, Claude. "The Permanence of the Theologico-Political?" In *Political Theologies: Public Religions in a Post-Secular World*, edited by Hent de Vries and Lawrence Eugene Sullivan, 148–87. New York: Fordham University Press, 2006.

Legislative Assembly of the Province of British Columbia. "The Black Rod Fact Sheet." Province of British Columbia, July 13, 2015. Accessed March 20, 2017. https://www.leg.bc.ca/learn -about-us/learning-resources.

Levine, Robert M. "Canudos in the National Context." *The Americas* 48, no. 2 (1991): 207–22.

———. "Mud-Hut Jerusalem: Canudos Revisited." In *The Abolition of Slavery and the Aftermath of Emancipation in Brazil*. Durham, NC: Duke University Press, 1988.

———. *Vale of Tears: Revisiting the Canudos Massacre in Northeast Brazil, 1893–1897*. Berkeley: University of California Press, 1992.

Lipka, Michael. "Some Major U.S. Religious Groups Differ from Their Members on the Death Penalty." Pew Research Center, July 13, 2015. Accessed March 13, 2017, http://www.pewresearch.org/fact-tank/2015/07/13/some-major-u-s-religious-groups-differ-from-their-members-on-the-death-penalty/.

Lloyd, Vincent. *Black Natural Law*. Oxford: Oxford University Press, 2016.

Locke, John. *Second Treatise of Government*. 1689.

Lonetree, Amy. "Museums as Sites of Decolonization: Truth Telling in National and Tribal Museums." In *Contesting Knowledge: Museums and Indigenous Perspectives*, edited by Susan Sleeper-Smith, 322–37. Lincoln: University of Nebraska Press, 2009.

Louis, William Roger, P. J. Marshall, and Alaine Lowe, eds. *The Oxford History of the British Empire*. Vol. 2, *The Eighteenth Century*. Oxford: Oxford University Press, 1998.

Macedo, Nertan. *Memorial de Vilanova*. Rio de Janeiro: Edições O Cruzeiro, 1964.

Macklem, Patrick, and Douglas Sanderson. *From Recognition to Reconciliation: Essays on the Constitutional Entrenchment of Aboriginal and Treaty Rights*. Toronto: University of Toronto Press, 2016.

Maier, Pauline. "The Revolutionary Origins of the American Corporation." *William and Mary Quarterly*, 3rd series, 50, no. 1 (1993): 51–84.

Makokis, Janice. "Envisioning an Indigenous Jurisdictional Process: A Nehiyaw (Cree) Law Approach." *LawNow*, March 2, 2017. Accessed March 20, 2017. http://www.lawnow.org/envisioning-an-indigenous-jurisdictional-process-a-nehiyaw-cree-law-approach/print/.

Maldonado-Torres, Nelson. *Against War: Views from the Underside of Modernity*. Durham, NC: Duke University Press, 2008.

Mamdani, Mahmood. *Citizen and Subject: Contemporary Africa and the Legacy of Late Colonialism*. Princeton, NJ: Princeton University Press, 1996.

Marciáno, João Evangelista de Monte. *Relatório apresentado pelo Revd. Frei João Evangelista de Monte Marciano ao Arcebispado da Bahia sobre Antonio Conselheiro.* Bahia: Typographia do Correio de Noticias, 1895.

Martin, Emily. *Flexible Bodies: Tracking Immunity in American Culture from the Days of Polio to the Age of AIDS.* Boston: Beacon, 1994.

Martschukat, Jürgen. "'The Art of Killing by Electricity': The Sublime and the Electric Chair." *Journal of American History* 89 (2002): 900–921.

Marty, Martin. *Religion and Republic: The American Circumstance.* Boston: Beacon, 1989.

Marx, Karl. *Zur Judenfrage.* 1844; Berlin: Ernst Rowohlt Verlag, 1919.

Matthews, Maureen. "We Are All Treaty People." Manitoba Museum, April 30, 2014. Accessed March 20, 2017. https://manitobamuseum.ca/main/we-are-all-treaty-people/.

McBride, Keally. *Mr. Mothercountry: The Man Who Made the Rule of Law.* Oxford: Oxford University Press, 2016.

McNally, Michael D. "Native American Religious Freedom beyond the First Amendment." In *After Pluralism: Reimagining Religious Engagement,* edited by Courtney Bender and Pamela E. Klassen, 226–51. New York: Columbia University Press, 2010.

Merback, Michael. *The Thief, the Cross and the Wheel: Pain and the Spectacle of Punishment in Medieval Europe.* Chicago: University of Chicago Press, 1999.

Merry, Sally Engle. *Getting Justice and Getting Even: Legal Consciousness among Working-Class Americans.* Chicago: University of Chicago Press, 1990.

Mignolo, Walter. *The Darker Side of the Renaissance: Literacy, Territoriality, and Colonization.* Ann Arbor: University of Michigan Press, 2003.

Miller, J. R. *Compact, Contract, Covenant: Aboriginal Treaty-Making in Canada.* Toronto: University of Toronto Press, 2009.

Miller, Monica K., Joseph Dimitrov, Brian H. Bornstein, and Ashley Zarker-Sorensen. "Bibles in the Jury Room: Psychological

Theories Question Judicial Assumptions." *Ohio Northern University Law Review* 39 (2013): 579–625.

Miller, Robert J. "American Indians, the Doctrine of Discovery, and Manifest Destiny." *Wyoming Law Review* 11, no. 2 (2011): 329–49.

Miller, William Ian. *Bloodtaking and Peacemaking: Feud, Law, and Society in Saga Iceland*. Chicago: University of Chicago Press, 1990.

Milloy, John S. *A National Crime: The Canadian Government and the Residential School System, 1879 to 1986*. Winnipeg: University of Manitoba Press, 1999.

Milton, Aristides A. *A Campanha de Canudos*. Rio de Janeiro: Imprensa Nacional, 1902.

Mitchell, Timothy. "The Limits of the State: Beyond Statist Approaches and Their Critics." *American Political Science Review* 85, no. 1 (1991): 77–96.

Modern, John. *Secularism in Antebellum America*. Chicago: University of Chicago Press, 2011.

"The Monarch." Government of Canada. Accessed May 22, 2017. http://canada.pch.gc.ca/eng/1444999464289/1444999464291?=undefined&wbdisable=true.

Montenegro, Abelardo F. *Antônio Conselheiro*. Fortaleza, Ceará: A. Batista Fontenelle, 1954.

Monture, Rick. *We Share Our Matters: Two Centuries of Writing and Resistance at Six Nations of the Grand River*. Winnipeg: University of Manitoba Press, 2014.

Morgan, Edmund. *Inventing the People: The Rise of Popular Sovereignty in England and America*. New York: W. W. Norton, 1988.

Morris, Norval, and David Rothman, eds. *The Oxford History of the Prison: The Practice of Punishment in Western Society*. New York: Oxford University Press, 1998.

Mullen, Lincoln. "America's Public Bible: Biblical Quotations in U.S. Newspapers." America's Public Bible, 2016. Accessed March 14, 2017. http://americaspublicbible.org/.

Murphy, Victoria. "Kate Middleton Dazzles in Scarlet Dress for Reception on Canadian Royal Tour." *Mirror*, September 27, 2016. Accessed November 1, 2016. http://www.mirror.co.uk/news/uk-news/kate-middleton-dazzles-scarlet-cocktail-8920911.

Murray, John Courtney. *We Hold These Truths: Catholic Reflections on the American Proposition*. New York: Sheed and Ward, 1960.

Nancy, Jean-Luc. "Church, State, Resistance." In *Political Theologies: Public Religions in a Post-Secular World*, edited by Hent de Vries and Lawrence Eugene Sullivan, 102–12. New York: Fordham University Press, 2006.

Nassau, Robert Hamill. *Fetichism in West Africa: Forty Years' Observation of Native Customs and Superstitions*. New York: Negro University Press, 1904.

Nelles, H. V. *A Little History of Canada*. New York: Oxford University Press, 2004.

Neuhaus, Richard John. *The Naked Public Square: Religion and Democracy in America*. Grand Rapids, MI: Eerdmans, 1988.

Niebuhr, Reinhold. *The Irony of American History*. New York: Scribner, 1952.

———. *Moral Man and Immoral Society: A Study in Ethics and Politics*. New York: Scribner, 1932.

Nogueira, Ataliba, ed. *António Conselheiro e Canudos, revisão histórica: A obra manuscrita de António Conselheiro e que pertenceu a Euclides Da Cunha*. São Paulo: Companhia Editoria Nacional, 1974.

Nogueira Galvão, Walnice, ed. *No calor da hora: A guerra de Canudos nos Jornais*. São Paulo: Editora Ática, 1994.

———. "Piedade e paixão: Os sermões do conselheiro." In *Breviário de Antonio Conselheiro*, edited by Walnice Nogueira Galvão and Fernando da Rocha Peres. Salvador da Bahia: Universidade Federal da Bahia, 2002.

Nogueira Galvão, Walnice, and Fernando da Rocha Peres, eds. "Apêndices." In *Breviário de Antonio Conselheiro*. Salvador da Bahia: Universidade Federal da Bahia, 2002.

———, eds. *Breviário de Antonio Conselheiro*. Salvador da Bahia: Universidade Federal da Bahia, 2002.

Noll, Mark. *In the Beginning Was the Word: The Bible in American Public Life, 1492–1783*. New York: Oxford University Press, 2016.

O'Brien, Jean. *Firsting and Lasting: Writing Indians Out of Existence in New England*. Minneapolis: University of Minnesota Press, 2010.

Ogletree, Charles, and Austin Sarat, eds. *From Lynch Mobs to the*

Killing State: Race and the Death Penalty in America. New York: New York University Press, 2006.

Oliviera, Thaís Reis, and João Batista Jr. "Janaína Paschoal: 'Não sou a menina pastora e prefiro Pink Floyd.'" *Huffington Post Brasil.* Accessed August 31, 2016. http://www.brasilpost.com.br/2016 /04/06/janaina-paschal-pink-floyd_n_9626466.html.

Orsi, Robert A. *History and Presence.* Cambridge, MA: Harvard University Press, 2016.

Ortiz, Fernando. *Cuban Counterpoint: Tobacco and Sugar.* Durham, NC: Duke University Press, 1995.

Otten, Alexandre. *Só Deus é grande: A mensagem religiosa de Antonio Conselheiro.* São Paulo: Loyola, 1990.

Pasternak, Shiri. "Jurisdiction and Settler Colonialism: Where Do Laws Meet?" *Canadian Journal of Law and Society / La Revue Canadienne Droit et Société* 29, no. 2 (2014): 145–61.

Peres, Fernando da Rocha. "Fragmentaria." In *Breviário de Antonio Conselheiro,* edited by Walnice Nogueira Galvão and Fernando da Rocha Peres. Salvador da Bahia: Universidade Federal da Bahia, 2002.

Pessar, Patricia R. *From Fanatics to Folk: Brazilian Millenarianism and Popular Culture.* Durham, NC: Duke University Press, 2004.

Peters, John Durham. "Calendar, Clock, Tower." In *Deus in Machina: Religion, Technology, and the Things in Between,* edited by Jeremy Stolow, 25–42. New York: Fordham University Press, 2012.

Provincial Archives of Saskatchewan. "King George III Medal." Provincial Archives of Saskatchewan, 2011. Accessed November 1, 2016. http://www.saskarchives.com/node/218.

Radforth, Ian Walter. *Royal Spectacle: The 1860 Visit of the Prince of Wales to Canada and the United States.* Toronto: University of Toronto Press, 2004.

Radosh, Daniel. "The Good Book Business: Why Publishers Love the Bible." *New Yorker,* December 18, 2006.

Reid, Jennifer. "The Doctrine of Discovery and Canadian Law." *Canadian Journal of Native Studies* 30, no. 2 (January 1, 2010): 335–59.

———. *Louis Riel and the Creation of Modern Canada: Mythic Dis-*

course and the Postcolonial State. Albuquerque: University of New Mexico Press, 2008.

Richland, Justin. "Hopi Tradition as Jurisdiction: On the Potentializing Limits of Hopi Tribal Sovereignty." *Law & Social Inquiry* 36 (2011): 201–34.

———. "Jurisdiction: Grounding Law in Language." *Annual Review of Anthropology* 42 (2013): 209–26.

Robertson, Lindsay G. *Conquest by Law: How the Discovery of America Dispossessed Indigenous Peoples of Their Lands*. Oxford: Oxford University Press, 2005.

———. "The Judicial Conquest of Native America: The Story of Johnson v. M'Intosh." In *Indian Law Stories*, edited by Carole Goldberg, Kevin Washburn, and Philip Frickey, 29–60. New York: Foundation, 2011.

Rodrigues, Raimundo Nina. *Coletividades anormais*. Brasilia: Edições do Senado Federal, 2006.

Romero, Sílvio. *Estudos sobre a poesia popular do Brasil*. Petrópolis: Vozes, 1977.

"Royal Commission on Aboriginal Peoples—Final Report." Vol .2, "Restructuring the Relationship." Accessed October 22, 2016. https://archive.org/details/RoyalCommissionOnAboriginal Peoples-FinalReport-Vol.2-Restructuring.

Rupp, Kathleen. "Capital Hypocrisy: Does Compelling Jurors to Impose the Death Penalty without Spiritual Guidance Violate Jurors' First Amendment Rights?" *American Criminal Law Review* 48 (2011): 217–240.

Sampaio, Consuelo Novais. *Canudos: Cartas para o barão*. São Paulo: EdUSP, 1999.

Sandys, Marla, and Adam Trahan. "Life Qualification, Automatic Death Penalty Voter Status, and Juror Decision Making in Capital Cases." *Justice System Journal* 29 (2008): 385–95.

Sandys, Marla, and Edmund McGarrell. "Beyond the Bible Belt: The Influence (or Lack Thereof) of Religion on Attitudes toward the Death Penalty." *Journal of Crime and Justice* 20, no. 1 (1997): 179–90.

Santner, Eric. *The Royal Remains: The People's Two Bodies and the*

Endgames of Sovereignty. Chicago: University of Chicago Press, 2011.

———. *The Weight of All Flesh: On the Subject Matter of Political Economy*. Oxford: Oxford University Press, 2015.

Santos, Eurides de Souza. *A música de Canudos*. Salvador: Coleção Selo Editorial, n.d.

Scalia, Antonin. "God's Justice and Ours." Institute on Religion and Public Life. *First Things*, May 2002. Accessed March 13, 2017. http://www.firstthings.com/article/2002/05/gods-justice-and-ours.

Scherer, Matthew. *Beyond Church and State: Democracy, Secularism, and Conversion*. New York: Cambridge University Press, 2013.

Schmidt, Leigh Eric. Review of *An American Bible: A History of the Good Book in the United States, 1777–1880*, by Paul C. Gutjahr. *Church History* 69, no. 2 (2000): 445–46.

———. *Village Atheists: How America's Unbelievers Made Their Way in a Godly Nation*. Princeton, NJ: Princeton University Press, 2016.

Schuback, Marcia Sá Cavalcante. *Olho a olho: Ensaios de longe*. Rio de Janeiro: Fundação Biblioteca Nacional, 2011.

Scott, James. *The Art of Not Being Governed: An Anarchist History of Upland Southeast Asia*. New Haven, CT: Yale University Press, 2009.

———. *Seeing Like a State: How Certain Schemes to Improve the Human Condition Have Failed*. New Haven, CT: Yale University Press, 1998.

Seed, Patricia. *Ceremonies of Possession in Europe's Conquest of the New World, 1492–1640*. Cambridge: Cambridge University Press, 1995.

Sheehan, Jonathan. *The Enlightenment Bible: Translation, Scholarship, Culture*. Princeton, NJ: Princeton University Press, 2005.

Shell, Marc. *Wampum and the Origins of American Money*. Urbana: University of Illinois Press, 2013.

Shusterman, Noah. *Religion and the Politics of Time*. Washington, DC: Catholic University of America Press, 2010.

Simpson, Audra. *Mohawk Interruptus: Political Life across the Borders of Settler States*. Durham, NC: Duke University Press, 2014.

———. "Subjects of Sovereignty: Indigeneity, the Revenue Rule, and Juridics of Failed Consent." *Law and Contemporary Problems* 71, no. 3 (2008): 191.

Simpson, Leanne. "Looking after Gdoo-Naaganinaa: Precolonial Nishnaabeg Diplomatic and Treaty Relationships." *Wicazo Sa Review* 23, no. 2 (October 8, 2008): 29–42.

Slattery, Brian. "The Royal Proclamation of 1763 and the Aboriginal Constitution." In *Keeping Promises: The Royal Proclamation of 1763, Aboriginal Rights, and Treaties in Canada*, edited by Jim Aldridge and Terry Fenge, 14–32. Montreal: McGill-Queen's University Press, 2015.

Smith, Jonathan Z. *Relating Religion: Essays in the Study of Religion*. Chicago: University of Chicago Press, 2004.

Soares, Henrique Duque Estrada de Macedo. *A Guerra de Canudos*. Rio de Janeiro: Philobiblion, 1985.

Sodré, Nelson Werneck. *Quem é o povo no Brasil*. Rio de Janeiro: Editôra Civilização Brasileira, 1962.

Stampp, Kenneth. *The Peculiar Institution: Slavery in the Ante-Bellum South*. London: Vintage Books, 1956.

Sullivan, Winnifred Fallers. *The Impossibility of Religious Freedom*. Princeton, NJ: Princeton University Press, 2005.

———. *Paying the Words Extra: Religious Discourse in the Supreme Court of the United States*. Cambridge, MA: Harvard University Press, 1995.

Sundby, Scott E. *A Life and Death Decision: A Jury Weighs the Death Penalty*. New York: St. Martin's, 2007.

———. "The True Legacy of *Atkins* and *Roper*: The Unreliability Principle, Mentally Ill Defendants, and the Death Penalty's Unraveling." *William & Mary Bill of Rights Journal* 23 (2014): 487–528.

Tavares, Odorico. *Canudos: Cinqüenta anos depois*. Bahia: Conselho Estadual da Cultura, 1947.

Taylor, Charles. *A Secular Age*. Cambridge, MA: Harvard University Press, 2007.

Taylor, Mark Lewis. *The Executed God: The Way of the Cross in Lockdown America*. Minneapolis: Fortress, 2001.

Temkin, Moshe. "The Great Divergence: The Death Penalty in the United States and the Failure of Abolition in Transatlantic Perspective." Faculty Research Working Paper Series. Harvard Kennedy School, July 2015.

Thuesen, Peter. *In Discordance with the Scriptures: American Protestant Battles over Translating the Bible*. New York: Oxford University Press, 1999.

Tidridge, Nathan. *Canada's Constitutional Monarchy: An Introduction to Our Form of Government*. Toronto: Dundurn, 2011.

———. *The Queen at the Council Fire: The Treaty of Niagara, Reconciliation, and the Dignified Crown in Canada*. Hamilton: Dundurn, 2015.

Tocqueville, Alexis de. *De la démocratie en Amérique*. Paris: C. Gosselin, 1811.

———. *Democracy in America*. Vol. 1. Translated by Henry Reeve. London: Longman and Roberts, 1862.

Truth and Reconciliation Commission of Canada. *The Final Report of the Truth and Reconciliation Commission of Canada*. Vol. 5, *Canada's Residential Schools: The Legacy*. Montreal: McGill-Queen's University Press, 2015.

Tully, James. *Strange Multiplicity: Constitutionalism in an Age of Diversity*. Cambridge: Cambridge University Press, 1995.

Turner, Jack. "John Locke, Christian Mission, and Colonial America." *Modern Intellectual History* 8, no. 2 (2011): 267–97.

Uzgalis, William. "'An Inconsistency Not to Be Excused': On Locke and Racism." In *Philosophers on Race: Critical Essays*, edited by Julie Ward and Tommy Lott, 81–100. Oxford: Blackwell, 2002.

Valente, Waldemar. *Misticismo e região*. Recife: MEC, 1963.

Valverde, Mariana. *Chronotopes of Law: Jurisdiction, Scale and Governance*. London: Routledge, 2015.

———. "The Crown in a Multicultural Age: The Changing Epistemology of (Post)colonial Sovereignty." *Social & Legal Studies* 21, no. 1 (2012): 3–21.

———. "The Ethic of Diversity: Local Law and the Negotiation of Urban Norms." *Law & Social Inquiry* 33 (2008): 895–923.

———. "'The Honour of the Crown Is at Stake': Aboriginal Land Claims Litigation and the Epistemology of Sovereignty." *UC Irvine Law Review* 1, no. 3 (2011): 957–74.

Vargas Llosa, Mario. *The War of the End of the World.* Translated by Helen Lane. New York: Picador, 1981.

Veer, Peter van der. *The Modern Spirit of Asia: The Spiritual and the Secular in China and India.* Princeton, NJ: Princeton University Press, 2013.

Villa, Marco Antonio. *Canudos: O povo da terra.* São Paulo: Editora Ática, 1995.

Waddington, Raymond B. "Elizabeth I and the Order of the Garter." *Sixteenth Century Journal* 24, no. 1 (1993): 97–113.

Walker, Andrea D. "'The Murderer Shall Surely Be Put to Death': The Impropriety of Biblical Arguments in the Penalty Phase of Capital Cases." *Washburn Law Journal* 43, no. 1 (2003): 197–223.

Wallerstein, Immanuel. "The Construction of Peoplehood: Racism, Nationalism, Ethnicity." In *Race, Nation, Class: Ambiguous Identities*, edited by Etienne Balibar and Immanuel Wallerstein, 71–86. London: Verso, 1991.

Weatherdon, Meaghan, and Pamela E. Klassen. "The Study of Indigenous Religions in North America." In *Oxford Handbook of the Anthropology of Religion*, edited by Simon Coleman and Joel Robbins. Oxford: Oxford University Press, forthcoming.

Webber, Jeremy. "We Are Still in the Age of Encounter: Section 35 and a Canada beyond Sovereignty." In *From Recognition to Reconciliation: Essays on the Constitutional Entrenchment of Aboriginal and Treaty Rights*, edited by Patrick Macklem and Douglas Sanderson, 63–99. Toronto: University of Toronto Press, 2016.

Weber, Max. "The Nature of Charismatic Authority and Its Routinization." In *Max Weber on Charisma and Institution Building*, edited by S. N. Eisenstadt, translated by Talcott Parsons. Chicago: University of Chicago Press, 1968, 48–65.

———. "Politics as a Vocation." In *From Max Weber*, translated and edited by Hans Gerth and C. Wright Mills, 77–128. New York: Oxford University Press, 1946.

Wenger, Tisa Joy. *We Have a Religion: The 1920s Pueblo Indian Dance Controversy and American Religious Freedom.* Chapel Hill: University of North Carolina Press, 2009.

"What's Happening in Muskrat Falls? Here's a Primer." *CBC News.* Accessed November 1, 2016. http://www.cbc.ca/news/indigenous/muskrat-falls-what-you-need-to-know-1.3822898.

Whiteley, Patrick. "Natural Law and the Problem of Certainty: Robert Bolt's *A Man for All Seasons.*" *Contemporary Literature* 43, no. 4 (2002): 760–83.

Whitman, James Q. *Harsh Justice: Criminal Punishment and the Widening Divide between America and Europe.* New York: Oxford University Press, 2005.

———. "Separating Church and State: The Atlantic Divide." *Historical Reflections* 34, no. 3 (2008): 86–104.

Wilson, Alan. *The Clergy Reserves of Upper Canada.* Canadian Historical Association Booklets 23. Ottawa: Canadian Historical Association, 1969.

Witte, John, Jr., and Frank S. Alexander, eds. *The Teachings of Modern Protestantism on Law, Politics & Human Nature.* New York: Columbia University Press, 2007.

Wolf, Eric R. *Europe and the People without History.* Berkeley: University of California Press, 1982.

Zama, César "Wolsley." *Libelo republicano acompanhado de comentários sobre a guerra de Canudos.* Bahia: Diário da Bahia, 1899.

Zilly, Berthold. "Flávio de Barros, o ilustre cronista anônimo da Guerra de Canudos," *Estudos avançados* 13, no. 35 (1999): 105–113.